MW00812371

Eternally Eve

For Aryeh and Flora with gratitude for your friendship and support

Anne Lapidus

HBI SERIES ON JEWISH WOMEN

Shulamit Reinharz, General Editor
Joyce Antler, Associate Editor
Sylvia Barack Fishman, Associate Editor

The Brandeis Series on Jewish Women is an innovative book series created by the Hadassah-Brandeis Institute. BSJW publishes a wide range of books by and about Jewish women in diverse contexts and time periods, of interest to scholars, and for the educated public. The series fills a major gap in Jewish learning by focusing on the lives of Jewish women and Jewish gender studies.

For the complete list of books in this series, please see www.upne.com and www.upne.com/series/BSJW.html

Anne Lapidus Lerner, *Eternally Eve: Images of Eve in the Hebrew Bible, Midrash, and Modern Jewish Poetry*

Margalit Shilo, *Princess or Prisoner? Jewish Women in Jerusalem, 1840–1914*

Marcia Falk, translator, *The Song of Songs: Love Lyrics from the Bible*

Sylvia Barack Fishman, *Double or Nothing? Jewish Families and Mixed Marriage*

Avraham Grossman, *Pious and Rebellious: Jewish Women in Medieval Europe*

Iris Parush, *Reading Jewish Women: Marginality and Modernization in Nineteenth-Century Eastern European Jewish Society*

Shulamit Reinharz and Mark A. Raider, editors, *American Jewish Women and the Zionist Enterprise*

Tamar Ross, *Expanding the Palace of Torah: Orthodoxy and Feminism*

Farideh Goldin, *Wedding Song: Memoirs of an Iranian Jewish Woman*

Elizabeth Wyner Mark, editor, *The Covenant of Circumcision: New Perspectives on an Ancient Jewish Rite*

Rochelle L. Millen, *Women, Birth, and Death in Jewish Law and Practice*

Kalpana Misra and Melanie S. Rich, editors, *Jewish Feminism in Israel: Some Contemporary Perspectives*

Judith R. Baskin, *Midrashic Women: Formations of the Feminine in Rabbinic Literature*

Eternally Eve

Images of Eve in the Hebrew Bible, Midrash, and Modern Jewish Poetry

Anne Lapidus Lerner

Brandeis University Press
WALTHAM, MASSACHUSETTS
...
Published by University Press of New England
HANOVER AND LONDON

Brandeis University Press

Published by University Press of New England,

One Court Street, Lebanon, NH 03766

www.upne.com

Designed by Dean Bornstein

© 2007 by Brandeis University Press

Printed in the United States of America

5 4 3 2 1

All rights reserved. No part of this book may be reproduced in any form or by any electronic or mechanical means, including storage and retrieval systems, without permission in writing from the publisher, except by a reviewer, who may quote brief passages in a review. Members of educational institutions and organizations wishing to photocopy any of the work for classroom use, or authors and publishers who would like to obtain permission for any of the material in the work, should contact Permissions, University Press of New England, One Court Street, Lebanon, NH 03766.

This book was published with the generous support of the Lucius N. Littaur Foundation, Inc.

LIBRARY OF CONGRESS CATALOGING-IN-PUBLICATION DATA

Lerner, Anne Lapidus.

 Eternally Eve : images of Eve in the Hebrew Bible, Midrash, and modern Jewish poetry / Anne Lapidus Lerner.

  p. cm.

Includes bibliographical references and index.

ISBN-13: 978-1-58465-553-4 (cloth : alk. paper)

ISBN-10: 1-58465-553-4 (cloth : alk. paper)

ISBN-13: 978-1-58465-573-2 (pbk. : alk. paper)

ISBN-10: 1-58465-573-9 (pbk. : alk. paper)

1. Eve (Biblical figure) 2. Eve (Biblical figure) in rabbinical literature. 3. Eve (Biblical figure)— In literature. I. Title.

 BS580.E85L47 2007

 222'.11092—dc22   2006035332

The author gratefully acknowledges permission to reproduce the following: "Ḥavvah," from *Poems* (in Hebrew) by Miriam Bat-Yokheved. Copyright © 1963 by Sifriyat Po'alim. Used by permission of Sifriyat Po'alim. "The Call," from *The Hunger Song* by Kim Chernin. Copyright © 1983 by Kim Chernin. Used by permission of the author. "Ḥavvah," from *A Corner of the Field: Poems* (continued on page 239)

This book is dedicated to the memory of a remarkable woman,

Dorothy Agnes Didofsky Stern (1910–2002),

a feisty protofeminist who valued her independence, as well as the love of her sister, husband, nieces, and nephews. She served as a role model for the wider family, inculcating in them her love of Judaism, of fashion, of family, and her sense of humor. May her memory be a blessing.

CONTENTS

PREFACE

This exploration of Eve is the outgrowth of a lifelong infatuation with Jewish texts, languages, and ideas. It presents an opportunity for me to bring together those pursuits with a strong feminist interest in the ways in which women are represented, particularly in texts that have a sacred aura.

Contending, as I do, that none of us approaches text in a totally objective manner, I would like to say a few words about what I necessarily bring to my readings. I have always been an observant Conservative Jew whose life is daily informed by Jewish tradition, and have long been an active, avowed feminist. My scholarly training in comparative literature has led me to examine the ways in which text and textual traditions interact and the ways in which society and text impact on each other. While I have attempted to shed my prejudices in working with these texts, I recognize that I do so only imperfectly.

This book has been a long time in the making and has been shaped by the many opportunities I have had to teach courses on reflections of Eve at Jewish Theological Seminary, at Harvard Divinity School, and in many congregational settings and lectures around the United States and in Europe. Wherever I have taken Eve, I have been rewarded with new insights and fresh references.

There are many to whom I am grateful for their reading of all or part of this manuscript, in some cases more than once. While I have benefited from their scholarship, wisdom, and insights, I hold myself responsible for whatever flaws this volume may retain. Colleagues who have freely and generously offered their support include: Janet Burstein, Stephen A. Geller, Edward L. Greenstein, Nathan Gross, Jon D. Levenson, and Naomi Sokoloff. Each has made countless helpful suggestions for improving the work, while suggesting other books and articles that have bearing on the subject. I have been blessed as well by family members who have, in addition to providing encouragement, served as readers: my husband, Stephen C. Lerner; my children, Rahel A. Lerner and David G. Lerner, and my daughter-in-law, Sharon Levin; my sister, Marcia L. Kaunfer, and my nephew Eliezer Kaunfer. Colleagues including Moshe Bar-Asher, Neil Gillman, Avraham Holtz, Joel Roth, Seth Schwartz, Michael Sokoloff, Zvi Steinfeld, and Devorah

Steinmetz have been generous in responding to my questions. Editorial consultants Muriel Jorgensen and Elisheva Urbas contributed to the accuracy and cogency of the text. Research assistants Jill Jacobs, Miriam Greenblatt Weidberg, Chris Cardullo, Sheridan Gayer, and Katy Schwalbe have taken on tasks great and small.

In many ways, the colleagues and students I have found in my more than three dozen years on the faculty of Jewish Theological Seminary have shaped my intellectual and religious development. I want to thank the staff of the JTS Library for their care in providing me with often obscure items. I am grateful, as well, for the support of its Maxwell Abell Fund.

The initial draft of much of this volume was written in 2001–2002 when I had the opportunity to participate in the Women's Studies in Religion Program at Harvard Divinity School. The program's director, Ann Braude, and my colleagues Joan Branham, Vijaya Nagarajan, Michelene Pesantubee, and Emilie Townes, served as a community with whom I could test my work and from whom I received much appreciated feedback and encouragement.

I express my thanks to Shulamit Reinharz, editor of the Brandeis Series on Jewish Women, and Phyllis Deutsch, editor in chief of the University Press of New England, for their encouragement, patience, and counsel.

I am also deeply grateful for the support of the Herbert and Barbara Goldberg Foundation.

My most profound gratitude goes to my parents, Lillian (Green) and Joseph Lapidus, whose memories are a blessing, who transmitted their love of Judaism, of culture, and of words to their children and grandchildren. Their unstinting support for me, their conviction that I could successfully undertake daunting tasks, and the care that they invested in my education are beyond measure.

I hope that this study will encourage others to continue the exploration of Eve and her impact on culture as we know it.

A. L. L.

A NOTE ON TRANSLATION, TEXTS, AND TRANSLITERATION

The translations here are, with the exception of some of the verses from the Hebrew Bible beyond Genesis 5, my own. In my translations I have endeavored to be as literal as possible in order to give the reader who may not understand the original language an experience close to the original. I am in no sense criticizing those who have rendered these texts into more felicitous English in order to fulfill other objectives.

I have used the masoretic biblical text for the Bible quotations, inserting a hyphen into the Tetragrammaton, the four-letter name of God, to follow the Jewish practice of not writing out God's name. I have transcribed the Tetragrammaton as *YHWH*.

Transliteration presents an overwhelming problem for these texts. I have, with the help of Miles B. Cohen, followed in large part the practice of *Prooftexts* for both modern and classical texts. Because the original Hebrew and Yiddish texts are included, I have opted for a relatively simple and uncluttered system of transliteration. This does result in some inconsistencies, particularly when quoting from other sources. When an author has a commonly accepted spelling of his or her name in English, I have used that, occasionally resulting in different transliterations of the same name. My goal is to facilitate comprehension for those who do not read Hebrew.

Eternally Eve

Introduction

The Significance of Eve

Eve seems ubiquitous in contemporary American popular culture. She is employed to market a diverse list of products, from bathroom fixtures and fruit juices to sex toys, Colombian coffee, and hand creams—an indication of the extent to which received notions about Eve have become devalued, common coin. Even more significant than her commercial pursuits is Eve's role in shaping society. Western civilization has for centuries used the biblical story of Eve to prescribe and justify the position and situation of its women.[1] It is "the very base of [the] Western perception of femininity."[2] The creation of the first woman has been viewed as secondary to the man's; her substance, derivative; her eating the fruit of the forbidden tree, culpable; her status relative to her man, subordinate. Her story, framed by her creation from a rib and by her banishment from the Garden of Eden, has been exploited to validate the dependent, circumscribed position of women.

As the first woman in the religious traditions of Judaism, Christianity, and Islam, Eve comes, in many contexts, to symbolize all women. Her onus is to serve as the archetype of the female, making her a paradigm of women's roles in the social structure of Western civilization, as well as the rationalization for them. To reconsider the texts, primary and critical, ancient and modern, in which Eve is a principal focus, to "reread Eve," then is not only to interpret them in a theoretical sense, but also to reexamine certain assumptions conventionally validated by the traditional readings of Eve.

Yet from the outset one must admit that the biblical texts relating to Eve cannot be forced into rigid uniformity. They rebel, eschewing unanimity and manifesting instead the gaps and contradictions in the account. Pious claims aside, the Genesis narratives constituting the primeval myths set forth competing concepts of the origin of the universe.[3] Gender plays an important role in these texts that tell and retell the story of the creation of human life and its purpose. Upon close examination the light they shine on the questions of gender and hierarchy subsumed within them proves to

1

be less a bright spotlight than the endlessly refracting light of a disco ball, illuminating a scene that is dynamic, constantly changing.

A Three-Way Conversation

Eternally Eve relies on critical scholarship and insights provided by rewriters, who narrate Eve's story afresh, filling gaps, adding details, and contributing new perspectives to the study of ancient biblical texts. The strands of Jewish text comprising the threefold textual cord that runs through this study comment on one another. While in modern literary studies we routinely uncover allusions to earlier sources, here we also reverse the process, turning the midrashic and modern sources back to add texture and depth to the reading of the biblical originals. The later, alluding midrashic and modern texts change our perception of the evoked biblical texts, even as their evocation contributes to our understanding of the later texts themselves. For the reader the texts change roles, evoking and alluding to one another without consideration of chronology.[4] We employ a variety of tools, including other texts, to release the range of interpretations inherent in each text, not to trace the history of an image or an allusion.

By bringing modern poetry and midrash into "virtual conversation" with Genesis, I have selected the current end point and an early point of Jewish biblical interpretation.[5] "Bookending" Jewish literary production in this way juxtaposes texts that are not often in conversation and allows us to see in them differences and similarities not often apparent. In so doing I propose that modern literature, particularly poetry, has to a large extent, intentionally or unintentionally, taken up the task of rewriting the Bible from a contemporary perspective that was, in their time, undertaken by the rabbis whose rewriting is collected in classical midrash. Significantly, the Bible, which to the postmodern reader seems almost porous in its polysemy, is restrained by the rabbis who counterbalance its polysemy through the relative lack of ambiguity in their own writing. While the rabbis of late antiquity rewrite various biblical passages in competing and contradictory ways, each of their statements tends to be in itself less subject to multiple interpretation than is the Bible. In contrast, modern poetry, almost by definition, often rivals the Bible in its multiple possibilities of meaning. The import of each word, phrase, or line, while lacking the imprimatur of the canonical text, resembles it in its complexity.

An intense reading of each of these strands of Jewish literature elucidates some of the many ways in which Eve's story can be understood.

2

There is little need to rehearse the manner in which faithful readers of Genesis, approaching the texts from varied perspectives, have seen in the biblical depiction of Eve a prescription for unequal gender roles in human society. For that reason this study privileges less traveled interpretive routes in order to present the complex possibilities inherent in this narrative. By remaining within the corpus of Jewish literature, I have chosen to look deeply into a single set of religious traditions, not to deny the fruitful cross-cultural forces that have always been at play, but to examine more closely their products.

Polysemy, the possibility of multiple meanings within a single text, abounds in the primeval history as narrated in Genesis—the repeated tale of the creation of man and woman is just one salient example. The complexity increases as later generations, whose worlds diverge markedly from the biblical, engage with these texts.[6] Layering strands of rewriting onto the biblical originals liberates the biblical texts and reveals the possibilities of meaning inherent in them.

Eve's story, so often cited as the definitive source for ultimate wisdom on human gender relations, proves to be obscure, not transparent. It has been frequently reinterpreted, although, surprisingly, *not* in the Hebrew Bible, where Eve never resurfaces after Genesis 5.[7] As a group, the rabbis of late antiquity, like their Christian contemporaries, read these texts long after their redaction and understood them within the perspectives of their worlds. Their readings, like ours, are framed in the world of the possible, shaped by specific, time-bound, social, and religious structures that are read back into the biblical text as though they were timeless. Lacking our contemporary sense of relativism and historical change, and our heightened self-awareness, they often fell into thinking that the world, in its most important and relevant features, had undergone little change[8]— leading them, for example, to place Jacob in a house of Torah study centuries before the institution developed.[9] Looking at the ways in which the rabbis understood the biblical texts highlights some of the issues in the texts and allows insights into the rabbinic worldview. Similarly, examining a selection of modern poetry about Eve leads us back to the biblical and rabbinic texts. This process allows alternative approaches to interpretation grounded, often quite self-consciously, in modern or postmodern constructions of society, particularly as they relate to gender. In this manner, modern poets and other rewriters continue the project of midrash; they mine the biblical texts to yield new treasures buried within them.

3

The rabbis seem more concerned than the biblical text itself to explain and justify male-dominant gender hierarchy; modern poets, as a group, have more often chosen to undermine or even to reverse it. In making this argument I want to avoid the temptation to blame previous generations for not having viewed these texts as possessing more opportunities for varied interpretations. We are reading their writings, not judging whether or not they constitute a plot against women. At such a wide gap in history, we can at best state that the rabbis, like Genesis itself, produced androcentric and occasionally misogynist texts that seem rooted in the patriarchal culture where they were originally written. But the timeless nature of the text of Genesis itself opens all these potential meanings, forged at the junction of text and reality, regardless of authorial intention.[10] It is precisely the exegetical possibilities inherent in the text, but not attended, that interest us as readers.[11]

What We Read and How We Read It

My examination of Eve assumes that Jewish literature can profitably be viewed whole, beyond the artificial division of texts into disparate domains. In addition to the Bible, we shall consider a selection of midrashic material, mostly from *Genesis Rabbah,* and a selection of modern Jewish poetry in English, Hebrew, and Yiddish. Lowering the partitions permits us to look at some of the multiplicity of Eves presented by the Jewish imagination without regard for their provenance, language, or age.

To understand this varied body of texts including the Hebrew Bible, rabbinic midrash, and modern poetry demands several approaches to literary analysis. Each non-English selection is presented in its original language, as well as in an English translation for those citations not originally written in English. Foundational to our comprehension of text are, of course, the words themselves, stripped, insofar as possible, of later accretions of interpretation. As a self-aware reader, I make no claim to presenting either an objective reading of the text or the exclusive reading. I seek to break open the texts to uncover some of the rich possibilities they offer. As a close reader, I work from the text itself, unpacking the various layers of meaning, looking for potential new interpretations that may, without violating textual integrity, make Eve's story resonate for early twenty-first-century readers.

Feminist approaches are useful in exploring the texts. While the woman in the Eve stories is not hard to find, she is also not easy to appreciate. As

4

heirs to a rabbinic tradition of interpretation that, despite its ambivalences, often sees the first woman as the source of society's ills, and to an ambient Christian tradition that casts Eve as the antithesis to Mary,[12] today's readers must make a determined effort to perceive the uninterpreted words of the biblical text itself.[13] Each of us also brings to the text's words the intellectual baggage derived from previous readings and our own experience—yet all must be set aside if we are to encounter Eve in the unencumbered text, in Genesis, and in later rewritings.

Paying particular attention to the voice and the agency of the woman in these texts goes counter to the traditional emphasis on the man and male culture. Some of the obscuring veneer of later interpretation is here systematically removed from the biblical text by devices such as never translating *adam* (human, man, Adam), except when it is unequivocally a proper noun, and eliminating the marriage, husband, and wife metaphors that have been superimposed on this story in which the words used in the text are simply "man" and "woman." Further, wherever possible and appropriate, I have used a neuter pronoun when its antecedent is *adam* on the grounds that the change, though jarring, helps the reader remember that the *adam* is not necessarily exclusively masculine.[14]

Alicia Ostriker proposes for "biblical revisionism" a feminist hermeneutic composed of three strands: suspicion, desire, and indeterminacy.[15] Suspicion leads the reader to question the accepted reading of a text; desire, to find in the text what one hopes to find; indeterminacy, to accept that no interpretation is exclusive of others. This study has consciously used both suspicion and a measure of indeterminacy sufficient to remind us that all human readings are fallible. Some desire, despite the best efforts to block it, has doubtless crept in.

Reading Modern Jewish Poetry

Twentieth-century Jewish literature in all its many manifestations presents a corpus of unparalleled creativity. Hebrew and virtually all the languages of the Jewish Diaspora have participated in this growth of imaginative literature. As the contemporary layer in this study of Eve, modern poetry transmits the encounter of some twentieth-century artists with the biblical figure.[16]

Selecting exemplary poems for this book is a daunting task. While one can start with some of the compilations and studies of Jewish poetry,[17] one ends up facing the challenge that there is an enormous range of material from which to choose and one can never know the full extent of the possibilities. My choices include material in the three major languages of twentieth-century Ashkenazic Jews: Hebrew, English, and Yiddish. I have also reached back to the first half of the twentieth century, before the second wave of feminism that has inspired so much new writing in this area. The poets whose works appear here include men and women, some of them well known, others less so. Other less objective criteria involved the poem's intrinsic quality, complexity, and ability to open interpretive paths into biblical and midrashic texts—to converse with them. Among the thirteen poems analyzed in detail, I have included voices ranging from those who seem rooted in the language and imagery of the Bible and midrash, to those who, in challenging their precursors, often seem remote from them.

Modern interpretations, particularly those that fuse poetry's creativity and ambiguity with an appreciation of the biblical text, pose a stimulating set of issues. Even without the further complication of its relationship to biblical antecedents, modern poetry often presents a polysemy of more than biblical proportions. While some ambiguity is purposeful, some seems unintentional, the product of a fluidity of meaning like that often found in the Hebrew Bible.

Further, the rabbis were familiar with their predecessors' approach and believed they had immediate access to the biblical world—those assumptions no longer obtain. While our Hebrew and Yiddish writers read the Bible in the original, the same is not necessarily true of those writing in English. All the midrashic material has been published in the Hebrew and Aramaic original, as well as in English translation, although some of it is not readily available. Availability, of course, provides readers with the possibility of access without indicating whether or not any writer actually read a specific text. But access is not limited to the printed page and many of these rabbinic interpretations of the Bible have become so intimately tied to the original text that the Bible is often taught as though the rabbinic interpretations were part and parcel of the text itself. The degree to which any writer makes that material her or his own varies widely. Similarly, the extent to which modern writers in various languages read one another's work in the original or in translation is also unpredictable.

In addition, some modern poetry, like some rabbinic midrash, is unambiguously polemical, arguing for a position in the battle for ownership of the biblical text. Further, as Robert Alter points out, modern, secularist explorations of the biblical text differ from traditional rabbinic exegesis: the moderns, unlike the rabbis, do not share "the ontological assumptions of the Bible."[18] Ḥ. N. Bialik and other Hebrew writers of the late nineteenth century ushered in what Alter refers to as an "age of multiple canonicities"[19] in which the traditional constraints on textual discussion no longer obtain.

Modern poetry also differs from the earlier strands of literature in its intended audience, its language, and the genre it exploits. Contemporary readers must grasp the meaning of words in modern poetry, along with the resonances and allusions they evoke. Modern poetry is read mostly by educated readers of the language. We come to poetry with a set of expectations about form, structure, rhyme, assonance, and figurative language. While a work's lack of transparency may challenge the reader, a set of familiar tools and techniques can make it comprehensible.

Reading Rabbinic Midrash

The Jewish midrashic tradition of biblical interpretation offers a wide range of ways to view a biblical text. Its view of the text has no need "to deny the pluriform character of the Hebrew Bible in favor of a uniform reading."[20] Rabbinic midrashic interpretations enable the reader to understand that the text has many potential readings. In order to comprehend how the rabbis approach the opening chapters of Genesis, one must consider that they saw it not merely as sacred, but as divine, a transcription of the words God spoke to Moses on Mount Sinai. They assumed that every written word had its purpose within the text beyond its rhetorical or syntactical function.[21] The divine nature of the text precluded the failings found in human discourse such as contradiction and repetition. Any element of the text that a modern reader might label a contradiction or repetition had to be explained in some other way.[22]

Moving from the relatively familiar world of modern poetry to rabbinic midrash multiplies the questions facing the reader. The two collections of *midrashim*[23] examined here represent different genres of midrash from separate historical periods. *Genesis Rabbah* is generally dated to the early fifth century in Palestine.[24] This exegetical collection links each midrash with the biblical verses in order. *Pirqei Rabbi Eliʿezer,* also known as *Pirkê de Rabbi Eliezer,* probably dates from eighth- or ninth-century Palestine.[25] *Pirqei Rabbi Eliʿezer* presents its material as a narrative, essentially retelling the biblical story.[26] Like *Genesis Rabbah, Pirqei Rabbi Eliʿezer* incorporates earlier material, some of which occurs elsewhere in rabbinic and other sources. Neither is reliably attributed to any known compiler, editor, or author.

While the roles of modern literary writing in our culture are familiar, the function of midrash is obscure. The collections we have were clearly developed over time but precious little is known about their composition. Current scholarly thinking suggests that *Genesis Rabbah*, like other similar compilations of *midrashim*, was intended not as biblical commentary or an aid to understanding the text, but as a handbook for preachers.[27] If that be so, it was a handbook for an elite, highly educated, male audience who instructed those who came to hear their sermons. The compilations were probably not intended to be widely read, but rather to serve as notes for longer sermons. Although women were sometimes present to hear the preaching based on these notes, they were excluded from the community in which they were developed.

Rabbinic Judaism developed in academies where the scholars who are cited in its literary sources studied and taught. As far as we know from the extant literature, no women were present. This absence of women would deprive their contemporaries and future readers of insights that women might have contributed.[28] In a womanless setting, a man never had to watch his tongue because his mother, sister, wife, or daughter might be drawn into the discourse. Groups of men conducted their deliberations and developed a series of texts often concerning the circumstances of women, describing them, and prescribing for them, but these texts were not intended for females.[29]

Midrash is often transmitted in the form of a discussion. Because learning took place in the context of dialogue or in a "multivocal dialectical structure,"[30] the modern reader presented with multiple perspectives on a particular text, or with different approaches to its understanding, may find unsettling the frequent lack of any clear outcome, tally of opinions, or resolution of apparently irreconcilable differences. The process is "primarily a religious rather than a literary"[31] mode of questioning assumptions and views with the expectation that the truth will somehow prevail. As the Talmud records in such a situation: *"eillu ve'eillu divrei Elohim ḥayyim,"* "both [opinions] are the words of the living God."[32]

The Judaism of late antiquity and the early medieval period—the world of rabbinic literature—seems strikingly distant from the religion of the Hebrew Bible. In the course of its evolution over time, Judaism, like other living religions, absorbed some of the social and philosophical views of the surrounding cultures. Thus, in the outlook and even in the vocabulary of these rabbinic texts, the impact of cultures of the Greek-speaking parts of the Roman Empire is perceptible.[33]

Eve figures prominently in the representative group of midrashic passages that I examine. Some are those often cited as misogynist; others present a more positive portrayal of Eve and of women in general. Although they often appear unequivocal, I give them the same attention to detail and language that I apply to the biblical and modern texts.

Reading Genesis 1–5

A large body of interpretation must have developed around any complex story that has been read and reread for thousands of years.[34] Eve's story is no exception. The biblical texts about Eve are few, clustered between Genesis 1:26 and 5:5. While I have translated the biblical text using current scholarly opinion as to the meaning of the words and the larger sense of the text, I have not delved into the ancient Near East parallels and precursors. This study concentrates on Eve's afterlife, not her gestation in literary or mythic antecedents. I treat the biblical text as a synchronic literary entity despite the acknowledged presence of contradictions and inconsistencies within it.[35] Indeed, these disparities contribute to the polysemy that makes these passages such a rich source for later rewriters, be they rabbinic or modern.

Modern biblical scholars have long resolved the major contradictions among these texts in Genesis by ascribing them to different sources or traditions that were brought together without harmonizing the inconsistencies among them. One salient feature of these sources, somewhat muted in translation, is that they do not refer to God with the same words. In the first and fifth chapters of Genesis, the predominant term for God is *Elohim,* considered a marker of the *P* or Priestly tradition, distinguished by an interest in genealogies and in being "heaven-centered."[36] The texts we have are the result of a long period of evolution within this tradition.[37] The passages in Genesis 2:4b–4:26 most likely derive from the *J* tradition, characterized by the use of the Hebrew word *YHWH* to refer to God and by its rich portrayal of humans, who often take center stage in *J* texts.[38]

The identification of various sources notwithstanding, the text we have is an amalgam, drawn from different traditions and pieced together in an artful and literary manner. Thus, for example, the framing of the lively narrative of creation and the experiences of the first humans coming from the putative J tradition with the majestic opening and dry genealogies of the probable P tradition produces a contrast in style that heightens the effect of these different sections. They were not interwoven in random fashion but reflect a high level of literary sensibility.

Other issues complicate our understanding of the biblical texts. In Hebrew every noun, pronoun, adjective, and verb is gendered, contributing to the ambiguity of this text. As Hebrew has only two genders, masculine and feminine, but no neuter, the noun representing the first human(s) is necessarily gendered. Either choice, masculine or feminine, would be open to question. It is also clear, however, that the "default position" of the biblical mind is male, even as the "default position" of the Hebrew language is masculine.[39]

The first context where this phenomenon is encountered concerns the grammatical gender of God. The nouns signifying God in the Hebrew Bible are overwhelmingly treated as masculine singular. Although metaphors portraying God with characteristics usually associated with women do occur,[40] the overall impression is that our texts generally portray God, although beyond gender or sex, as male.[41] Thus, although the theology implicit in the Bible, like the theology more clearly developed by the rabbis, does not assign God any human form, God's anthropomorphic and metaphoric representations are most often, though not exclusively, masculine. In this work every effort has been made to avoid gendering God, except in the biblical and rabbinic texts where God is perceived as having predominantly masculine characteristics.[42] Referring to God as "It" sounds awkward to me and does violence to the way in which the original writers and readers of the classical texts would have imagined the terms.

Ultimately the attempt to present an objective reading is doomed; the material cannot be stripped of accretions of previous readings. Neither can readers be forced to forget what they know of the text. As Robert Alter suggests, ancient Hebrew writers may have intended "to produce a certain indeterminacy of meaning, especially in regard to motive, moral character, and psychology."[43] Reuven Kimelman proposes that "given the frequent indeterminate nature of the Hebrew, its meaning is likely to be resolved on literary grounds rather than solely on grammatical or linguistic ones."[44] In providing new translations I have opened new interpretive possibilities for a series of texts that many readers believe they have long understood in the only manner possible. To encourage rethinking, I have retranslated.

Eve Studies

Interest in the figure of Eve is hardly a new phenomenon. The rabbis of late antiquity were involved in a pursuit that had developed long before the compilation of collections like *Genesis Rabbah*. Writers like Philo and books like the pseudepigraphic Book of Jubilees evince more than a passing curiosity about the first woman.[45] But concentration upon Eve among Jewish writers did not achieve the prominence it received in the Christian world. A simple explanation of this disparity may be found in Eve's place in Christian theology as the anti-Mary and in the Jewish interest in Abraham and Sarah, rather than Eve, as common ancestors.[46]

As for "Eve studies," the growth of interest in feminism and feminist scholarship since the late 1960s has produced a wide range of scholarly research that examines biblical characters, texts, themes, and structure from new perspectives. Eve has certainly benefited from that renewed interest and from other developments in biblical scholarship. Although in the second wave of feminism, Jewish feminists often initially looked at Eve disdainfully—reflecting their assumption that her purported predecessor Lilith better exemplified their values[47]—Eve is experiencing a revival of interest.

Feminist interpretations of Genesis are taking their place alongside more traditional Christian and Jewish commentaries. For example, in "Depatriarchalizing in Biblical Interpretation" (1976),[48] Phyllis Trible peels away some of the accretions that the biblical text of Genesis 1 and 2 has acquired over time and forces the reader to confront the text itself. In her essay "A Love Story Gone Awry,"[49] Trible goes further: she examines the texts through the eating of the fruit and offers an approach to Genesis that suggests alternatives to the prevalent notion that it projects—even prescribes—male primacy. Mieke Bal in *Lethal Love* (1987)[50] examines the development of Eve as a character and attacks Paul's reading of the texts as prescriptive. In her *Countertraditions in the Bible* (1992), Ilana Pardes examines precursor feminist readings and underscores the significance of Eve's naming speech (Genesis 4:1). By reading beyond the conventional Christian framework of the Eve story—creation, temptation, sin, and banishment—Pardes reveals some of Eve's power. *Eve and Adam: Jewish,*

Christian, and Muslim Readings on Genesis and Gender, edited by Kristen E. Kvam, Linda S. Schearing, and Valerie H. Ziegler, presents sources from the three major monotheistic religions with commentary, but includes only one twentieth-century poem.[51] Our work adds to its predecessors an examination of how later rewriters have uncovered multiple dimensions in Eve's story.

Two books in particular have been helpful in setting Eve in her time and place. In *Discovering Eve* (1988),[52] Carol Meyers situates women in ancient Israelite society. Using tools from archaeology and anthropology, she examines a range of biblical texts to uncover the many critical roles played by women. Tikva Frymer-Kensky's *In the Wake of the Goddesses: Women, Culture, and the Biblical Transformation of Pagan Myth* (1993)[53] discusses in detail ancient Near Eastern religions, and articulates the ways Israelite religion transformed the nature of earlier cults and supplanted their multiple gods and goddesses with a single God, Who alone was to be responsible for all divine functions. Frymer-Kensky examines the concomitant changes in the concept of "human" as portrayed in the opening chapters of Genesis. Both these books have provided much valuable context for my own biblical studies.

Eve studies extend beyond the Bible. In the field of midrash, two scholars who focus on Eve arrive at divergent conclusions. In *Carnal Israel: Reading Sex in Rabbinic Culture* (1993),[54] Daniel Boyarin analyzes rabbinic texts in order to explore sexuality in rabbinic culture. Within that context he carefully reads a number of midrashic passages that discuss Eve, concluding that while rabbinic culture was androcentric, it was not, with few exceptions, misogynist. Judith R. Baskin, on the other hand, asserts in *Midrashic Women: Formations of the Feminine in Rabbinic Literature* (2002)[55] that alterity is essential to the rabbinic conception of woman. Eve helps both Boyarin and Baskin understand the ways in which the rabbis construct gender.

Eve's role in modern literature is examined in Nehama Aschkenasy's *Eve's Journey: Feminine Images in Hebraic Literary Tradition* (1986)[56] and Pamela Norris's *Eve: A Biography* (1999).[57] They look seriously at the biblical Eve stories as a prelude to a discussion of the depiction of women in literature. Presenting all women as Eve's descendants, these books cut across Hebrew and English literatures, respectively, without regard for the extent to which a given author may have grappled with the biblical Eve. Unlike these two works, mine consistently focuses on imaginative religious and literary rewritings of Eve, explicating the ways understandings of gender and religion are informed by and influence the rewriting of Eve. In the works to be considered here Eve is identified by name, or by role as the first woman or as the companion of Adam, or as living in the Garden of Eden, or as mother of Cain and Abel.

Structure

Proceeding chronologically through Eve's biblical, midrashic, and modern texts, incorporating the scholarship on each in order, is not the route I have chosen. Each chapter focuses on a distinct phase of Eve's life: Creation, In the Garden, and Life in the Real World. What is exciting about this structure is precisely that the different writers and rewriters, biblical, midrashic, and modern, are brought into contact with one another, developing a conversation—or a confrontation—among the texts, creating "a transhistorical textual community."[58] Some would argue that the biblical text itself may not be narrated in chronological order—that is yet another question of interpretation—but it is the only order we have. Although rabbinic and modern rewriters often combine in one work incidents drawn from all parts of Eve's life, I have dealt with each work within one chapter.

Eternally?

The texts concerning Eve's creation are well known; her death, however, is unrecorded. This lacuna seems anomalous as we have records for the deaths, but not the births, of three of the four matriarchs; Rebecca's birth is recorded in the genealogy in Genesis 20:24. The matriarchs become significant when they are of marriageable age. Their most important function is assuring proper succession; having achieved that, they are mourned at their deaths. Eve's birth, like Adam's, is recorded because it signals a significance that extends beyond procreation to the establishment of gender roles, of culture, of civilization broadly construed. Adam's death is recorded as a link in the patriarchal genealogies (Genesis 5:5). Eve never dies, she slips away, leaving no mark except in the Western imagination where her story seems always to be with us, fascinating in its many facets and drawing the attention of generations of interpreters, scholars, and rewriters.

The three strands of literature examined in this study are linked by the significance of the biblical text. For later writers, rabbinic and modern, the story of the creation of humans as transmitted in the Hebrew Bible remains "a value-laden, imaginatively energizing body of texts."[59] They are fascinated and inspired by the biblical texts, which they engage in dialogue and revisit and reshape, acknowledging and honoring their central role in the construction of the human. This wealth of imaginative writing adds new layers of meaning, keeping the biblical text itself ever living.

Chapter One: The Creation of Woman

אמר ר' ירמיה בן לעזר בשעה שברא הקב"ה את אדם הראשון
אנדרוגינוס בראו שנ' זכר ונקבה בראם (בראשית ה ב), אמר ר'
שמואל בר נחמן בשעה שברא הקב"ה אדם הראשון דיפרוסופון
בראו וניסרו ועשאו גביים לכאן וגביים לכאן, מתיבין ליה והא כת'
ויקח אחת מצלעותיו (שם ב כא), אמר להם מן סטרוי היך מה דאת
אמר ולצלע המשכן וגו' (שמות כו כ).

R. Yirmeyah ben Le'azar said: "At the time when the Holy One,
blessed be He, created the first *adam*,[1] He created him an androgyne, as is said, 'Male and female He created them,' etc.
(Genesis 5:2)."[2]

R. Shemu'el bar Naḥman said: "At the time when the Holy
One, blessed be He, created the first *adam,* He created him
double-faced, then He sawed him apart and made him two backs,
a back on this side and a back on the other side."

To this they object: "But it is written, 'and He took one of
tsal'otav ['its sides,' usually translated as 'his ribs']' (Genesis 2:21)?"

He responded to them: "[*mitsal'otov* means one] of its sides, as
is written, 'And for the other side wall [*tsela'*] of the Tabernacle,'
etc. (Exodus 26:20)."[3]

This rabbinic midrash engages one of the biblical texts describing
the creation of humans in an attempt to resolve a troubling contradiction
presented in the biblical primeval history. How, it asks, was that ostensibly
single *adam* both male and female? R. Yirmeyah ben Le'azar suggests that
the first human was an androgyne, incorporating both male and female
genitalia; R. Shemu'el bar Naḥman conjectures that the *adam* was essentially conjoined twins, sharing a back. The passage next includes a brief
dialogue about the meaning of the Hebrew word *tsela'*, which by the rabbinic period had come to mean "rib," as well as "side," but, in the Hebrew
Bible, overwhelmingly means "side."[4]

Ostensibly we are reading a brief discussion of physiology, followed by one of philology. But lurking behind these questions is another one, one that had more relevance to life in the period of late antique Judaism: gender hierarchy. Is the first female part of the original creation of human? Is she subsidiary to the male or his equal?

Kim Chernin (1940–), a contemporary American Jewish writer, provides us with another way to frame the creation of woman. Chernin's writing includes essays, novels, and nonfiction, much of it exploring the situation of women from a psychological perspective.

The Call

Was I summoned?
Or did I rise
from my own emergency?
Dreaming of a dark and formless thing
5   that had no eyes
and fashioned mine.
Remembering:
waters, the disquieting wind
dark earth and dismembering fire:
10   A servile arc
that roared disquietude,
wakened from slumber;
and breath,
ribbed with mortality.[5]

Unlike the rabbis or the Bible, Chernin gives Eve voice, providing readers access to the first woman's musings on her own creation. In its first telling of the creation of the *adam* the Bible offers us God's thoughts on the creation of the *adam,* which includes the first woman, as well as on its purpose (Genesis 1:26–30). The second version of creation includes both God's thinking in advance of the creation of woman (Genesis 2:18) and the male's reaction to her creation (Genesis 2:23). Nowhere in the Bible, neither directly nor indirectly, do we hear the woman's thoughts on her coming into being. Questioning the circumstances of her own birth, her literal raison d'être, Chernin's Eve attempts to reach back into time, recalling the four elements—air, earth, fire, and water—to ask our universal human questions of origin. Here too, however, these are but pretext. The real issues concern agency and hierarchy. If she was "summoned," her birth was not self-directed but other-directed; the need she fills would not be her own but another's. On the other hand, if her own "emergency," her own crisis, or her own need to emerge, propelled her into life, then she is a creature of independent stature and value.

The Biblical Stories of the Creation of Woman

Our conventional Western familiarity with Eve's story often proves to be an obstacle to confronting the words of the Bible itself. Whether acquired in religious school or in a course on seventeenth-century English litera-ture, our readings have most likely blurred the line between text and inter-pretation. Thus, in the popular imagination, the creation of woman fol-lowed the creation of man. He was created out of the dust of the earth; she, out of the man's rib.[6] Her secondary, derivative status has been cited as a proof text to explain and justify the secondary status in which women often find themselves or to which they are often relegated. If, indeed, the prototypical first woman was an afterthought, not included in God's origi-nal plan for humanity, why would a woman be entitled to a status equal to that of a man?[7]

To begin understanding the texts that tell Eve's tale we must confront the words of the Bible, acknowledging that a careful reading of the three clusters of verses in Genesis describing the creation of the first woman—Genesis 1:26–27; 2:21–22; 5:1–2—may provide a greater sense of ambigu-ity than of clarity. While, as has been discussed,[8] Bible scholars generally account for these three versions and the disagreements among them by ascribing them to the P (Genesis 1–2:4a and 5) and J (Genesis 2:4b–4) documents or traditions, that is not the only suggestion for resolving the pronounced differences between the P and J versions.

Three other approaches to resolving these apparent contradictions are important in the interpretive history but less significant for our reading. The most traditional finds no contradiction at all. The second version simply fills in details of the first, essentially repeated in the third with minor changes in the order of the elements.[9] Edward L. Greenstein has effectively refuted the argument that the second telling merely completes the first. He sees the second as a "competing" account representing a "contrasting worldview."[10] With so many significant inconsistencies these stories obviously derive from different sources.

A second group of readers proposes that these contradictions, so apparent to the modern reader, were either imperceptible or not troubling to the Bible's original audience. We cannot evaluate this thesis, given our inability to get into the mind of any putative early listeners or readers. Similarly, we consider it dangerous to assume that apparent inconsistencies, which may not have seemed problematic at the time of the redaction of this text, result from poor editing.[11]

A third theory, currently enjoying something of a revival of interest, assumes two creations of two women, thus allowing for the existence of a first "first woman" and a second "first woman"—an approach reflected in the stories surrounding Lilith who was supposedly the first "first woman."[12] The invention of yet another figure, whose existence is not confirmed in the text, complicates rather than clarifies. The Lilith texts, all extrabiblical, constitute a separate body of work.

The first report of the creation of the first humans concludes the sequence of the six days of Creation. It follows the creation of animals and is, as Ilana Pardes claims, "primarily a poetic celebration of the special status of humanity as the climax of creation."[13]

כו א וַיֹּאמֶר אֱלֹהִים נַעֲשֶׂה אָדָם בְּצַלְמֵנוּ כִּדְמוּתֵנוּ וְיִרְדּוּ בִדְגַת הַיָּם
וּבְעוֹף הַשָּׁמַיִם וּבַבְּהֵמָה וּבְכָל־הָאָרֶץ וּבְכָל־הָרֶמֶשׂ הָרֹמֵשׂ עַל־הָאָרֶץ:
כז א וַיִּבְרָא אֱלֹהִים אֶת־הָאָדָם בְּצַלְמוֹ בְּצֶלֶם אֱלֹהִים בָּרָא אֹתוֹ זָכָר
וּנְקֵבָה בָּרָא אֹתָם:

1:26 God said: "Let us make an *adam* in our image, according to our likeness. They shall rule over the fish of the sea and the fowl of the heavens and the cattle and all the earth and all the crawling things that crawl on the earth."   1:27 And God created the *adam* in His [or "its"] image, in the image of God He created it, male and female He created them. (Genesis 1:26–27)

Even these verses themselves are replete with problems, particularly regarding the number and kind of creature or creatures created.

The second version of the creation of the first woman is the most specific and the most memorable.

כא ב וַיַּפֵּל יְ-הֹוָה אֱלֹהִים תַּרְדֵּמָה עַל־הָאָדָם וַיִּישָׁן וַיִּקַּח אַחַת מִצַּלְעֹתָיו
וַיִּסְגֹּר בָּשָׂר תַּחְתֶּנָּה: כב ב וַיִּבֶן יְ-הֹוָה אֱלֹהִים אֶת־הַצֵּלָע אֲשֶׁר־לָקַח
מִן־הָאָדָם לְאִשָּׁה וַיְבִאֶהָ אֶל־הָאָדָם:

2:21 Lord God caused a slumber to fall upon the *adam,* and it slept and He took one of *tsal'otav* [its sides, usually translated as "ribs"] and closed the flesh in that place.　2:22 And Lord God built the *tsela'* [side or rib] He had taken from the *adam* into an *ishah* [woman] and brought her to the *adam.* (Genesis 2:21–22)

Drawn from the second telling of Creation, which is considerably less orderly than the first, these two verses present the creation of woman with equal ambiguity. The major source of confusion is the meaning of the Hebrew word *tsela'*.

The third, somewhat summary account appears at the conclusion of the Creation stories, as prelude to the genealogy of the ten generations that span the period between the first humans and Noah.

ה 1 זֶה סֵפֶר תּוֹלְדֹת אָדָם בְּיוֹם בְּרֹא אֱלֹהִים אָדָם בִּדְמוּת אֱלֹהִים עָשָׂה אֹתוֹ: ה 2 זָכָר וּנְקֵבָה בְּרָאָם וַיְבָרֶךְ אֹתָם וַיִּקְרָא אֶת־שְׁמָם אָדָם בְּיוֹם הִבָּרְאָם:

5:1 This is the record of *adam*'s lineage: On the day God created *adam* in the likeness of God He made it [*oto*].　5:2 Male and female He created them and He blessed them and called their name *adam* on the day of their creation. (Genesis 5:1–2)

The language echoes the words of Genesis 1 with minor differences, the most salient being that the number confusion of the first story is more pronounced. The verses before us explicitly describe this new creation as plural, "male and female," before recording their naming with a term suggesting a single creature: *adam.*

Comparing the three texts clarifies that in the first and third versions, a single creature, an *adam,* is created, who moves from singular to plural, male and female. In the second, an *adam* is created and a woman is created from its side. Each text, however, even when read alone, remains subject to multiple interpretations. One could scarcely contrive a series of texts to demonstrate polysemy as well as the biblical story of the creation of humans.

Before examining the ambiguities and complexities of the stories of the first woman, let us consider the common qualities of the Eve stories. The creation of humankind is the only part of the sweeping Creation story where one may catch a glimpse of the divine thought-process; only here are we given the purpose of an act of creation that, going beyond itself and drawing together the previously created elements, delineates a hierarchy.[14] Further, regardless of whether the being created starts out as singular or plural, gendered or genderless, it clearly ends up plural and gendered.

Three linked but separable issues become lenses through which we can view the story of the creation of woman. They permit an understanding of those issues of gender hierarchy that the biblical Creation accounts raise and that rabbinic midrash and modern poetry pursue. Plurality is the first issue: Is the human product of God's initial creation one creature or two? A second concern is the substance of the woman: What is the source of the woman's real corporeal being? The final question posed: What is the purpose of woman's creation? The layering of these issues leads us ultimately to envision gender hierarchy as a critical theme underlying the stories of human creation.

Plurality

Number provides a useful approach to the polysemy of the biblical stories of the creation of the first woman. Is the *adam* initially one creature incorporating both male and female? Or one male creature? Or is it two separate creatures, one male and one female? The ramifications of this issue are considerable. If the first is a single male, then the female is clearly second. If, on the other hand, the *adam* is two from the moment its creation is contemplated, then the female is completely contemporaneous with the male. There is no simple answer.

HOW MANY GODS?

Complexity also blurs the identification of those responsible for the creation. The seamless slide from singular noun[15] to plural verb in the cases of both the divine and the human complicates our perception of the Creator and the created. The confusion of singular and plural regarding the Creator becomes the prelude to the confusion of singular and plural regarding the *adam,* created in the divine image. Did God create one creature or more than one? The noun *adam* denotes the singular in both meaning and form; yet the verbs and pronouns that refer to it are, for the most part, plural in these passages. In passages as carefully constructed as these there must be some purpose and meaning attached to the presumably deliberate grammatical contradictions.

The first account of the creation of the human includes the unusual use of a first-person plural verb and first-person plural possessive pronominal suffixes with reference to God. The very same divine statement constitutes the shift between singular and plural regarding the *adam.*

א 26 וַיֹּאמֶר אֱלֹהִים נַעֲשֶׂה אָדָם בְּצַלְמֵנוּ כִּדְמוּתֵנוּ וְיִרְדּוּ בִדְגַת הַיָּם
וּבְעוֹף הַשָּׁמַיִם וּבַבְּהֵמָה וּבְכָל־הָאָרֶץ וּבְכָל־הָרֶמֶשׂ הָרֹמֵשׂ עַל־הָאָרֶץ׃

1:26 God said: "Let us make an *adam* in our image, according to our likeness. They shall rule over the fish of the sea and the fowl of the heavens and the cattle and all the earth and all the crawling things that crawl on the earth." (Genesis 1:26)

The opening words of this verse, "God said," are those that introduce each new step in the story of Creation in Genesis 1. Their recurrence with formulaic regularity serves as a poetic anaphora linking the elements in this progression.[16] The verb "said" is singular. Until this point, a third-person hortatory verb consistently followed, for example, "Let there be light" (Genesis 1:3) or "Let the earth bring forth every kind of living creature" (Genesis 1:24). The first-person statement "Let us make . . ." breaks the pattern, signaling an imminent change.

The Creator, singular to this point, suddenly adopts a plural to relate the intention to create *adam,* but reverts to the singular when describing the act of creation itself. Insofar as this somewhat anomalous shift may indicate that others, besides the one God, were part of the divine realm, it undercuts the picture of absolute monotheism that the opening chapter of Genesis labors to establish. The conundrum is further complicated by the next words: "in our image, according to our likeness."[17] If the plural subject of the verb "let us make" does include other beings, they must occupy some middle ground, sharing an image and likeness with God, as well as with humans.

Although this is the only occasion in the *P* creation document where the plural is so used, it does recur at a critical juncture recorded by *J.* Having banished the *adam* from the Garden of Eden, God bars reentry, voicing the concern that the *adam* "has become like one of us, knowing good and bad" (Genesis 3:22). Structurally these matching uses of the plural at creation and expulsion frame the narrative of the first humans that precedes their entrance into the world east of Eden.

Several scholars have responded to this issue as exclusively syntactic. Surprisingly, E. A. Speiser summarily dismisses the issue. Translating the verse: "Then God said, 'I will make man in my image, after my likeness,'" he notes that the use of plural possessives in the Hebrew is a grammatical point here, "without a direct bearing on the meaning."[18] He indicates its connection to the word for God used here, *Elohim*, which is "plural in form." The two parallel texts he adduces, Genesis 20:13 and 35:7, have *Elohim* govern plural verbs, but they differ from our verse; in neither is God the speaker. Cassuto's assertion, which he admits is not widely accepted, that "we have here the plural of exhortation,"[19] is undercut by the absence of a parallel first-person plural hortatory verb referring to God elsewhere in the Hebrew Bible. Similarly, Trible proposes that the words constitute a "plural of deliberation."[20] But there is no indication of whether the deliberation was inner or included others.

Substantive explanations tend to draw upon non-Israelite ancient Near Eastern theology. As Tikva Frymer-Kensky cogently demonstrates in *In the Wake of the Goddesses: Women, Culture, and the Biblical Transformation of Pagan Myth*, the Israelite adoption of monotheism was not instantaneous. The prophets and Deuteronomy eventually "eliminat[ed] the heavenly court, . . . leaving only human beings and God."[21] Texts like Psalm 82 bear remnants of the belief in a tier of godlike beings, intermediaries between humans and the greatest gods in the ancient Near East pantheons.[22] The plural in Genesis 1:26, according to this school of readers, represents a remnant of an earlier period when such beings interposed between humanity and God were assumed to exist. The development of radical monotheism reduced this belief.

Sarna sets the scene in the context of a "heavenly court"; that is, "the Israelite version of the polytheistic assemblies of the pantheon— monotheized and depaganized."[23] Similarly, F. J. Stendebach, in his article on the word *tselem*, suggests that the plural here represents "a coalescence of God with his heavenly court." He counters the objection that the P traditions emphasize the uniqueness of God by making the "mythical source" with which P was working responsible for this deviation from P theology.[24]

Edward L. Greenstein sees in the *Elohim* powerful forces in the world who take pride in a "good" creation, pleasing to them, rather than one that is morally or absolutely good.[25] They are responsible for both the good in the world and the evil, as is evident in the story of the "divine beings" (literally, sons of *Elohim*) and the "daughters of man" (literally, daughters of the *adam*) in Genesis 6:2. This bold suggestion helps resolve the theological issue of evil emanating from a good God.

Stephen A. Geller proposes that the *P* texts as a whole represent a stage in the development of Israelite religion when there was significant residual resistance to the radical monotheism of the Deuteronomic texts.[26] These texts from Genesis 1 may also represent the remnant, embedded in this *P* text, of an Old Cult belief in a group of minor divinities, reflecting the ambivalence toward absolute monotheism.[27] W. Randall Garr carefully evaluates all the data regarding occurrences of *Elohim* meaning God as a plural noun and concludes that in the *J* texts it appears "only at times when the divine and human worlds meet" with the concomitant danger that humans will breach the human/divine barrier.[28] For Garr, the appearance of the divine plural in Genesis 1:26 (a *P* or Priestly document) is a conundrum because it is both unique and in opposition to the Priestly theology.[29] The solutions he proposes are either that it is unintentional or that it is the part of "*P*'s creation story that specifies the relationship between humanity and God."[30] In that sense it would be foundational to Israelite monotheism.

If, as Garr proposes, the divine plural is an artifact here in a *P* text, the question of its persistence remains open. The most startling aspect of this unexpected divine plural is that this relic of an ancient Near Eastern worldview surfaces at this particular moment in the narrative rather than in the overwhelming number of occasions, both here and elsewhere, when God refers to God's self in the singular. One can see this usage as a redactional choice that parallels the appearance of *Elohim* referring to God at points of human/divine contact. Surely this moment of the divine creation of the human brings them into intimate contact. More specifically, the unidentified creatures included in the plural pronouns clearly share an image and likeness with God, Who is now proposing expanding the group to include humans. Are they designed to replace or to rival the divine court traditionally seen as God's "partners" in this verb and these pronouns? The sudden intrusion of the plural may signal the heavenly court's collusion in its own displacement. As a literary device the placement of this jarring plural after the introduction: "And God said," enables us to infer the tone of this statement. In all the previous acts of creation we have found in this syntactical location a third-person hortatory form of the verb. The syntax here precludes seeing God's proposal as a question open for real discussion.[31] Its purpose is

rather to inform the "inner circle" of the next step. The parallel occurrence of the plural at the end of the Garden story (Genesis 3:22) indicates that just as the humans are to be walled out of the Garden, so are
the *Elohim* to be walled in. When they breach the wall, as recorded in
Genesis 6:4, the consequences are dire.

Understanding the significance of this intentional plural referring to
God, which comes laden with ambiguity, will help us understand the parallel shift from singular to plural in the verses that refer to the creation of
humans. They remind us that the one God will assume all the many roles
previously filled by these mediating figures. In moving our focus to humans, we are mindful that they, too, are both diverse and singular.

HOW MANY HUMANS?

Although the word *adam* conforms to everything expected of a masculine
singular Hebrew noun, it generally functions like a plural in these verses.
Every verb it governs before and after its creation is plural, from the first
in God's planning stage to the last in the blessing.[32] The pronouns that
refer to *adam* shift from singular (*oto*, him/it) in the middle of Genesis 1:27
to plural (*otam*, them; *lahem*, to them; *lakhem*, to you [pl.]) at the end of
that verse and in the subsequent two verses. The nearly consistent use of
the plural referring to the *adam* in these verses presents a strong argument
for a plural creation.

Number confusion regarding the *adam* is most apparent in the poetic,
triple verse (Genesis 1:27) that describes the actual creation:

כז וַיִּבְרָא אֱלֹהִים אֶת־הָאָדָם בְּצַלְמוֹ בְּצֶלֶם אֱלֹהִים בָּרָא אֹתוֹ זָכָר א
וּנְקֵבָה בָּרָא אֹתָם:

> 1:27 And God created the *adam* in His image,
> in the image of God He created it,
> male and female He created them.

Here we see the problem in almost algebraic elegance. At its simplest, it
contains three parallel declarative statements:

God	created	*adam*
God	created	it
God	created	them

24

Thus, *adam* = it = them. The singular "it," or, as usually translated, "him," becomes the equivalent of the plural "them." How are we to understand this anomaly?

The third clause of the verse forcefully confronts us with the question of number that was present in the previous verse where God, too, seems to be plural. If God's stated intention is to create an *adam* and a single *adam* is created, how does it become plural?[33] As Cassuto points out, it does not suffice to say that the *adam* was a hermaphrodite with male and female facets: the pronoun *otam* is distinctly plural and a hermaphrodite is necessarily singular.[34] This verse is generally read as a complicated report of a single act of creation; as such it is hopelessly, perhaps even dizzyingly,[35] ambiguous.

One approach would have *adam* serve as a collective noun. In his detailed article on *adam* in the Hebrew Bible, Fritz Maass indicates that the word "predominantly occurs as a collective singular designating a class (as 'man' in English),[36] and therefore can be translated by 'mankind' or as a plural 'men.'"[37] In his annotations to these verses, Jon D. Levenson further suggests that the account of the creation of humans in Genesis 1 "seems to speak of groups of men and women created simultaneously."[38] This reading also resolves the conundrum of humans who are apparently not among the descendants of Adam and Eve and become the wives of their descendants.

Although Maass does not comment on the use of plural pronouns or verbs with the noun, he does point out that the word itself never appears in the plural form. As Robert Alter puts it, *adam*, after Genesis 1:27 "consistently with a definite article, which is used both here and in the second account of the origins of humankind, is a generic term for human beings, not a proper noun."[39] This schema allows no role for primacy in hierarchy because no primacy would occur where the species *adam* is created at once as a collective.

Another possibility is that the *adam*, while created singular, became plural shortly after its creation, before it/they started to act. The plurality, inherent in the original *adam*, would have come into being only later and the woman would have been part of the original creation.

Before looking at the different portrayal of the creation of woman in Genesis 2, we turn to the set of verses at the opening of Genesis 5 that presents language, themes, and provenance similar to those in Genesis 1, although less poetically stated.

ה 1 זֶה סֵפֶר תּוֹלְדֹת אָדָם בְּיוֹם בְּרֹא אֱלֹהִים אָדָם בִּדְמוּת אֱלֹהִים
עָשָׂה אֹתוֹ: ה 2 זָכָר וּנְקֵבָה בְּרָאָם וַיְבָרֶךְ אֹתָם וַיִּקְרָא אֶת־שְׁמָם אָדָם
בְּיוֹם הִבָּרְאָם:

5:1 This is the record of *adam*'s lineage: On the day God created
adam in the likeness of God He made it.   5:2 Male and female
He created them and He blessed them and called their name
adam on the day of their creation. (Genesis 5:1–2)

Considered in their location in the Genesis narratives, these verses are piv-
otal, both summarizing the tale of the creation of humanity as told in the
first P version in chapter 1 and introducing the genealogy that follows.[40] Here
the text presents no image of a potentially plural God, but does retain the
ambiguity regarding the number of the created. As in the first telling of the
story, the singular noun *adam* is the antecedent initially of a singular pronoun (*oto*, him/it) and, in the following verse, of a plural pronoun (*otam*,
them). Along with the plural number comes gender: male and female.

The introduction of a sense of time is one element clearly distinguish-
ing these verses from those in Genesis 1. Translating *beyom* in Genesis 5:1
and 5:2 literally as "on the day," rather than following the NJPS "when,"
allows more room for interpretation while introducing an emphasis on
time that is handled differently in Genesis 1. The schema of creation divided into six days of work and one of rest—each labeled a *yom* (day)—
that undergirds Genesis 1 makes it clear that the creation of the *adam* is
but one of the acts of the sixth day. Genesis 5 brackets the story of the
creation of humans with the element of time as if to emphasize the exceptional character of this act of creation, producing a single *adam* that
becomes plural, male and female.

This précis of the P creation narrative in Genesis 1 has two features
linked to Eve's story that are worthy of note. The focus of creation has
become the humans; there is no room for the creation of anything else in
this introduction to the human-centered genealogies. God both blesses
the plural male and female creatures and formally names them *adam*.
Here *adam* seems to have become humanity, male and female. Further,
God's blessing of all humanity, male and female, is repeated here without
the specific details of dominion it carried in Genesis 1:28.

The issue of time, so well defined in Genesis 1 and 5, is significant in its
absence from Genesis 2. Naturally, reading it against the template of the

days of creation in Genesis 1, we may fail to recognize that Genesis 2 provides only a sense of sequence and no sense of time limits. Reading Genesis 2:4b–24 as an independent unit would allow no basis for determining whether the creation of the *adam* in 2:7 immediately preceded the creation of woman in 2:21–22 or whether the actions narrated in the intervening verses took hours, days, or years.

A consequence of the indeterminacy of time in Genesis 2, so different from the time frames of Genesis 1 and 5, is the indeterminacy of number. This *J* text presents us with a singular *adam*. Whether this *adam* becomes plural only with the separate, presumably later, creation of the woman in Genesis 2:22, or whether the *adam* incorporated the woman from the outset, is connected to the reader's sense of how much time has elapsed between verses 7 and 22. This distinction has major implications for our discussion of the creation of woman. So strong is the disparity between the narratives of the creation of humans in Genesis 1 and 5, on the one hand, and in Genesis 2, on the other, that one might conclude we are witness to an ancient argument that no mere human editor dares reconcile.

While leaving a fuller discussion of Genesis 2 for later, we have discovered that no unambiguous answer can be found to the ostensibly simple question: "Was the *adam* singular or plural?" A close reading of the versions of the story in Genesis 1 and 5 leaves us with the question unanswered and unanswerable. What we read into that answer will affect our readings of all subsequent texts bearing on the first man and woman.

Long before the advent of modernity and the concomitant critical approach to sacred texts, careful readers noticed the contradiction inherent in the verses from Genesis 1 and 5.[41] At least as far back as *Genesis Rabbah*, in statements ascribed to two third-century Palestinian *amora'im,* R. Yirmeyah ben Le'azar and R. Shemu'el bar Naḥman, the possibility of the simultaneous creation of the first man and woman, of a first man/woman, is raised.[42]

אמר ר' ירמיה בן לעזר בשעה שברא הקב"ה את אדם הראשון
אנדרוגינס בראו שנ' זכר ונקבה בראם (בראשית ה ב), אמר ר'
שמואל בר נחמן בשעה שברא הקב"ה אדם הראשון דיפרוסופון
בראו וניסרו ועשאו גביים לכאן וגביים לכאן, מתיבין ליה והא כת'
ויקח אחת מצלעותיו (שם ב כא), אמר להם מן סטרוי היך מה דאת
אמר ולצלע המשכן וגו' (שמות כו כ).

R. Yirmeyah ben Le'azar said: "At the time when the Holy One, blessed be He, created the first *adam,* He created him an androgyne, as is said, 'Male and female He created them,' etc. (Genesis 5:2)."

R. Shemu'el bar Naḥman said: "At the time when the Holy One, blessed be He, created the first *adam,* He created him double-faced, then He sawed him apart and made him two backs, a back on this side and a back on the other side."

To this they object: "But it is written, 'and He took one of *tsal'otav* [its sides, usually translated as 'his ribs']' (Genesis 2:21)?"

He responded to them: "[*mitsal'otov* means] one of its sides, as is written, 'And for the other side wall [*tsela'*] of the Tabernacle,' etc. (Exodus 26:20)."[43]

Nor does this explanation exist in only one source. Part of the Jewish imagination for centuries, it also occurs at least twice in the Babylonian Talmud and in The Fathers According to Rabbi Nathan, probably from the same period.[44]

This midrash in *Genesis Rabbah* provides two slightly different models for a singular creation of the human that became plural. Each statement contains the possibility of primal androgyny, implying that the created *adam* was a single creature and allowing for woman as part of the divine plan from its inception, not as an afterthought.

Although R. Yirmeyah ben Le'azar's version is not specific enough for us to visualize it in detail, the sage seems to imagine a hermaphrodite, a person created with both male and female genitalia.[45] That he does not specify how that creature would become two, if it is originally a single creature, does not detract from the necessary, logical conclusion: No subsequent primacy can be said to exist between male and female; any hierarchy implicit in primacy is precluded. The very absence of a description of separation emphasizes the simultaneity of the creation of "male and female."

R. Yirmeyah ben Le'azar's choice of proof text is not without significance. He uses Genesis 5:2, which, when standing alone, contains no reference to the creation of a single creature, only to the plural. In other words, taken out of its context, this verse would indicate the creation of two creatures, male and female. But verse divisions are not significant enough to dictate this choice. R. Yirmeyah ben Le'azar would not have seen 5:2 in isolation; he knew that the verses in the Genesis 1 story contain every element he wanted to include in his proof text. Might he have made his odd choice based on context? Genesis 1 describes origins; Genesis 5, with its genealogies, looks to the future.[46] To this relatively terse, forward-looking summary these rabbis have affixed their comments.

The language of the midrash does not indicate whether R. Shemu'el bar Naḥman's view constitutes elaboration or dissent. His comment, presented in greater detail, implies the equal, simultaneous creation of conjoined twins, connected at the back, allowing their sexual differentiation to be apparent; the front of each would face out. At the same time, God would be able to separate them by creating the same missing feature, a full back, for each of them.[47] But it does not state, for example, that God removed one side that became a woman, possibly implying that the initial creature was essentially male. In this passage, neither male nor female is "finished" before the other.

When R. Shemu'el bar Naḥman is challenged by the anonymous citation of Genesis 2:21, the verse most easily read to render woman secondary by positing the earlier creation of a single male *adam,* he retorts that the woman was created from a side, not a rib, drawing on the usage in Exodus 26:20 with regard to the Tabernacle. As the Tabernacle was a building with different parts, so was the original *adam* a single creature with different parts.[48]

To make his bold statement, R. Shemu'el bar Naḥman must ignore some elements of the second Creation story. His view renders somewhat improbable the scene in which God declares that it is not good for the *adam* to be alone (Genesis 2:18). If woman was incorporated in the primal human, why would God pause to consider her creation? Surprisingly, no such objection is proffered to either R. Shemu'el bar Naḥman's hypothesis or R. Yirmeyah ben Le'azar's original premise. The inclusion of these unchallenged suggestions in *Genesis Rabbah* and other rabbinic collections indicates that the midrashic tradition was elastic enough to entertain the possibility of the simultaneous creation of woman and man.

Modern scholars have attempted fully to explicate these rabbinic retellings. Judith R. Baskin sees in this text a "vision of a primal androgyne, which imagines human male and female sexual characteristics as originating in one simultaneous creation, [in which] the primary being [is] still constructed as male. Only afterwards, as R. Samuel b. Naḥmani elaborates, did God separate the female 'side' from the male entity to create a new and independent being."[49] This reading is problematic, as both these descriptions present the creation of woman and man as simultaneous, not sequential. The similar midrash appearing in B. Berakhot better supports Baskin's thesis; it goes on to discuss the ambulation of this two-fronted creature, concluding that the male face must lead.[50]

The question of how this doubly faced creature might function has also exercised twentieth-century philosophers. Emmanuel Levinas couches the question in terms of the balance of power within a couple. Taking as text for a lecture on the Talmud the long aggadic section in B. Berakhot 61a that includes this passage, he states that a truly equal relationship between man and woman is untenable. Declaring true equality so dysfunctional it would probably lead to war, Levinas arrives at much the same conclusion as do the rabbis, assuming male dominance without so much as a nod to any possibility that the female might be in charge.[51]

Baskin emphasizes the way in which this midrash melds the two versions of the creation of the *adam,* concluding: "In these interpretations, both biblical versions of human creation are accounted for, while any possibility of imagining an initial female creation separate from the original man is obviated. The idea of an essentially male being with male and female characteristics is as close as the rabbis will come to acknowledging the simultaneous and co-equal creation of man and woman described in Genesis 1:26, and even this view is a decidedly minority opinion."[52] Baskin claims that the rabbis could not conceive of "an initial female creature." The androcentricity of both their worldview and the Hebrew language precludes their doing so. Because masculine is the "default position" of Hebrew, they have no space for considering that possibility, unlikely as they might have been to adopt it. If one sex comes first, it must be the male. But Baskin's assertion that male primacy in creation is the dominant view among the rabbis ultimately cannot be demonstrated.[53] Daniel Boyarin, who in *Carnal Israel* had argued that simultaneous creation was "the more common rabbinic view," explicitly corrects that "methodological error" in his *Unheroic Conduct: The Rise of Heterosexuality and the Invention of the Jewish Man.* He maintains that it is impossible to determine which rabbinic ideology is dominant, which subordinate.[54] It is impossible definitively to assess what opinions a minority or a majority of the rabbis held. The records we have are clearly fragmentary. Where Baskin sees misogyny, Burton L. Visotzky sees the rabbis "coming down now on one side, now on the other, to create a wholly balanced anthropology."[55] What can be stated with some degree of certainty is that the rabbis whose views have survived were more attached to the second Creation story with its rib or side than to the first or the third.

Most modern poetic rewriters of the creation of Eve also take as their basic text the "rib" version of the story. It provides a measure of graphic detail absent from the first, but at the cost of possibly implying that the creation of Eve was second and therefore secondary. As we have seen, Kim Chernin's "The Call" takes an altogether different approach. Her focus is entirely on the woman whose thoughts she records as though she is articulating them upon first finding herself in the world.

The Call

Was I summoned?
Or did I rise
from my own emergency?
Dreaming of a dark and formless thing
5   that had no eyes
and fashioned mine.
Remembering:
waters, the disquieting wind
dark earth and dismembering fire:
10   A servile arc
that roared disquietude,
wakened from slumber;
and breath,
ribbed with mortality.[56]

The only reference to the Deity describes God as a clearly singular "dark and formless thing / that had no eyes / and fashioned mine." No *adam* is explicitly mentioned. Despite the allusive use of "ribbed," the poem, in contrast to the biblical text, is completely gynocentric, focusing only on the woman, with no implication that anything or anyone else might also have emerged into life. In fact, were it not for its placement in the cycle "The Uncertainty of Eve," this poem would not necessarily be read as part of the story of the first woman. Once the connection to Eve is established, however, allusions to the biblical text become apparent. The "dark and formless thing," for example, while a reference to God, reminds the reader of *tohu vavohu*, the "unformed and void" state of the world preceding the initial acts of creation. Further, the memory of water, wind, and earth—though not of fire—also recalls the precreation state of the world (Genesis 1:2).[57]

Proleptically emphasizing her eyes as the only part of the woman's physical body specifically mentioned in the poem, while noting the absence of eyes in "the dark and formless thing," Chernin has her Eve allude to the conversation between the first woman and the serpent—a conversation in which sight plays a significant role. Finally, the closing lines refer both to the Creation story in Genesis 2 and to the threatened punishment for eating of the Tree of Knowledge. The penultimate line, "and breath," the shortest line in the poem, refers to God's creating the *adam* from both the "dust of the earth" and the "breath of life" (Genesis 2:7). Setting those words in a separate line makes the point that the woman partakes of the divine breath of life, often connected with the soul.

That "breath of life" is, however, not presented as eternal in Chernin's poem; it is "ribbed in mortality." In this final line Chernin forcefully brings closure to the poem. The underlying image of the lung as the locus of breath, under the ribs, evokes a physical image more concrete than the amorphous imagery of the rest of the poem. At the same time it recalls the "rib version" of Eve's creation (Genesis 2:21–22). The last word of the poem, "mortality," brings the poem, which opens with Eve's creation, to its end. In so doing, Chernin echoes those who argue that the death God threatened in the admonition not to eat of the Tree of Knowledge (Genesis 2:17) was not the specific death of the transgressor, but death itself. For Chernin's readers, the graphic image of the woman's life force caged or limited by mortality encapsulates Eve's story.

The contemporary American Jewish literary scholar, midrashist, and poet, Alicia Suskin Ostriker (1937–), having made her mark in the field of English literature, has gone on to become an award-winning poet who also writes modern midrash. Her "In the Beginning the Being,"[58] in addressing all of creation, not merely the creation of man and woman, takes yet another route. From the title on, the poem sets its own agenda. Referring to God as the Being, Ostriker degenders our usual God language, while remaining faithful to the connection between God's sacred name *YHWH* and the Hebrew verb "to be," *h.y.y.*[59] The Being, distinctly singular and always capitalized, is never designated by a pronoun. No divine council precedes the creation of humans. Ostriker's presentation is straightforward and concise.

35 The Being created the world   without
Language   without pronoun   then
The Being created man and woman
In the image
The distant image
40 Of itself
And blessed them.

Throughout her poem Ostriker uses gaps within lines as a visual reminder of God's separating things to make order out of chaos in the early
stages of creation. The gap in line 35 sets the word "without" apart, giving it additional weight. As one reads sequentially the "world without"
seems to be implicitly juxtaposed to the "world within." Continuing to
read, one quickly locates "language," the object of the preposition, in
the next line. "Language without pronoun" would then be another creation of the Being, with the clear implication that pronouns, which often
gender a text, are not part of the divine plan, despite their presence in
the biblical text.

Although many lines exemplify, through the gaps within them, creation by differentiation,[60] the creation of humans does not. The dramatic
effect of God's deliberation in the biblical text is captured in the one word
"then," hanging at the end of the previous line (36). Ostriker's version of
the creation of humans is plural and simultaneous, captured in one verb,
followed by two separate nouns. It is striking that such an unabashedly
feminist poet, who is ready to take liberties with the biblical text, does not
put woman before man. Might the conventions be too strong for her to
flout hierarchy altogether?

The importance of the divine aspect of the humans is underscored by
the repetition of "image." Its reiteration is in italics, which emphasizes its
significance, but the insertion of "distant" (39) leaves the reader wondering about the distance between the human and the divine realms. In any
case, both the man and the woman share that precious aspect, implying
that they are created separately and simultaneously.

As we follow Eve's course, the ambiguous issue of number becomes paramount. It will bear on a host of questions including the order of creation, the divine plan in creating humans, and whether or not the woman

heard the divine command not to eat the fruit of the Tree of Knowledge directly from God. It will shape our thinking about the relations among the three different biblical versions of the story of the creation of humanity. At the same time, it helps shape the way we see gender hierarchy in our contemporary world.

The Form and Substance of the First Woman

Having considered the vexing question of the plurality of the *adam* and whether the male and female were simultaneously or sequentially created, we turn to the form and substance of the first woman. What was her relationship to the divine likeness? From what material was she shaped? We are, again, dealing with the issue of hierarchy, albeit from a somewhat different perspective.

IMAGE AND LIKENESS

Since the *adam* may include the woman as well as the man, the first task is to analyze the form of the *adam* in relation to the Creator's opening words in Genesis 1:26–28. God initially proposes making the creature "in our image [*tselem*] according to our likeness [*demut*]" (Genesis 1:26). This brief description stands out in the spare narratives of Genesis 1 and 5.[61] Visotzky astutely observes that the very comparison to God or to God and the divine entourage explains anthropology through theology. Most texts choose the opposite route, explaining God in human terms.[62]

As the story of the creation of the *adam* unfolds, *tselem* appears twice and *demut* is omitted (Genesis 1:27). While neither word appears in the second account in Genesis 2, *demut* alone does reappear in the opening verses of the genealogy that closes the narrative of the primal family (Genesis 5:1).[63] Both F. J. Stendebach and H. D. Preuss, in their respective articles on *tselem* and *demut* in the *Theological Dictionary of the Old Testament,* see the terms as close in meaning.[64] Helen Schüngel-Straumann suggests that both words are used, despite their similarity, because no single word adequately conveys the nature of the human[65]—but if both words are needed, why does one or the other occasionally suffice?

Several groups of texts that include *tselem* and/or *demut* relate to the creation of the *adam*. God first proposes the creation of the human and immediately creates it in a pair of verses. (Genesis 1:26–27)[66]

א 26 וַיֹּאמֶר אֱלֹהִים נַעֲשֶׂה אָדָם בְּצַלְמֵנוּ כִּדְמוּתֵנוּ וְיִרְדּוּ בִדְגַת הַיָּם
וּבְעוֹף הַשָּׁמַיִם וּבַבְּהֵמָה וּבְכָל־הָאָרֶץ וּבְכָל־הָרֶמֶשׂ הָרֹמֵשׂ עַל־הָאָרֶץ:
א 27 וַיִּבְרָא אֱלֹהִים אֶת־הָאָדָם בְּצַלְמוֹ בְּצֶלֶם אֱלֹהִים בָּרָא אֹתוֹ זָכָר
וּנְקֵבָה בָּרָא אֹתָם:

1:26 God said: "Let us make an *adam* in our image, according to
our likeness. They shall rule over the fish of the sea and the fowl
of the heavens and the cattle and all the earth and all the crawling
things that crawl on the earth."
    1:27 And God created the *adam* in His image,
        in the image of God He created it,
        male and female He created them.

As has been discussed, the object of God's address in Genesis 1:26 is not
clear; it is clear, however, that they (or it?) share both image and likeness
with God.

Genesis 1:27 poetically records the actual creation of the *adam*. The
twelve Hebrew words,[67] using only seven roots,[68] are divided into three
clauses of four words, each with a form of the root *b.r.'* as its main verb.
This emphasis on this act of creation is unparalleled in Genesis. While Cassuto argues that "[t]he poetic structure of the sentence, its stately diction
and its particular emotional quality attest the special importance that the
Torah attributes to the making of man—the noblest of the creatures,"[69] the
text falls short of ascribing supreme nobility to the *adam*. The majestic progression of these clauses dramatically slows the action and allows the
reader to ponder what we are told and are not told in each of them. The
first emphasizes the similarity between God and the *adam*. The second
clause unambiguously states that the single human is created in the image
of God. The third both clarifies by providing the new information regarding gender and obfuscates by using the plural pronoun as the direct object.[70]

Most interpreters see these three clauses as parallel. For example, citing Mesopotamian and Egyptian sources where the king is compared to a
god using terms parallel to one or both of these Hebrew words, Nahum
M. Sarna suggests that the use of these terms is designed to bestow upon
every human the qualities that in most other contemporary cultures are
the special prerogative of royalty.[71] As a corollary, Sarna points out, humans become the symbols and witnesses of God's involvement in the

world.[72] Bird claims that "the notion of the divine image serves here to validate and explain the special role of *adam* among the creatures."[73] Cassuto argues even more explicitly that these three clauses function in parallel to emphasize three different aspects of the creation of the first human: "The first line speaks, in general terms, of man's *creation;* the second draws attention to the fact that he was created in the *Divine image;* the third notes the creation of *two sexes.*"[74]

These verses also sustain an alternate reading, one that, seeing these clauses as sequential rather than parallel, locates them within the larger schema of creation. The first two clauses together constitute a two-stage creation of the human. The first step is to create the human in the human image.[75] Grammatically speaking, the word *betsalmo,* "in its image," could mean that the *adam* was created either in the image of God, as it is conventionally read, or in the image of the *adam,* that is, in the image appropriate for a human.[76] The latter reading assumes that the antecedent of "its" in *tsalmo* (its image) in Genesis 1:27 is not God, but "the *adam.*" Immediately following that necessary first step, which indicates that a fundamental human core inheres in the *adam,* comes the second, the provision of a divine aspect, or "image of God."[77] The *adam* once complete, incorporating both human and divine elements, is ready for the final step, the creation of two distinct sexes by separating the *adam* into two parts, hence the plural pronoun.

This understanding of Genesis 1:27 implies a parallel to the two-stage creation of the *adam* in Genesis 2. There the *adam* is initially created of two elements: *'afar min ha'adamah* (dust of the earth) and *nishmat hayyim* (the breath of life) (Genesis 2:7). These parallel respectively *tsalmo* (the image of the *adam*) and *tselem Elohim* (the image of God) in Genesis 1. The *adam* subsequently becomes two gendered entities (Genesis 2:21–22).

The account of the creation of humans is a separable microcosm, following the paradigmatic pattern of creation through separation. As Fishbane clearly indicates, creation overall in Genesis 1 is a two-stage process: "The first three days present the creation in its generalities, and the second three present those of its features which specifically impinge upon the human habitat."[78] Each element created in the last three days is connected by location or by source to something created in the first three.[79] This neat schema does not, however, account for the special nature of the creation of humankind. Taking Genesis 1:27 out of the general schema, to which it does not conform, enables us to see in it the elements of a larger, three-stage creation process. First, we have the two-part creation of the general: the *adam,* undifferentiated regarding gender. That *adam* becomes through division the source of male and female. This division makes possible God's plan to have the humans populate, regulate, and care for the rest of creation.

Much the same pattern of division is observable in the summary of creation in Genesis 5 that precedes the genealogy.

ה 1 זֶה סֵפֶר תּוֹלְדֹת אָדָם בְּיוֹם בְּרֹא אֱלֹהִים אָדָם בִּדְמוּת אֱלֹהִים עָשָׂה אֹתוֹ: ה 2 זָכָר וּנְקֵבָה בְּרָאָם וַיְבָרֶךְ אֹתָם וַיִּקְרָא אֶת־שְׁמָם אָדָם בְּיוֹם הִבָּרְאָם:

5:1 This is the record of *adam*'s lineage: On the day God created *adam* in the likeness of God He made it.   5:2 Male and female He created them and He blessed them and called their name *adam* on the day of their creation. (Genesis 5:1–2)

After the introductory phrase, we learn that *adam* resembled God. Here the sole element of the phrase "image and likeness" is "likeness." There is no room for the detailed and repetitious language of Genesis 1 in this terse account.[80]

The shift of pronouns referring to the singular *adam* from singular to plural is also reminiscent of the same phenomenon in Genesis 1. The plural again follows the notion of male and female, indicating that a division has taken place — or, perhaps, that the plurality of the human is to be seen in regard to sexual function.

MALE AND FEMALE

Whatever the *adam* is intended to be, it is clearly not exclusively male. As a signifier, *adam* has all the attributes of a Hebrew masculine singular noun, but that alone does not render the signified male, particularly in a language with no neuter. To cite Robert Alter, *adam* "does not automatically suggest maleness, especially, but not without the traditional prefix *ben,* 'son of,' and so the traditional rendering 'man' is misleading, and an exclusively male *adam* would make nonsense of the last clause of verse 27."[81] The meaning of *adam* here includes "female" as surely as it includes "male."

The same phenomenon is most clearly apparent in the summary verses preceding the genealogy in Genesis 5. Although one might assume that *adam* is here a masculine singular proper noun[82] because in the first two verses the noun *adam* appears three times, never with the definite article,[83] it is described as "male and female" and referred to by plural pronouns four times, all in Genesis 5:2. The naming formula—"and He called X name Y"[84]—is clear; however, it is not the singular *adam* who is being named here but the plural one. Cassuto sees God functioning here like a human parent because this naming parallels the human naming speeches where one of the parents gives the name.[85] In Genesis 5:1–2, the word *adam* moves seamlessly from androgyny to masculinity, from generic signifier to proper noun.[86]

The phrase "male and female" may easily be construed as a standard binary polarity. Male and female are on opposite sides.[87] Opposing the view that the *adam* is initially of dual sexuality, R. E. Clements sees the phrase as an indication that "the two sexes together form the species."[88] Thus the two words together include all of humanity with no indication of any hierarchical relationship between them. Male precedes female in the verse, but that is without significance in terms of their relative power or importance.

RAW MATERIAL

One feature that distinguishes the second or *J* version in Genesis 2 is its sheer physicality.[89] In order to see the creation of the woman in context we must first turn to the creation of the *adam* from which she was taken. In this regard, the *J* version differs greatly from the *P* version, which contains no indication of what raw material, if any, may have been used in the creation of the *adam* or of what part of the world was the place of the *adam*'s creation. The God Who opens the sixth day by declaring: "Let the earth bring forth every kind of living creature, cattle, creeping things, and wild beasts of every kind" (Genesis 1:24), indicates no source for the human. The *adam* of Genesis 1 seems almost an abstraction embedded among the products of the land, sea, and sky.

Genesis 2, in contrast, turns our attention sharply to the concrete:

ב 7 וַיִּיצֶר יְ-הֹוָה אֱלֹהִים אֶת־הָאָדָם עָפָר מִן־הָאֲדָמָה וַיִּפַּח בְּאַפָּיו
נִשְׁמַת חַיִּים וַיְהִי הָאָדָם לְנֶפֶשׁ חַיָּה:

2:7 The Lord God formed the *adam* from the dust of the earth [*adamah*]. He blew into its nostrils the breath of life, and the *adam* became a living being. (Genesis 2:7)

As we have seen, the text is quite explicit in regard to the way the *adam* is formed. Differentiating the *adam* from the *adamah,* much as God had separated components of the universe in order to create in Genesis 1,[90] God combines two disparate elements: "dust from the earth [*adamah*]" and the "breath of life" into "a living being." The tactile metaphor of God as potter, shaping the dust moistened by the flow of groundwater, differs markedly from the God Who creates by fiat in P.[91]

The very word *adam* links this new creature with the *adamah.* As Speiser indicates, biblical "names were regarded not only as labels but also as symbols, magical keys as it were to the nature and essence of the given being or thing (cf. vs. 19)."[92] While *adam* is here not a personal name but a generic noun, its use continues to emphasize the connection of the *adam* to the *adamah* each time the word appears.[93]

Unlike both P versions, *J* does not mention gender. An *adam* whose gender is apparently irrelevant replaces the "male and female" creature(s) of those two versions. This distinction has major implications for our discussion of the creation of woman, and for the issue of culpability regarding the Tree of Knowledge.

RIB OR SIDE?

Like its version of the creation of the *adam,* the depiction in Genesis 2 of the creation of the woman is specific and palpable. It may be read as a syntactic parallel to the story of the creation of the *adam.*[94] After recording the creation of the *adam* and its placement in the Garden of Eden,[95] the text states:

ב 21 וַיַּפֵּל יְ-הֹוָה אֱלֹהִים תַּרְדֵּמָה עַל־הָאָדָם וַיִּישָׁן וַיִּקַּח אַחַת מִצַּלְעֹתָיו וַיִּסְגֹּר בָּשָׂר תַּחְתֶּנָּה: ב 22 וַיִּבֶן יְ-הֹוָה אֱלֹהִים אֶת־הַצֵּלָע אֲשֶׁר־לָקַח מִן־הָאָדָם לְאִשָּׁה וַיְבִאֶהָ אֶל־הָאָדָם:

2:21 And Lord God caused a slumber to fall upon the *adam,* and it slept and He took one of *tsal'otav* [its sides, usually translated as "ribs"] and closed the flesh in that place.   2:22 And Lord God built the *tsela'* [side, rib] He had taken from the *adam* into an *ishah* [woman] and brought her to the *adam.* (Genesis 2:21–22)

The woman is described as created from the *tsela',* most often translated as "rib," of the previously created *adam.*[96] This passage is conventionally read as leaving the woman derivative in substance and second in sequence, leading to her status as secondary in role.

But even this telling is not as unequivocal as it seems. A crux of the ambiguity in the second Creation story concerns the word *tsela'*, denoting the part of the *adam*'s body from which the woman was formed. Whatever the *tsela'* was, it was inherent in the *adam*'s body from the time of its creation. Although the second description of the *adam*'s formation, unlike the first and the third, does not specify that it was "male and female," the *adam* held within its grammatically male body the raw material for the creation of the female.

As for the meaning of *tsela'*, the Hebrew Bible includes thirty-eight other uses of the word.[97] Twenty-three seem to mean "a side"; fifteen, "a side room." The only two verses in which this word is regularly translated as "rib" occur in the description of the creation of the woman in Genesis 2:21–22. This rendering is remarkably consistent in English: virtually all English translations, from the 1530 Tyndale on, use "rib."[98] Reuven Kimelman, in his essay on Eve, attempts at length to track down the origins of this translation.[99] He proposes that the first occurrence may be in Jubilees 3:5, where "rib" appears without any comment. Most dictionaries cite both meanings for the word.[100] In his comprehensive article on *tsela'* as it appears throughout the Hebrew Bible, Heinz-Josef Fabry points to the Septuagint's reading of Genesis 2:21–22 as *pleuron*, or "side," as "an interesting early reading."[101] While "rib" and "side" are not without parallel qualities, suggesting that these two meanings may once have had a common origin, Fabry concludes that, given the fact that *tsela'* is seen as meaning "rib" only in the context of the creation of woman, it is unlikely that it is a correct reading.[102] The Vulgate uses *costa*, which can mean either "side" or "rib." The confusion may stem from a mistranslation of *pleuron* and/or *costa*, which can mean both "side" and "rib."[103]

Because the Genesis 2 version of the Creation story is overwhelmingly the dominant one in the minds of those familiar with the text, it is important to define its terms as carefully as possible. "Side" makes at least as much sense as "rib" and implies that the woman was created out of a part of the *adam*'s body more substantial than a rib,[104] in fact, out of the same material that had been used to shape the *adam*. Hailing her as "bone of my bones / And flesh from my flesh," the *adam* makes the same claim: she is made not made merely out of its/his bone, but also from its/his flesh. Fabry makes the fascinating suggestion that the use of *tsela'*, a term drawn from the semantic field of sacred architecture might, in this context, have made the introduction of "bone" and "flesh" necessary to clarify the meaning.[105] He further proposes that the use of the sacred term is "designed to evoke associations with the construction of the sanctuary."[106] At the time of the text's composition, this usage would have responded to "the anticipated construction of the temple of Solomon."[107] As we have seen in the midrash opening this chapter, some rabbis of late antiquity entertain the notion that the woman was created out of a *side* of the *adam*, without indicating that this reading is in any way revolutionary. Given the evidence of the Septuagint, there was no reason to do so. This reading implies that the man and the woman have the same status.

The man and the woman are clearly made of the same material, the combination of dust of the earth and the breath of life that made *adam* a living being, as described in Genesis 2:7. Whether we consider it rib or side, it is clearly of the same material that became the *adam*. The salient difference is that he was the vehicle for its original combination; she was formed from material that already existed.

In short, the translation of *tsela'* is a critical issue in understanding the kind of creature the woman is. Depending on one's reading of this text one can consider the woman to be of significance lesser or greater than, or equal to, that of the man.[108] For that reason one can consider this passage to be completely indeterminate because of its high degree of polysemy, or prescriptive if one reads it as though it had one clear meaning, whatever that might be. For millennia it has been overwhelmingly understood to demean the woman of Genesis 1–5 and, through her, all women to come. Whatever one's social or religious agenda, it must be absolutely clear that such an interpretive leap is, in fact, a leap into the unknown.

This verse gives us few clues, beyond the question of raw material, as to the kind of creature the woman is. She is an *ishah*, a "woman," a word that first appears in Genesis 2:22. N. P. Bratsiotis divides the meanings of *ishah* into "woman" and "wife,"[109] allowing the reader a choice. In this verse, however, the narrator's voice contrasts *ishah* and *adam*.[110] As there is no indication of the nature of the relationship between the *ishah* and the *adam*, "woman" suits this context. The triple repetition of *adam* in verses 21–22 emphasizes that, before the *adam* recognizes the *ishah*, there is no *ish*.[111]

Speech is a vehicle for conveying the relationship between the two creatures. To this point in Genesis, the only voice we have heard directly is God's; we assume that the *adam* uttered words to name the animals, but we do not hear these words.[112] The first human words spoken are the *adam*'s and they lay claim to the woman:

בּ 23 וַיֹּאמֶר הָאָדָם זֹאת הַפַּעַם עֶצֶם מֵעֲצָמַי וּבָשָׂר מִבְּשָׂרִי לְזֹאת
יִקָּרֵא אִשָּׁה כִּי מֵאִישׁ לֻקֳחָה־זֹּאת:

2:23 The *adam* said,
> "This [*zot*] one, this time,[113]
> is bone from my bones
> and flesh from my flesh.
> This one [*zot*] shall be called woman [*ishah*],
> for from man [*ish*] this one [*zot*] was taken."
> (Genesis 2:23)

One of the striking features of this verse is the doubling, even tripling, of words. All but four of the thirteen Hebrew words in the *adam*'s direct speech are repeated.[114] Three pairs of words emphasize the sameness of the woman and the man; none indicates her uniqueness.[115] Two, referring to the raw material—'*etsem me'atsamai* (bone from my bones) and *basar mibesari* (flesh from my flesh)—constitute a kinship formula.[116] These phrases represent the *adam*'s understanding of the components of the woman. The third pair, *ish* (man) and *ishah* (woman), is a popular etymology[117] connecting these two words. In a sense, the dismemberment implicit in "bone" and "flesh" is restored. Thus word repetition links the two creatures both in the physical sense, as they are constituted of the same materials, and in a linguistic sense, through this play on words.[118]

The *adam*'s first recorded attempt at speech is marked by a lack of clarity, as seen in his threefold use of *zot* (this one), referring at least twice to the woman. The tone one reads into it is somewhat ambiguous. Although *zot* frames the *adam*'s speech, it is not clear whether it indicates the same thing in the opening and the closing. The second and third iterations of *zot* clearly refer to this new creature. The first may be a time reference. On the negative side, this double or triple vague designation of the new creature could be read as dismissive, or denigrating. Even after the *adam* calls her *ishah*, he closes his statement with yet another *zot*.

Alter points out that the word *zot* "is the first and last word of the poem [Genesis 2:23] in the Hebrew as well as the linchpin in the middle." Whatever or whomever the *adam* may have named, "in the poem, man and his bone and flesh are syntactically surrounded by this new female presence, a rhetorical configuration that makes perfect sense in the light of their subsequent history together." This view emphasizes the complexity of their relationship, the difficulty in establishing hierarchy.[119]

On the positive side, Sarna reads *zot* as a "cry of ecstatic elation."[120] The repetition of *zot*, which can be read as "pointing" to its object, could represent the intensity of the male's gaze as he focuses on this new creature. Another possibility is suggested by Bratsiotis who sees the *adam*'s characterization of this new thing as *zot* as an attempt "to recognize that she is a fellow creature."[121] More likely, the *adam*'s inability to find the right word is born of confusion and surprise at finding a creature so like himself, yet different.[122] This reading would complement the view of the *adam* as "a lost and confused child."[123]

No physical act, loving or menacing, is mentioned here. The woman is first to be defined as a gendered creature; the man is designated as her source.[124] Her response to the words of the newly defined *ish*, if any, is not recorded.

The *adam* seems to have attempted to arrogate to himself the role of namer. God has brought the woman to the *adam* without indicating what their relationship is to be. Unlike the scene when God brings the animals explicitly to be named, here the text is silent. To the extent that the namer asserts power over the named, the *adam* has rushed in to take on that role; as Trible points out, however, he does so ineptly, as indicated by the omission of the critical word "name."[125]

While the *adam* seems to be dominating this moment, it is important to realize that his power is not unalloyed. After all, the *adam* is not the prime namer of the woman: God has already referred to her as *ishah* in the previous verse. Moreover, when she is named, she also defines him through her very existence. As Pardes puts it, "although man is the first to speak and differentiate, the woman is the first to be differentiated."[126] Her creation results in his definition.

In this verse and the following one, "Therefore a man [*ish*] will leave his father and his mother and cling to his woman [*ishto*]"(Genesis 2:24), it is difficult to assess the balance of power between the man and woman. The excitement with which the man seems to greet the woman is linked to his willingness to follow her. This hint of matrilocality is offset by the power of his naming. Hierarchy is at the core here but neither creature seems to dominate absolutely.

The rabbis attached significance to the choice of the *tsela'*, the rib to many of them, as the part of the *adam*'s body that would be built into a woman.

ר' יהושע דסכנין בשם ר' לוי ויבן כת' התבונן מאיכן לברותה, אמר
לא נברא אותה מראש שלא תהא מוקרת ראשה, ולא מן העין שלא
תהא סוקרנית, ולא מן האוזן שלא תהא צייתנית, ולא מן הפה שלא
תהא דברנית, ולא מן הלב שלא תהא קונתנית, ולא מן היד שלא
תהא משמשנית, ולא מן הרגל שלא תהא פורסנית, אלא ממקום
צנוע באדם אפילו בשעה שאדם עומד ערום אותו מקום מכוסה,
ועל כל אבר ואבר שהיה בורא היה אומר לה אשה צנועה אשה
צנועה, אפעלפיכן ותפרעו כל עצתי ותוכחתי לא אביתם (משלי א
כה), לא בראתי אותה מן הראש והרי היא מוקרת ראשה ותלכנה
נטויות גרון (ישעיה ג טז), ולא מן העין והרי היא סוקרנית ומסקרות
עינים (שם שם), ולא מן האוזן והרי היא צייתנית ושרה שומעת
פתח האהל (בראשית יח י), ולא מן הלב והרי היא קונתנית ותקנא
רחל (שם ל א), ולא מן היד והרי היא ממשמשנית ותגנוב רחל את
התרפים (שם לא יט), ולא מן הרגל והרי היא פרסנית ותצא דינה
(שם לד א).

R. Yehoshua' of Sikhnin said in the name of R. Levi: "*Vayiven* is written, [meaning] that He contemplated well (*hitbonen*) from what [part of the *adam*] to create her. Said He: 'We will not create her from [the *adam*'s] head, that she not be swell-headed [literally, overvalue her head]; and not from the eye, that she not be painting her eyes with red [to entice men]; and not from the ear, that she not be listening in; and not from the mouth, that she not be talking too much; and not from the heart, that she not be envious; and not from the hand, that she not be touching [things that are not hers and steal them]; and not from the foot, that she not be gallivanting; but from the modest part of man, for even when he stands naked, that part is covered.'

"And about each limb He created He would say to her: 'A woman is modest, a woman is modest.'

" 'Nonetheless, "You spurned all my advice, / And would not hear my rebuke" (Proverbs 1:25). I did not create her from the head, yet she is swell-headed, as it is written, "They [the daughters of Zion] walk with heads[127] thrown back" (Isaiah 3:16); nor from the eye, yet she is curious and paints her eyes with red:[128] "With roving eyes" (ibid.); nor from the ear, yet she listens in: "Sarah was listening at the entrance of the tent" (Genesis 18:10); nor from the heart, yet she is envious: "She [Rachel] became envious of her sister" (ibid., 30:1); nor from the hand, yet she touches things: "And Rachel stole her father's household idols" (ibid., 31:19); nor from the foot, yet she does gallivant: "Now Dinah . . . went out," etc. (ibid., 34:1).' "[129]

R. Levi, as quoted by R. Yehoshua' of Sikhnin,[130] presents us initially with an image of God's stopping to consider what material to use in constructing woman. Choosing the "rib" definition of *tsela'*, he assumes that God considered only various parts of the *adam*'s body. The midrash comprises a brief introduction followed by two lists of body parts. Reading into the text by linking two Hebrew verbs that actually are not from the same root,[131] a common rabbinic exegetical tool, R. Levi introduces a considered selection of the parts of the *adam*'s body that might be used to create the woman—an element that thus was apparently not designed ab initio for that purpose. Woman is an afterthought.

Yet it is not the woman who is dismembered here; she is yet to be created. The *adam* is the one who is taken apart. A different interpretive goal or view of gender relations might have expanded that notion into a positive evaluation of woman, but such is not the case here. As Judith R. Baskin asserts, "In this literal excursus on the construction of the female body, God is described as attempting to build a woman who would personify what the framers of rabbinic Judaism believed to be ideal female qualities of humility, sexual modesty, domesticity, discretion, and passivity."[132] Baskin's clear summary of the import of this midrash vis-à-vis women should not blind us to the fact that all the traits that God tried to avoid are actually inherent in the *adam*. Are they, in the rabbinic view, acceptable in a man? Or is God actually trying to make improvements in what is viewed as the second creation of a human?

This midrash presents an essentialist, misogynistic catalogue of women in general and, specifically, of biblical women. First, woman is reified by being associated with a particular part of *adam*'s body, moving from head to foot. Whatever part of *adam* is to be chosen, woman would take on the characteristics of that body part. God is depicted as seeing woman prone to unacceptable behavior. In explaining the list of limbs God rejected, this midrash manages to produce a substantial inventory of negative stereotypes of women. But even God's considered plan is subverted: each of the negative qualities that God tries to preclude does, nonetheless, become a characteristic of women, as demonstrated by proof texts from other biblical stories. Overall, one can almost hear God repeating, mantralike, as each limb is considered: "Be a modest woman." Leila Leah Bronner sums up the situation succinctly: "The masculine discourse simultaneously creates an ideal of female virtue and a stereotype of feminine shortcomings and culpabilities."[133] Even God cannot prevail when dealing with inherently flawed females.

In the second list, that of the female subversion of the divine plan, the first proof text, Proverbs 1:25, sets the tone for what is to follow. In the context of the midrash it would seem that God is the speaker, indicating that human free will limits God's ability to control the world. God's plans do not always work out because humans sabotage even the divine plan. In fact, however, Proverbs 1:25 is part of a section of that first chapter that is spoken by Wisdom, ḥokhmah, who is presented in the form of a woman.[134] It is not God but Wisdom whose sage counsel is rejected. By choosing this proof text, the author of this midrash presents women as undermining the divine plan while effacing the positive female figure of Wisdom.

How do R. Yehoshuaʿ of Sikhnin and R. Levi document women's rejection of the sage counsel they were given? They adduce specific empirical evidence from the lives of biblical women. First, a verse from Isaiah predicting the destruction of Zion because of the vain and flirtatious behavior of its wealthy women accounts for the deleterious effects of the head and the eye.[135] This broad indictment is followed by specific references to Sarah, Rachel, and Dinah, as well as general criticism of the "daughters of Zion." These objects of condemnation are not always seen as similar in the rabbinic tradition. Dinah is frequently cited by the rabbis as a woman who brought about her own ruin and the shaming of her family by her "going out."[136] Rachel and Sarah are generally seen in a much more positive light in which minor lapses such as those cited are more than balanced by their virtues. The double mention of Rachel, Jacob's beloved wife and the mother of Joseph, the hero of the last section of Genesis, serves to remind us how one-sided this presentation is. The message of this midrash is Woman is Other; her creation, secondary; her behavior, reprehensible. Clearly she neither hierarchically dominates the man nor serves as his equal. As all the actions cited here are independently undertaken by the women, the subliminal warning is that women need to be controlled.

Even more remarkable than the negative singling out of Sarah, Rachel, and Dinah[137] as named exemplars of immodest and inappropriate behavior, however, is the absence of Eve herself. Surely, one might have expected to find Eve taken to task for her disobedience, despite her creation from the modest, hidden rib. In fact, Eve could easily have served to exemplify disobedience using the mouth,[138] which is curiously omitted from the litany of bad behavior, although it is present in the first list of possibilities. But Eve is glaringly missing.

While the preceding midrash omits Eve where we might most readily expect to find her, the rabbis do occasionally bring the first woman's experience to bear on matters we might consider distant from her purview. One such case is the following riff on perceived physical and social distinctions between men and women:

שאלו את רבי יהושע מפני מה האיש יוצא פניו למטה והאשה יוצאת
פניה למעלה, אמר להם האיש מביט למקום ברייתו והאשה למקום
ברייתה, ומפני מה האשה צריכה להתבסם והאיש אינו צריך להתבסם,
אמר להם אדם נברא מאדמה והאדמה אינה מסרחת לעולם, אבל
חוה נבראת מעצם, משל אם תניח בשר ג' ימים בלא מלח מסריח
הוא מיד, ומפני מה האשה קולה הולך ולא האיש, אמר להם משל
אם תמלא קדירה בשר אין קולה הולך, כיון שתתן בתוכה עצם אחד
מיד קולה הולך, ומפני מה האיש נוח להתפתות ולא האשה, אמר
להם אדם נברא מאדמה, כיון שאת נותן עליה טיפה שלמים מיד
היא שותה אותה, וחוה נבראת מעצם אפילו את שורה אותו כמה
ימים במים אינו נשרה, ומפני מה האיש תובע באשה ואין האשה
תובעת באיש, אמר להן משל למה הדבר דומה לאחד שאיבד אבידה
הוא מבקש אבידתו ואבידתו אינה מבקשתו, מפני מה האיש מפקיד
זרע באשה ואין האשה מפקדת באיש זרע, אמר להן לאחד שהיה
בידו פיקדון ומבקש אדם נאמן שיפקידנו אצלו.

They asked R. Yehoshuaʿ, "Why does the man come out [with] his face down and the woman comes out [with] her face up?" He said to them, "The man looks to the place from which he was created [the earth], and the woman [looks] to the place from which she was created [the rib]."

"And why does the woman have to perfume herself, and the man does not have to perfume himself?" He said to them, "Adam was created from earth and the earth never stinks, but

Eve was created from a bone. An analogy: if you leave meat for three days without salt it will stink immediately."

"And why does the voice [qol][139] of a woman carry and not [that of] a man?" He said to them, "An analogy: if you fill a pot with meat, its sound will not carry, whereas [if] you put one bone into it its sound immediately carries."

"And why is the man readily pacified,[140] but not the woman?" He said to them, "Adam is created from the earth, once you put on it a drop of water, it immediately drinks it up. Eve is created from a bone; even if you soak it for several days in water, it is not absorbed [lit., steeped]."

"And why does the man demand of the woman and the woman does not demand of the man?" He answered, "To what is the matter similar, to a person who has lost something; he seeks the lost object, but the lost object does not seek him."

"Why does the man deposit seed in the woman, but the woman does not deposit seed in the man?" He answered, "[It is] like one who had in hand a valuable deposit; he searches for someone [adam] who is faithful to deposit it with him."[141]

This text, focusing on men and women as binary, constitutes in large part a distinctly misogynistic series of questions and answers. Daniel Boyarin, who in *Carnal Israel* generally exonerates the rabbis on the grounds that they are androcentric rather than misogynistic, concedes that R. Yehoshuaʿs responses in this first section of the midrash are "obnoxious in tone" but "do not necessarily depict vicious contempt for the female."[142] Nonetheless, he labels *Genesis Rabbah* 17:8 as a whole "the only examples of misogynistic diatribe in all of the classical rabbinic literature."[143] I read this text as using the purported material of the first woman's creation as an excuse for blatant misogyny. This string of questions and responses essentializes woman, pointing to qualities, real and imagined, socially and physically constructed, that, by and large, portray woman negatively.[144] Using the first woman's purported origin in the *adam*'s rib as its starting point or pretext, it underscores a rabbinic view of woman as the unfamiliar Other.[145]

The first of these questions rests on the factually dubious assertion that *ha'ish yotzei panav lematah veha'ishah yotzeit paneha lemaʿlah* (the man comes out [with] his face down, while the woman comes out [with] her face up). R. Yehoshuaʿ, who appears to be no closer to the birth process than his anonymous questioner, explains that both men and women, as they emerge at birth, look to their respective places of origin, *mekom beriyato* or *beriyatah*.[146] Setting aside the flawed gynecological evidence, we could imagine another explanation for this assumed disparity, one that might have woman looking to God, while man looks to the ground. This first midrashic assertion is not, on its surface, particularly negative toward women; it stresses difference and the importance of origin.[147] But this line of reasoning lays the groundwork for considering women as "a nation unto themselves,"[148] collectively tainted by the misdeeds of the first woman—an absurd assertion, given that, in the biblical account, all humans, both male and female, are descended from the primal couple.

The following two assertions are linked by the clear message that, from the beginning, woman is essentially and negatively Other. Even as the first woman was created from a bone, so will all women throughout time retain the unfortunate malodorous quality of bone. Therefore, *ha'ishah tzrikhah lehitbassem* (the woman has to perfume herself). Irrelevant is her origin in man—therefore also, logically, the source of her smell. It is perhaps useful to remember that, in a time and place where frequent bathing may not have been de rigueur, both men and women may well have been more odiferous than they are today. For men who spent much of their working lives in the company of men and not women, women's scent may well have seemed strange and requiring camouflage in the form of perfume.[149] Once more, it is the essential Otherness of the woman that underlies this statement. Once more, we are instructed to look to origins, here to the raw material, for the explanation of woman's Otherness. Even as the first woman was created from a bone, a male's bone, to be specific, so will all women throughout time be malodorous, retaining this unfortunate quality of bone.

Similarly, the issue of a woman's voice is raised with the assumption that it carries farther, or perhaps is shriller, than a man's. Once more, R. Yehoshua' looks to woman's origins in the bone to explain an apparent conundrum in human experience. Human discourse takes on a quiet tone when conducted only among men just as meat cooks quietly unless an *etsem* (a bone) is added to the pot. Expanding this analogy, what is cooking is meat, or, metaphorically speaking, male; adding the bone, or the woman, increases the noise, may even add a bit of unwanted flavor, but does not enhance the basic nutritional quality of the meat or the meatiness of male discourse.[150]

The following example is harder to categorize because the meaning of the key word—*lehitpattot*—is unclear. One reading would have it mean that, in comparison to the woman, the man is *noah lehitpattot* (more readily pacified), once again favoring men. Like bones, impervious to liquid, women do not absorb their hurts; men, like earth, do. Being readily pacified, like not bearing a grudge, would be a positive quality in a person, particularly in the domestic setting described here. If that is the meaning of *lehitpattot*, then this question and answer are of a piece with the two preceding exchanges and, predictably enough, favor men.

If, however, *lehitpattot* means to be seduced, then being readily seduced is a quality of a *peti*, a fool. The man would be guilty of being easily seduced or led astray. On one level that is critical of men and, in the setting here envisioned, might imply that they are likely to have relations with women outside of marriage. Within a society that allows polygamy and permits, though does not encourage, nonmarital sexual relations, as long as they are not with married women, the relative sexual freedom of men may have been, as Baskin claims, viewed as an advantage that women do not share.[151]

Further complicating the understanding of this passage is the Adam and Eve dimension lurking in the background of this text. There Adam, the prototypical male, ate the forbidden fruit without an argument, whereas Eve argued with the snake. In that sense, as we shall see, Adam is more the fool than Eve, bringing us back to the core meaning of *lehitpattot*, to make oneself a fool.

There are three divergent readings of this passage proposed here. To determine which is the dominant reading, the analogy proves helpful. Water or rain that lands on the earth and remains on the surface is of little use; once absorbed, it becomes part of the process of fructification. Particularly in the dry climate of Palestine where *Genesis Rabbah* was compiled, water absorption was critical. For that reason, I propose that the first reading—which indicates that men, like the earth, absorb water and are to be praised for that—is dominant.

Even men's sexual solicitation of women, rather than the reverse, can be directly connected to the bone from which the first woman was created. In this case it is the missing bone that is being sought by the male—who, presumably, continues to feel the loss.[152] While the binary quality of gender is clear here, how one assesses the impact of this distinction is more complex. A man has agency, a woman is passive; a man has more opportunities, a woman is restricted to her husband. But man is flawed, lacking something, while woman is sought after—she may even be the prize.

Thus, the first five of this series of questions and answers about the assumed differences between men and women are resolved by looking back to the bone that is the origin of the woman. It is an essentialist argument of the purest kind: a bony origin is in no way reversible or malleable—and it is for all women for all time, at least theoretically, traceable to Eve.

Only the last of this series attributes to the woman some positive quality. The woman is considered a trustworthy keeper of the male *zera*ʿ (seed),[153] without reference to her bony origins. Only in connection with procreation does the woman finally have an attribute worthy of respect. But that respect is predicated on her passively receiving and holding on to the fetus, which, according to medical theory at the time, had been completely formed by the male.[154] This positive view is grounded in the rabbinic advocacy of procreation—which, however, was not, as some claim, the principle that underlies rabbinic treatment of women.[155] In fact, the previous five questions and answers have little to do with woman's role in procreation. Woman as Other shapes the rabbinic view, as well as woman as mother.

Two words leap out of R. Yehoshuaʿ's last, positive response: *piqqadon* (deposit) and *ne'eman* (trustworthy). The word *piqqadon* and verbs formed from the same root occur in four of the five clauses in this exchange.[156] This analogy between pregnancy and the world of commerce carries us back to the mishnaic discussion of the situation of the owner of an object who requests that someone else keep it for him without recompense—for example, having the keeper take care of an animal while the owner is away.[157] What characterizes this relationship? The Mishnah does not even mention the obvious fact that the owner is well advised to seek out a trustworthy person for this task. Implicit, but not explicit, is the keeper's agreement. Ultimately, however, the object remains entirely the possession of the owner, who must be compensated if the object is damaged due to the keeper's negligence. So it is within the realm of pregnancy: the father is the sole owner of the fetus, which has essentially become commodified; the mother should be a person who can be trusted to do the fetus no harm and to return it to the father's control upon birth. There is a moral dimension to the description of the woman as trustworthy, but it is limited by its origin in the commercial arena of laws of ownership.

The unalterable nature of woman's alterity lies at the heart of this midrashic passage in which the rib story provides a platform for reinforcing, explaining, or perhaps justifying the perception of woman's difference. But this difference is in no way a case of "separate but equal." Woman's alterity marks her as hierarchically inferior.

The Genesis 2 story of the creation of woman, particularly when one translates *tselaʿ* as "rib," seems, at first reading, to provide an irrefutable context for establishing the secondariness of the woman. As we have seen in the texts from *Genesis Rabbah,* it is fairly easy to create such a reading. For that reason, it is noteworthy that contemporary poets like Linda Pastan and Kim Chernin find within that essentialist "rib" reading an independent, powerful woman.

In the title poem of her 1975 collection *Aspects of Eve* the contemporary American Jewish poet Linda Pastan (1932–) challenges the conventional reading of Genesis 2.

> *Aspects of Eve*
>
> To have been one
> of many ribs
> and to be chosen.
> To grow into something
> 5   quite different
> knocking finally
> as a bone knocks
> on the closed gates of the garden—
> which unexpectedly
> 10   open.[158]

Pastan does not engage the biblical text as a scholar might, comparing the versions of the story in Genesis 1, 2, and 5, or examining the recurrences of *tselaʿ* in the Hebrew Bible. Instead she accepts the rib but transforms the image generally perceived as demeaning into one replete with meaning. She "steals the metaphor," to adapt Alicia Ostriker's rendering of Christine Herrmann's characterization of women writers as *"voleuses de langue,"* or "language thieves."[159]

Unlike some of Pastan's other poems about Eve,[160] this one incorporates her name only in the title; no name, of course, is needed to identify the subject of the poem, given the centrality of the rib. Despite the focus on the rib, traditionally interpreted as a sign of secondariness and lack of agency, Pastan presents Eve actively and purposefully taking the initiative. The title "Aspects of Eve" communicates openness, promising no more than noncommittal notes or thoughts, eschewing a thesis. The poem's structure reflects this open quality. Although capital letters and full stops would seem to indicate a division of the ten lines into two sentences, neither unit actually is a sentence; each is a mere fragment, opening with an infinitive. The absence of any indication that these two elements are related further underscores a lack of structural precision.

But the imprecise nature of these two thoughts belies their boldness in engaging Genesis and their poetic complexity. Taking an essentialist approach, focusing on the material used in creating the woman, Pastan emphasizes the importance of choice. The selection of one specific rib from among the dozen pairs of possibilities suggests that some unique, perhaps privileged, quality inheres in the one chosen. Ending the first line with the word "one," contrasting with "many ribs" at the end of the second line, reinforces the notion of uniqueness. With "chosen" in line 3, a word Sanford Pinsker describes as "a charged word—perhaps the charged word—of Jewish history,"[161] Pastan poetically opens multiple conceptual possibilities that may be inferred from the comparison of the Jews as a "chosen people" with the rib as a chosen element with a mission.[162] The passive infinitive form of "to be chosen" indicates a state of being that is ongoing.

How differently the issue of choice plays out here and in the text attributed to R. Levi. Implicit in Pastan's presentation is a "chooser," who considered all the ribs before singling one out of many. For the rabbis, too, the issue of the choice of rib is significant, not as one among many ribs, but as God's choice of one body part among many possibilities. The text from *Genesis Rabbah* 18:2 is completely focused on curbing the evil nature of woman; Pastan's text is one in which chosenness is prized.

Pastan's approaching the creation of woman from the perspective of the rib is innovative; the second element, describing that rib's function, takes entirely by surprise any reader familiar only with the biblical text and its classic interpretations. The focus is exclusively on the bone. The phrase "To grow into something / quite different" is itself entirely different from the familiar description of God's careful construction of the rib into a woman in Genesis 2:22. The active voice of "to grow" contrasts sharply with the passive "to be chosen." While I prefer to interpret that as making the growth of the rib resonate as self-directed and positive, another tenable reading would have the growth of the bone inherent, perhaps the very reason for the choice. The only possible reference to "woman" as the final product of this growth is embedded in the phrase "something quite different," which delineates the alterity of the woman while echoing positively the sense of value in the difference—as the French would say, "Vive la différence!" Even when it has become "something quite different," the bone has only a limited role; the final product can "knock as a bone knocks."

The location of the bone adds ambiguity to this poem. If we place the "bone" and, metonymically, the woman outside the Garden and its Edenic pleasures, we interpret her actions as a successful attempt to reverse the divine decree. This reading underscores the unexpectedness of the opening of the gates as nothing in the biblical text would lead us to anticipate success.[163] If, however, we picture the bone, and thus the woman, within the Garden of Eden, prior to the expulsion, attempting to get the gates to open, we see her as a knowledge-seeker, chafing at her confinement in the Garden, looking for something new, different from what she already knows. This reading, bolstered by its coherence with some of Pastan's later poetry, is the stronger one.[164] Following this second interpretation, the last line, the only line consisting of just one word—"open"—concludes the poem with a sense of the possibilities lying ahead, beyond the confines of the Garden of Eden. This somewhat ironic closing with openness leaves the reader anticipating, rather than dreading, what is to come.

The rib develops without losing the essential, hard "boniness," enabling it to knock, to bang on the Garden gates. The repetition of "knock," the only word of significance repeated in the poem, onomatopoetically echoes the bone's repetitive, persistent knock on the gates of Eden. The unexpected opening of the gates stands in contrast to another set of gates, doubtless known to Pastan, namely the Christian gates of salvation. To quote the Sermon on the Mount: "Ask, and you will receive; seek, and you will find; knock, and the door shall be opened."[165] Unlike Jesus' door with its promise of ready, faith-based salvation, Pastan's gates require a repeated knock; nonetheless, when confronted with human persistence, they, too, do open.

Pastan's unconventionally essentialist portrayal of the woman prompts the reader to reconsider the implications of the story of the creation of woman as portrayed in Genesis 2. By taking a direction unlike that usually taken by essentialist readers, it raises the question of agency; it depicts the rib/bone as the growing and active force in the story. Eve's story is often read as establishing gender hierarchy, with the man almost always granted more significance than the woman. Pastan's version omits the *adam,* and God too, for that matter, leaving the woman with enough independence and power to cause the gates to open—allowing her either back in or out.

In addition, Linda Pastan's "Aspects of Eve" presents us with a transgressive reading of the "rib story" of the first woman's creation that underscores its polysemous nature, allowing for reading gender in multiple ways. This reading relies heavily on the slang meaning of the terms Pastan uses. Each of the two syntactical units in this poem posits a different word at its center of meaning: the first, rib; the second, bone. In our first reading we treat them as identical, using as our rationale the *adam's* poetic first reaction to the woman, addressing her as *'etsem me'atsamai* (bone of my bones) (Genesis 2:23). But rib and bone are not necessarily identical. In American English, the language of the poem, they can be read oppositionally, as gendered and binary.

Based on Genesis 2:21, "rib" is used as an expression for "woman" or "wife" in American slang.[166] "To have been one / of many ribs / and to be chosen" would then be a description of a woman singled out among many. For what purpose and by whom she is chosen is an open question. While the meaning "wife" connotes a sexual aspect to the choosing, it does not limit the possibilities, as "woman" and even "girl" are also acceptable definitions. As we saw in our first reading, the rib/woman/wife is not active at first; but she seems to be the prize, as she appears to be for R. Yehoshua'. In this reading, "bone" is also understood in its slang resonance: "an erection of the penis."[167] Thus, while the poem's first syntactical fragment revolves around a woman, the second concerns a man. The "bone," read as gendered female at the opening, has crossed a permeable gender barrier and become male.

From this point, the rest of the poem falls into place rather smoothly. The repeating word, "knock," connotes "to copulate or copulate with"—a "vulgar" usage.[168] The garden is not the "Garden of Eden," but the garden of female sexuality or female genitalia common as a topos in sources as diverse as the biblical Song of Songs and the medieval French *Roman de la Rose.* The opening of the garden to the knocking bone is where we see her agency; but it is reactive, a response to the bone's knocking. Further, from whose perspective is the opening unexpected? Does the man repeatedly knock despite his expectation that the woman will remain closed off from him? Is it the woman, who had decided to resist his advances, but, given his persistence, succumbs?

Combining these two parts of the poem, we have a somewhat explicit text about human copulation in which the woman values chosenness, having been picked out of the crowd, as it were, by a man, while the male sees penetrating the woman's metaphoric gates as the value or goal and persists until he reaches it, making him the more active partner. The woman, on the other hand, has ultimate control; it is her choice to open in response to his knocking.

But poetry, meant to be read aloud, possesses an aural quality that transcends the printed page. The poem's first line, when heard, is telling us that two have been one; in other words, that the two, man and woman, were originally one. Reunited in their sexual relationship, they now exemplify the biblical statement *"vehayu levasar eḥad"* (and they shall become one flesh) (Genesis 2:24). Although I am not suggesting that this is the definitive reading, the confluence of all these elements in a poem of only thirty-two words suggests that it is a tenable one.

Finally, if this is all about hierarchy, the second, transgressive reading paradoxically undermines the first reading, which presents the woman, metonymically represented by the bone, as the prime agent in the poem. The male, absent from our first reading, dominates the second, without achieving complete mastery. Pastan's poem then can function like Gustave Verbeck's early twentieth-century comic strip "Upside Downs of Little Lady Lovekins and Old Man Muffarroo"—in which, when the page is rotated, the male and female characters change places.[169]

But the rabbis could also find positive qualities in the texts in which the construction of the woman is described. Not all rabbinic imaginings of women are negative. The selection we are about to examine opens with a discussion that seems to praise woman's probity. As the discussion continues, however, the text becomes more ambivalent, leaving the modern reader to locate the text on the spectrum of rabbinic attitudes toward women. Like *Genesis Rabbah* 18:2, which dismembers the *adam* in order to warn women to be modest, this midrash is based on an intentional mistranslation of the word *vayiven* (and he built or and he fashioned), which is the term used for God's creation of woman in Genesis 2:22.

ויבן י"י אלהים את הצלע וגו', ר' אלעזר בשם ר' יוסי בן זימרא ניתן
בה בינה יותר מן האיש דתנינן תמן בת אחת עשרה שנה ויום אחד
נדריה נבדקין, בת י"ב שנה ויום אחד נדריה קיימין ובודקין כל י"ב,
בן י"ב שנה ויום אחד נדריו נבדקין, בן י"ג שנה ויום אחד נדריו
קיימין, ובודקין כל י"ג שנה, ר' ירמיה בשם ר' שמואל בר רב יצחק
אית דמחלפין, דרכה שלאשה להיות יושבת בתוך ביתה ודרכו שלאיש
להיות יוצא לשוק ולמד בינה מבני אדם, ר' איבו ואמ' לה בשם ר'
בניה ותני לה בשם ר' שמעון בן יוחי קישטה ככלה והביאה לו, אית
אתרין אמרין לקלעיתא בנייתא, אמר ר' חמא בר' חנינא מה את
סבור שמתחת חרוב אחד או מתחת שקמה אחת הביאה לו, אלא
משקישטה בכ"ד תכשיטין ואחר כך הביאה לו.

"And Lord God built [*vayiven*] the *tsela'* [side, rib], etc." (Genesis
2:22).

R. Ele'azar [said] in the name of R. Yose ben Zimra: "She was
given more understanding [*binah*] than the man. As we have
learned elsewhere: 'The vows of a girl of eleven years and one
day are examined; [those of] a girl twelve years and one day are
binding, and we examine [her] the whole of the twelfth year. The
vows of a boy twelve years and one day are examined; [those of]
a boy of thirteen years and one day are binding, and we examine
[him] in the whole of the thirteenth year' [M. Niddah 5:6]."

R. Yirmeyah [said] in the name of R. Shemu'el ben R. Yitshaq:
"Some reverse it, [because] a woman's way is to be staying at
home, and a man's way is to go out into the marketplace and
learn understanding [*binah*] from [other] people."

R. Aibu—others state the following in R. Bannayah's name,
and it was also taught in the name of R. Shim'on ben Yohai—said:
"He [God] adorned her like a bride and brought her to him [the
adam], for there are places where [hair] braiding is called building
[*beniyyata*]."

R. Hama ben R. Hanina said: "What do you think, that He
brought her to him from under a carob tree or a sycamore tree?
Rather He [first] decorated her with twenty-four pieces of jewelry and then brought her to him."[170]

This midrash, unlike the previous ones we have cited, involves an aspect
of Jewish law or halakhah. Connecting the root of the verb for building or

fashioning, *b.n.y*, with the root for wisdom or understanding, *b.y.n*, R. Ele'azar quoting R. Yose ben Zimra suggests that one may infer that God gave the woman more *binah* (understanding) than a man has. He cites as evidence the mishnah that states that from the time a girl reaches the age of eleven and one day until she becomes twelve and one day, should she make a vow, she is to be questioned to ascertain whether she understands to Whom the vow is made, or the significance of her action. If she does, her vow has legal standing (M. Niddah 5:6). However, once she reaches the age of twelve years and one day, she is considered an adult and thus, even if she declares that she does not understand the legal implications of her vow, it still stands. The same is true of boys, but their time frame is a year later. In other words, at twelve and thirteen and one day, respectively, women and men are automatically given the responsibilities and rights of adults. Thus, women apparently reach intellectual maturity earlier than do men.[171]

The statement that women have more wisdom or understanding than men, based on their earlier intellectual development as demonstrated by M. Niddah 5:6, is not without its opponents. Two somewhat different considerations of this mishnah are recorded: one is in the midrash we are discussing,[172] the other in the Babylonian Talmud. In each of these instances a suggestion is made that the situation is reversed, in other words that boys actually acquire wisdom earlier than girls, based on empirical evidence. In the text in *Genesis Rabbah* 18:1, R. Yirmeyah cites R. Shemu'el bar R. Yitshaq, who says that women generally stay at home whereas men go out into the marketplace and learn wisdom from their contacts with and observations of others. One might posit that men go out into the marketplace of ideas, but it seems more likely that even their forays into the bustling physical marketplace would give them better understanding. From this we also learn that the kind of wisdom under discussion is not Torah knowledge—which, in the circles of the rabbinic elite, is the summum bonum—but rather the kind of wisdom one gains from life experience. Thus, even the notion that women may have more understanding than men in the sense of "street smarts" is being challenged.

The Babylonian Talmud uses a different word for intellectual achievement and a different setting to challenge the notion of women's earlier mental maturity. There R. Shemu'el bar R. Yitshaq is quoted as saying that the reverse of the mishnah is true because a boy spends his time sitting in the house of his teacher where he develops *'armumit*, perhaps best translated as cleverness, earlier (B. Niddah 45b). In neither case does the challenge prevail, as is demonstrated by the fact that twelve and thirteen do become the ages of majority for girls and boys, respectively.

Perhaps because continuing in this vein would lead to a profound disconnect between law and life, the next suggestion in the midrash takes another direction entirely. It returns us, by citing the actual root of *vayiven*, from the intellectual world of wisdom or understanding to the physical world of fashioning or building. It cannot resolve the apparent contradiction between the legal and the empirical evidence, so it moves instead directly to the physical aspects of woman. The ensuing discussion is unarguably androcentric and based on an underlying marriage metaphor. Although Jewish law does require the bride's consent to her marriage, this section of midrash is focused solely upon the ways to make the woman presentable; that is, sufficiently attractive for the man to accept her. There is no parallel concern expressed for the impression the *adam* might make on the woman. From the rabbis' perspective, one may deduce that men need no further embellishment; they are intrinsically attractive to women. Alternatively, one may conclude that the rabbis were not concerned with understanding what aroused women.

The ensuing discussion gives us some insight into the wedding practices of the time. According to the tradition R. Aibu reports, the use of the verb "build" is explained by God's having constructed an elaborate braided hairdo for the first woman before presenting her to the man, implying that she would otherwise have been unacceptable.[173] R. Ḥama bar R. Ḥanina concurs, perhaps sarcastically, that it is inconceivable that God would have brought her to the man as she was created; she must have been first adorned with jewelry. On the surface this is a compliment to the first woman for whom God served as hairdresser and wardrobe attendant. But, lest the reader see the process as entirely positive, there is an intertext lurking here. Isaiah 3:18–24 follows the description of the vain and arrogant wealthy women of Zion who are responsible for its destruction,[174] with an enumeration of the twenty-four types of ornamentation God will strip off them. In other words, before God has formally introduced the first woman to the first man, the sins of women are subtly present between the lines.

One may choose to see this passage as harmlessly androcentric or as pointing to deficiencies inherent in the woman that God must rectify. It is, however, apparent that she, unlike the man, needs improvement. While these rabbis may well have made their suggestions in an effort to emphasize the significance of the woman, today these statements are as likely to be read as indications of her insufficiency. Unlike the man, who, as reported in this midrash, seems to require no barbering, the woman clearly needs work, even on the physical level. Woman is inferior. She may be decorated, but she may not be taken seriously as an equal. She remains ultimately Other, needing God's help to attract her man, even when she is the only woman on earth.

In a parallel flight of metaphor, Cassuto suggests that "just as a builder builds, with the raw materials of stones and dust, an edifice of grace and perfection, so from an ordinary piece of bone and flesh the Lord God fashioned the most comely of his creatures."[175] In ranking the woman first in physical perfection Cassuto counters the strand in the rabbinic tradition that sees the gap between the beauty of the man and the woman as parallel to the gap between the man and an ape.[176] Trible's imagination is also engaged in this scene as she describes God's shift from "anesthesiologist and surgeon" in the previous verse to "architect, designer and builder."[177] It is a tribute to the power of the biblical text that it continues to fire the creativity of modern scholars. At the same time, it is significant that it is the creation of the woman that gives rise to these bursts of hyperbole. It leads one to wonder whether or not it is inspired by a perceived problem in the biblical text.

LOVE AND MARRIAGE

The temptation to read love and marriage into Genesis 2:22–24 seems close to irresistible. The rabbis of late antiquity are not alone in reading a full-blown wedding into the story of the first woman. Many a twentieth-century scholar, some prominent feminists included, follows that course.[178] Sarna goes so far as to declare that Genesis 2:22 "conveys the idea that the institution of marriage is established by God Himself."[179] It is difficult to resist the temptation to read marriage into this proposed union between the first two creatures and its replication throughout the generations.[180]

One of the most extensive and elaborate analyses of these verses is presented by Bratsiotis, who also sees here God instituting marriage. He suggests that before God and the woman "the man acknowledges . . . the equality of the partnership between *ish* and *ishah* which God had established, and before God he makes a covenant with the woman," a "covenant of God." He further reads into Genesis 2:24 a "marriage formula" and "monogamy."[181] Evidently this equality does not include allowing the woman to speak or to voice her vision of this relationship. That is something that comes more naturally to a modern rewriter like Kim Chernin, in her poem "The Call," which was discussed above.[182] This biblical text provides quite a one-sided view of equality.

Nevertheless, as Carol Meyers points out in a later context, marriage "does not fit the archetypal literary setting of the Eden story."[183] Further, Phyllis Bird states that Genesis 1:27 "describes the biological pair, not a social partnership; male and female, not man and wife."[184] There is no mention of love at all in the text; in fact, love between a man and a woman who form a couple first appears in Genesis regarding Isaac's love for Rebecca.[185] Linking love and marriage is largely a modern phenomenon.

If one is looking for marriage in Genesis 1–5, the best place to look is: "Therefore a man [ish] will leave his father and his mother and cling to his woman [ishto] and they become one flesh" (Genesis 2:24). Sarna characterizes this verse as "an etiological observation on the part of the Narrator," which explains "some interrelated and fundamental aspects of the marital relationship."[186] While there is no institution established here, the verse implies a lasting bond, or perhaps a need, strong enough to move a man to leave his family of origin. That it is the man who leaves to be with the woman makes this text quite different from the devaluing of woman that is often read into the Creation story. While some reject the notion that it is the remnant of a matrilocal society,[187] it is a verse made all the more puzzling by the texts of the patriarchal/matriarchal narratives in which each of the matriarchs ultimately leaves her family of origin, whether with her husband, as in the case of Sarah, Leah, and Rachel, or to marry, as in the case of Rebecca.[188] If this is etiology, it serves the unusual function of explaining something that does not exist in the text in which it appears.

BLESSING

Although the content of the divine blessing given to the *adam* in Genesis 1:28 will be discussed in greater detail in the context of the role the *adam* is designed to play, blessedness is part of the nature of the *adam*. Both Genesis 2:28 and 5:2 record that God "blessed them." The blessing seems to devolve upon the *adam* only after it has become plural.[189] This is the moment in the biblical text Ostriker uses when she chooses to close her poem "In the Beginning the Being," with the line "And blessed them." For Ostriker the Being's blessing the newly created man and woman is in itself adequate; there is no need to articulate the contents of that blessing.[190]

Notions of gender hierarchy dictate one's reading of the creation of the first woman. Although the biblical texts can be read as indicating that the first woman and the first man were created out of the same material, they have generally not been read that way. The focus on the "rib" version of woman's creation has often led premodern readers to see the very substance out of which woman was created as inferior, rather than as an integral part of the *adam*. Modern feminist rewriters have gone back to the first Creation story or have capitalized on the "rib" version, seeing in it a positive rather than a negative.

Yet, in order to understand the root of the issue of gender hierarchy as read into the story of the creation of woman, number and substance are not sufficient. The third and most significant element is that of purpose.

The Purpose of the Creation of Woman

The single most important index of any potentially hierarchical relationship between the first woman and the first man is the role they were designed to fill. Again, aware that the man and woman were created out of the same material, most likely at the same time, we take as our starting point the role of the *adam* as a whole before entertaining the separate role that might have been assigned to the woman.

Why was the *adam* created? In Genesis, the ultimate raison d'être for the *adam* is discussed a number of times: Genesis 1:26, 28; 2:5, 15; and 2:18, 24. Some of these passages are regularly adduced to demonstrate the superiority of man and the concomitant inferiority of woman. The first pair of passages seems to be concerned with the undifferentiated *adam;* the last, clearly, with the woman. The second appears, on first reading, also to refer to the undifferentiated *adam,* but that assumption becomes less reasonable as we reread it in light of the later texts referring to the creation of woman.

The creation of the *adam* in Genesis 1 is bracketed by two statements clearly delineating God's intentions. In the same verse in which God proposes forming a human "in our image, according to our likeness," God goes on to state the mission of this creature: to "rule over the fish of the sea and the fowl of the heavens and the cattle and all the earth[191] and all the crawling things that crawl on the earth" (Genesis 1:26). Similarly, immediately after the *adam* is created as male and female, God restates this role in the context of the divine blessing.

א 28 וַיְבָרֶךְ אֹתָם אֱלֹהִים וַיֹּאמֶר לָהֶם אֱלֹהִים פְּרוּ וּרְבוּ וּמִלְאוּ אֶת־
הָאָרֶץ וְכִבְשֻׁהָ וּרְדוּ בִּדְגַת הַיָּם וּבְעוֹף הַשָּׁמַיִם וּבְכָל־חַיָּה הָרֹמֶשֶׂת עַל־
הָאָרֶץ:

1:28 And God blessed them and God said to them: "Be fertile and
increase and fill the earth and subdue it; and rule over the fish of
the sea, the fowl of the sky, and all the living things that creep on
the earth." (Genesis 1:28)

Much of the language in God's postcreation blessing is identical with the
previous declaration of intention. These complementary statements
would have the *adam* responsible for taking charge of life on earth. The
object of this blessing is both the male and the female, with no distinction between their respective roles. No division of labor is addressed,
leaving them to determine it in whatever manner they find useful.[192]

The significant difference between these two iterations of the role of
the *adam*[193] is the four-verb sequence that opens the blessing: "be fruitful
and multiply and fill the earth and subdue it," which appears only in Genesis 1:28. The first three verbs are the same ones previously used in connection with the blessing of the fowl of the skies and all that lives in the sea
(Genesis 1:21–22) and will reappear in the blessing God gives Noah and his
sons (Genesis 9:1). For the *adam,* this shared task becomes relevant after
the division into male and female; sexuality is requisite for procreation.

The verb that appears in this verse, but neither in the blessing on the
fifth day in Genesis 1:21–22, nor in the intentional statement in 1:26, is
vekhivshuha, "and subdue it." As usually translated, it extends the power
of the *adam,* linking the previously used phrases and signaling the addition of power over the earth in general, leaving the specifics as examples.
But an orthographic anomaly offers an opening for further interpretation. Although the masoretic vocalization[194] of *vekhivshuha* indicates a
plural subject for that imperative, the written text omits the letter *vav*
that would normally, but not always, serve as the marker of the plural.
The Masoretes, reasonably reading this word as one of a series of plural
imperatives, vocalized the word as a plural.[195]

Some of the rabbis, however, used the original spelling as an opportunity
to make a statement about the power differential between men and women.
Following a discussion in *Genesis Rabbah* 8:12 of the appropriate day of the
week for the marriage of a virgin, one finds the following passage:

63

ר' לעזר בשם רבי יוסי בר זמרא וכבשוה וכבשה כת', האיש מצוה
על פריה ורביה אבל לא האשה, ר' יוחנן בן ברוק' אומר אחד האיש
ואחד האשה על שניהם הוא אומר ויברך אותם וגו', וכבשה כת',
האיש כובש את אשתו שלא תצא לשוק, שכל אשה היוצאה לשוק
סופה להיכשל, מנ' לן מדינה דכת' ותצא דינה וגו' (בראשית לד א)
ר' יצחק בשם ר' חנינא (אמר) הלכה כר' יוחנן בן ברוק'.

R. Le'azar in the name of R. Yose bar Zimra said: "[Why do we
read] 'vekhivshuha' [you (masculine plural)[196] subdue it (feminine)]? 'Vekhivshah' [you (masculine singular) subdue it (feminine)] is written. The man is commanded regarding procreation
but not the woman."

R. Yohanan ben Beroqah says: "It is the same for the man and the
same for the woman [because] the text says regarding both of
them, 'And He blessed them, etc.'"

"[Why do we read] 'vekhivshuha' [you (plural) subdue it (feminine)]?—It is written 'vekhivshah' [you (masculine singular) subdue
it (feminine)]. A man should subdue his wife so that she not go out
to the market, for every woman who goes out to the market will
end up stumbling. From where do we know this?

From [the story of] Dinah, as it is said, 'Now Dinah . . . went
out, etc.' (Genesis 34:1).

R. Yitshaq in the name of R. Hanina [said]: "The law follows R.
Yohanan ben Beroqah."[197]

This excerpt from *Genesis Rabbah* 8:12 records a difference of opinion
between two sages. It opens as though the participants in the discussion
were trying to ascertain the correct reading of the Hebrew text of Genesis 1:28, but its real subject is gender hierarchy. Citing the authority of R.
Yose bar Zimra, R. Le'azar says that the word should be read as a singular: *vekhivshah*, as it might have been were it not in a series of unambiguously plural verbs.[198] On the surface, this does not seem to make much
difference, but the midrash tells us otherwise. Reading the word as a
masculine singular verb and the direct object suffix as referring to the
land, as it most logically does, R. Yose bar Zimra connects this verb with
the previous two, which refer to human procreation. It is through procreation that humans will come to subdue the land.[199] If the subject of
vekhivshah is understood as masculine singular, the prototypical first man

bears responsibility for procreation.[200] R. Yoḥanan ben Beroqah retorts by taking us back to the text. As he points out, the blessing—of which *vekhivshuha/vekhivshah* is one component—is given to both the man and the woman. For that reason he concludes that the man and the woman are equally responsible for fulfilling the commandment to "be fruitful and multiply." Baskin claims that his opinion "remained a minority view."[201] But at the end of this midrash, as we shall see, R. Yitsḥaq in the name of R. Ḥanina states that the law follows the opinion of R. Yoḥanan ben Beroqah.

Rabbinic discussions of this type often end up with unresolved issues. In this dispute, there are those who claim that the obligation is only the man's and those who claim that it is both the woman's and the man's; no one maintains that it is only the woman's.[202]

But this midrash continues to explicate the difficult word *kh.v.sh.h.* How does our anonymous speaker arrive at a reading of this text so removed from its context? It is a two-step process. First, he must agree with R. Yose bar Zimra that *vekhivshah* should be read as "you (masculine singular) subdue it (feminine)," despite its position in a series of plural verbs. In addition, however, he reads the feminine direct object pronoun suffix of that verb as "the woman," rather than "the land," despite the position of "the land" as its grammatical antecedent.

By setting Dinah, who is, as we have seen in *Genesis Rabbah* 18:2, condemned by the rabbis for having ventured forth, as the warning of what happens to women who are not kept at home, our anonymous speaker would seem to be countering the egalitarian position of R. Yoḥanan ben Beroqah. Not only is a woman not obligated in the commandment of procreation; she is also not to be trusted to go out alone. At the very point where R. Yoḥanan ben Beroqah sees parity for the man and the woman, the anonymous speaker sees the absolute control of the husband over the wife, who may not be trusted to go even as far as the marketplace.

But the last word in the passage is not that R. Yoḥanan ben Beroqah's stance is beyond the pale, but that it represents the final position, which is to be embedded in Jewish law or halakhah. This passage is another example of the "wholly balanced anthropology" Visotzky attributes to the rabbis,[203] allowing the reader to weigh a spectrum of relationships for the man and the woman. They may be equal, or the woman may be slightly less responsible, or she may be so irresponsible as to require constant supervision; each of these possibilities exists within the midrashic structure.

The role of the *adam* in the second Creation story seems, at first, to be largely agricultural. Following the statement that the earth and heaven have been created, we find the following: "when no bush of the field was yet on the earth and no grass of the field had yet grown, because the Lord God had not caused rain [to fall] upon the earth and there was no *adam* to work the soil" (Genesis 2:5). Although not explicitly stated, the implication of this statement is clear: the role of the *adam,* after its creation, will be to till the soil. There is no indication that its responsibilities will be limited to the Garden that is yet to be planted. The gap between the perception of the need and the creation of the *adam* parallels God's hesitation before taking action that we see in Genesis 1:26.

Once the *adam* is placed in the newly formed Garden, its role is unambiguously, but tersely, indicated: *le'ovdah ulshomrah,* "to work it and to preserve it" (Genesis 2:15). It does seem to be a modest expansion of the previous statement that the absence of an *adam* to work it resulted in an *adamah* or "earth" that yielded no vegetation.[204]

What does the *adam* actually do? God seems to have preempted some of its responsibilities by planting the Garden with trees (Genesis 2:8–9) and providing a flow of groundwater sufficient to water them (Genesis 2:10–14). How much tending do the trees need? Does the *adam* do any of it? We are not told anything about the *adam's* actions until the naming of the animals.

In this description the *adam* seems to be a single creature. All the verbs and pronouns referring to the *adam* in Genesis 2:5–20 are masculine singular in form. Were it not for the fact that the reader of Genesis 2 is likely to have read Genesis 1, there would be no reason to suspect that the creature may be plural. We have no space to read a separate woman into this text.

The first hint of a woman is God's declaration: *Lo tov heyot ha'adam levaddo e'eseh lo 'ezer kenegdo,* "It is not good for the *adam* to be alone; I will make for it a helper fitting for it" (Genesis 2:18). This text, calling something in Creation "not good," contrasts sharply with the string of "good" that God has seen in Creation to this point.[205] It unambiguously links the creation of woman with a need of the *adam* perceived by God and would seem to make the position of woman secondary to that of man. It again parallels the first Creation story where God pauses long enough to reveal the plan to create the *adam* and indicates the goals of that act of creation (Genesis 1:26).[206] The creation of woman is thus defined as a separate, deliberate, and significant act.

But what does this indicate about the nature of the relationship between the *adam* and the "helper"? Classifying the woman as a helper of the *adam* serves, at first glance, further to reinforce the impression that woman exists to fill a need for the *adam* and to support it. The text itself seems to put her in the position of a support for a person who is helpless, in need of help.[207] But, once more, the seemingly unequivocal text of the Bible becomes polysemic when examined closely. Is God addressing the situation of the *adam* as lonely or as singular, as unique? Loneliness is not an issue that attracts a great deal of attention in the Hebrew Bible. Most of the 158 uses of various forms of *levad* seem to focus on singularity rather than loneliness. Clearly, when it describes inanimate objects the word does not mean "lonely," but its uses relating to humans are also likely to describe uniqueness. For example, when, as Greenstein indicates, Jethro tells Moses that it is *lo tov*, "not good" for him to serve as sole magistrate for the Israelites (Exodus 18:17–28), he uses *levaddo* to mean "alone," "without help."[208] Similarly, Moses twice complains that, given the large number of Israelites and the complexities of their situation, he cannot carry the burden of leadership by himself, using the word *levaddi* (by myself) to indicate his position as the one unique, but not necessarily lonely, authority (Numbers 11:12; Deuteronomy 1:9, 14).[209] As we have seen, the *adam* was created, at least in part, because there was a need for some being who could help the earth realize its potential. That reasoning renders the *adam*'s position similar to Moses's in that there was too much work for one human to complete.

For manifold reasons, the rabbis perceive human solitude as less than ideal. As is apparent in the following selection from *Genesis Rabbah* 17:2, this biblical text was read as though it meant that the *adam* were lonely rather than presenting the *adam* as overworked, unable to tend the Garden unassisted.

לא טוב תני כל שאין לו אשה שרוי בלא טובה בלא עזר בלא שמחה בלא ברכה בלא כפרה, בלא טובה, לא טוב היות האדם לבדו, בלא עזר אעשה לו עזר כנגדו, בלא שמחה ושמחת אתה וביתך (דברים יד כו), בלא ברכה להניח ברכה אל ביתך (יחזקאל מד ל) בלא כפרה וכפר בעדו ובעד ביתו (ויקרא טז יא), ר' סימון בשם ר' יהושע בן לוי (אמר) אף בלא שלום שנ' וביתך שלום (ש"א כה ו), ר' יהושע דסכנין בשם ר' לוי (אמר) אף בלא חיים דכת' ראה חיים עם אשה אשר אהבתה (קהלת ט ט), ר' חייא בר גומדי אמר אף אינו אדם שלם שנאמר ויברך אתם ויקרא את שמם אדם (בראשית ה ב), ויש אומ' אף ממעט את הדמות כי בצלם אלהים עשה את האדם (שם ט ו) ומה כת' אחריו ואתם פרו ורבו (שם שם ז).

67

"It is not good [Genesis 2:18]." It was taught: "Anyone who is in a wifeless state is without goodness, without help, without happiness, without blessing and without atonement."

"[What is the source for] 'without goodness?' " "It is not good for the *adam* to be alone [Genesis 2:18]."

"[What is the source for] 'without help?' " "I will make for it a helper fitting for it [Genesis 2:18]."

"[What is the source for] 'without joy?' " "And you shall rejoice, you and your household [Deuteronomy 14:26]."

"[What is the source for] 'without blessing?' " "That a blessing may rest upon your house [Ezekiel 44:30]."

"[What is the source for] 'without atonement?' " "And he shall make atonement for himself, and for his house [Leviticus 16:11]."

R. Simon said in the name of R. Yehoshuaʿ ben Levi: "Also without peace, for it is said: 'Peace be to your house' [1 Samuel 25:6]."

R. Yehoshuaʿ of Sikhnin said in the name of R. Levi: "Also without life, for it is written: 'Enjoy life with a woman you love.' [Ecclesiastes 9:9]."

R. Ḥiyya bar Gomdi said: "He is also not a complete person [*adam*], [for it is written], 'And He blessed them, and called their name "*adam*" [Genesis 5:2].' "

Some say: "He even diminishes the [Divine] likeness [*demut*]: [as it is written], 'For in the image of God He made the *adam*' [Genesis 9:6]. What is written after that? 'And you [plural], be fruitful and multiply' [Genesis 9:7]."[210]

This clearly androcentric—but just as clearly not misogynistic—midrash reads the value of marriage into Genesis 2:18 by examining, from the man's perspective, the benefits that accrue from marriage. Fully half of the ten proof texts are connected with Creation, the first two from the very verse in Genesis that is under discussion.[211] The anonymous speaker in this midrash considers the word *tov*, which is translated in the Bible as the adjective "good," to be a noun. Thus, having an *adam*, here appropriately translated as "man," without a spouse implies that he is without good, or, perhaps, goodness, in his life. Although not cited here, Proverbs 18:22a, "He who has found a wife has found goodness," may underlie this discussion. If the solution is to provide him some assistance in the form of a female partner, then, without that partner, he would also be largely without help.

R. Ḥiyya bar Gomdi's statement near the end of this midrash is based on the text of the third, summary telling of the Creation story in Genesis 5:1–2:

ה 1 זֶה סֵפֶר תּוֹלְדֹת אָדָם בְּיוֹם בְּרֹא אֱלֹהִים אָדָם בִּדְמוּת אֱלֹהִים עָשָׂה אֹתוֹ: ה 2 זָכָר וּנְקֵבָה בְּרָאָם וַיְבָרֶךְ אֹתָם וַיִּקְרָא אֶת־שְׁמָם אָדָם בְּיוֹם הִבָּרְאָם:

5:1 This is the record of *adam's* lineage: On the day God created *adam* in the likeness of God He made it.   5:2 Male and female He created them and He blessed them and called their name *adam* on the day of their creation. (Genesis 5:1–2)

As we have seen, here the order is different from that of Genesis 1 so that it appears that the singular creature, which becomes gendered and plural, is called by the singular name *adam* only after it has been created as man and woman. Thus, R. Ḥiyya bar Gomdi claims that the male and the female together constitute a complete *adam,* a thought that reflects the way in which the biblical text restores the sundered *adam* to wholeness.[212]

The other five proof texts adduced here present us with sources from Leviticus, Deuteronomy, I Samuel, Ezekiel, and Ecclesiastes. With the exception of the verse from Ecclesiastes, each of these texts uses the word *bayit* (house, home, or household), rather than a specific reference to a woman or a wife. This practice is attested to in the Mishnah, where, for example, the High Priest was directed, on the Day of Atonement, to ask forgiveness first for himself and *beito* (his house).[213] The mishnah goes on to say that "his house" means "his wife." But that is not the only source. R. Yose claims that he always referred to his wife as his house.[214] One might understand this to be a sign of respect to the wife, unless one checks the source in the Talmud, where he describes his similar practice of calling his ox his field. Nonetheless, for the rabbis, without a wife, there could be no house or household—certainly none that would include joy, blessing, atonement, or peace.

The context of the reference from 1 Samuel, the only one referring to a specific woman, is striking, even jarring. After the death of the prophet Samuel, David sets his eye on the property of Nabal and on Abigail, his wife, who is characterized as intelligent and beautiful, literally, "a woman good in intelligence and beautiful of form" (1 Samuel 25:3). Abigail does succeed in bringing peace into Nabal's household by interceding with David after her husband has refused him "protection money." But that peace is short-lived; Nabal dies shortly after Abigail reveals that she has stealthily plied David and his troops with food. Subsequently, Abigail becomes David's wife. From this we may deduce that a woman has, as R. Simon says, the power to placate as demonstrated by Abigail's having mollified David. But we might bear in mind that she acts through devious and deceptive means to undermine Nabal's household.[215] David's household, to which she moved, was anything but peaceful—a fact R. Simon conveniently overlooks.

But, although *levad,* when referring to humans, can mean either "lonely" or "unique," it is also frequently used in the Hebrew Bible to describe God.[216] While a Heschelian might read into these passages God's search for humans,[217] the plain meaning of the text itself simply emphasizes God's uniqueness or singularity. The notion of human uniqueness is thus doubleedged. On the one hand, it sets the human apart from the animal and plant world as a sentient, intelligent being; on the other, it can threaten the status of God Whose uniqueness and singularity are important attributes.

Building on the image of God as alone and unique, *Pirkei Rabbi Eliʿezer* presents us with a radically different rationale for the creation of woman. The context is a description of the *adam*'s responsibilities within the Garden of Eden.

והיה מטייל בגן־עדן כאחד ממלאכי השרת. אמר הקדוש־ברוך־הוא,
אני יחיד בעולמי, וזה יחיד בעולמו. אני אין פריה ורביה לפני, וזה
אין פריה ורביה לפני. לאחר כן יאמרו הבריות, הואיל ואין לפניו
פריה ורביה, הוא שבראנו, לא־טוב היות האדם לבדו אעשה לו עזר
כנגדו (בראש' ב יח).

And [the *adam*] would stroll in the Garden of Eden, like one of the ministering angels. Said the Holy One, blessed be He: "I am unique[218] in My world and this one [the *adam*] is unique in his[219] world. I have no one with Me [with whom] to procreate and this one has no one with him [with whom] to procreate. Hereafter all the creatures[220] will say: 'Since he [the *adam*] has no connection with propagation, it is he who has created us.' It is not good for the *adam* to be alone; I will make for him a helper fitting for him (Genesis 2:18)."[221]

Instead of the *adam*- or male-centered view of the situation presented both by the anonymous voice at the beginning of *Genesis Rabbah* 17:2 and by R. Ḥiyya bar Gomdi at its end, *Pirkei Rabbi Eliʿezer* assesses the situation from the perspective of the Divine. The portrayal of God here as insecure, vulnerable to the threat of another being who might be mistaken for divine, is not that of an omnipotent Creator. It is closer to the picture of a God Who is threatened by humanity that may overstep its bounds.[222] God's anxiety should not be mistaken for baseless paranoia. According to a previous passage in *Pirkei Rabbi Eliʿezer,* the animals had already worshiped the *adam* shortly after its creation.[223] If the creation of woman answers God's need, rather than the *adam*'s, she is on a par with the *adam,* rather than subsidiary to him.[224]

No exploration of the purpose of the creation of woman can be based solely upon the first hemistich of Genesis 2:18; it must also involve the second. There is less room for interpretation in the words: *eʿeseh lo ʿezer kenegdo,* "I will make for it a helper fitting for it." Following the Hebrew word order, the first problem is the word *lo,* "for it." Whatever way that word is turned, it unequivocally refers to the *adam,* not God, Who, as the speaker, indicates that woman is created for the *adam,* though not necessarily secondary to him. At the same time it does not preclude providing a creature for the *adam* who will also, or even primarily, serve God's need.

The real issue is the connotations of the word *ʿezer,* which apparently derives from the root *ʿ.z.r,* meaning "help."[225] The root occurs as various forms of the noun *ʿezer* twenty-one times in the Hebrew Bible, twice in these verses (Genesis 2:18, 20). Of the remaining nineteen occurrences, sixteen clearly refer to God or to help from a divine source, only three to humans or help from a human source.[226] The overwhelming preponderance of references to God as the *ʿezer* makes it unlikely that the word in Genesis is signaling that the woman was created for a secondary role, despite the fact that the relegation of woman to a subordinate role has clearly found support over the centuries in just such a reading.[227]

The obscurity of *kenegdo* underscores the ambiguity of *ʿezer.* Because this is the only place in the Hebrew Bible where the preposition *neged* is joined to the preposition *ke-,*[228] its meaning is not clear. While its import is relational, the nature of the relation is not apparent. It probably implies an equal relationship, as the underlying meaning of *neged* includes "opposite, facing."[229] Speiser's translation, "an aid fit for him," also suggests an equal, rather than a subordinate. He claims that the Hebrew "means literally 'alongside him,' i.e., 'corresponding to him,'" rather than "helpmeet, appropriate help," which has become "helpmate."[230] Edward L. Greenstein explains "a helper alongside it" as meaning: "Just as YHWH God made the first human to help him, he made the pair of humans to help each other."[231]

Thus, the common view that the woman created in Genesis 2 is un-equivocally designed to be subservient to the man is not supported by the words used to describe the relationship. It is at least equally possible that the phrase *'ezer kenegdo* describes a creature of status equal to that of the man. The possibility that woman may have been created to improve the situation of man does not necessarily mean that she is in any way inferior.

God brings the woman to the *adam* and disappears, reappearing only after the primal couple have eaten the fruit and covered their nakedness. In presenting this new creature to the *adam*, God does not indicate any purpose. Unlike the animals brought to the *adam* in order to be named, this creature's relationship to the *adam* is unspecified. "She belongs to a new order that will by itself transform the earth creature."[232]

The nature of the power relationship between the first man and the first woman seems to be of more interest to the readers of the biblical text than to its writer or redactor. Genesis 2 is often misread as linking the *adam*'s naming the woman with his domination of her—a major reinterpretation of the plain sense of the Bible. There is no inherent parallel between the *adam*'s giving names to the animals and calling the woman *ishah*. Human domination over the animals was part of the divine plan from the very beginning (Genesis 1:26). When God brings the animals to the *adam* it is so that it can name them; when God brings the woman to the *adam*, there is no explicit indication of what God has in mind. The *adam* arrogates to himself the power to name her not with a personal name, but with a generic[233] that had already appeared in the previous verse (Genesis 2:22). Unlike the naming of the animals—where the *adam* has the prerogative of choosing a name and God waits upon the *adam*'s selection—in the case of the woman, the *adam* is, in his excitement, essentially confirming the preexisting no-menclature. This does not necessarily give him power over her.

The only context clue we are provided emphasizes the power of women. The very next verse describes a matrilocal culture in which a man will leave his parents to cling to his woman. In this case, women would appear to have the upper hand.

God's purpose in creating the first woman is fraught with ambiguity. Whereas the slipperiness of pronouns causes many of the ambiguities relating to number in the P description of the creation of the *adam* in Genesis 1 and 5, when one looks at the divine purpose in Genesis 2, the words themselves seem opaque. That lack of transparency occurs in part because our associations for these words, whether in Hebrew or in English, are far wider than the text of the Hebrew Bible. Thus, the semantic field of "help" in English extends well beyond the Hebrew Bible. Similarly, the word *'ezer* ("help," in modern Hebrew) is as likely to echo with its military use in the context of auxiliary forces, as it is to recall divine help. Staying within the semantic field of the Bible helps narrow the possibilities, but does not exclude all variant understandings of the text.

A close examination of the words of the biblical text yields a picture different from many of the understandings the rabbis—also close readers—found in these texts. Like their rabbinic predecessors, modern rewriters are likely to bring to the biblical text a sense of the myriad possibilities of meaning that can be drawn from it.

Chronology and Hierarchy: A Conclusion

As we have looked at number, substance, and purpose in connection with the creation of woman and man, we have been circling the issue of hierarchy. The various biblical versions of the Creation story have often been cited in justification of a subservient role for women. That subordination would be seen as inherent in women from the moment of the creation of the first woman. Considering the first woman a paradigm, commentators, ancient and modern, have suggested that women are created second or secondary, derivative in substance and underling in purpose.

The issue of number is really a wrestling with order. If, indeed, the original creation of the man and the woman included two separate acts, there was an order to those acts. While the Creation story in Genesis 1 and 2 does not clarify the issue of whether or not the woman was created second, most readers and rewriters agree that the man was not second.[234] If the man and the woman were discretely created, the man must have been first.

Being first, however, does not necessarily imply primacy in importance. If it did, the crawling things would be more important than the humans because they were created a day earlier according to Genesis 1. In the primeval history recorded in Genesis, the role of precedence in determining hierarchy is so fraught with ambiguities that we shall have to move to later parts of the Pentateuch to gain some insight. Reframing our question regarding the impact of primacy on hierarchy, we might state it as: Does "birth order" have an impact on the "inheritance"? The legal sections regarding laws of inheritance give the advantage to the firstborn.[235] The message embedded in the narrative, on the other hand, is quite different. From the first instance of siblings, Cain and Abel, through the Genesis narratives and even into Exodus and 1 and 2 Samuel, God seems never to prefer the firstborn.[236] The divine pleasure in the sacrifice of Abel (Genesis 4:4) is replicated again and again.

Although conventional wisdom, aided in this case by sources like Paul,[237] assumes that second is secondary, we must conclude otherwise. In the context of the Genesis narratives, woman's not being created first would be tantamount to giving her the preferred place. Nor is it entirely counterintuitive to have the second preferred over the first. In our computer age surely we know that each successive version of hardware and software is, at least in theory, improved over its predecessor. Once more, the biblical text proves, upon examination, to be more ambiguous than it seems at first glance.

In fact, there is yet another reason to see the second place in this text as positive, rather than accepting the facile negative valence usually attached to it. The story of Creation in Genesis 1 is not static. Clearly the order goes from the less complex things to more complex beings. In other words, it seems to go from lower to higher. If, as people popularly do, one were to conflate Genesis 1 and 2, one would find that, because woman is created later, she is further away from the inanimate parts of Creation and, as Trible has pointed out,[238] closer to its pinnacle, namely, the Sabbath.[239]

The very physical substances from which the first woman and man were created would appear to be quite different. According to Genesis 2, the only account to provide any details, the *adam* is created out of clods of moist earth and the breath of life. The woman, on the other hand, is created from a side of the *adam*. Rabbinic discussions notwithstanding, there seems to be no inherent reason to think that a creature formed out of "dust of the earth" and "the breath of life" is necessarily superior to one created out of earth and breath that had been made human. Further, if the *adam* includes both the male and female, created at once, then they are necessarily of the same material when separated.

Finally, a close reading of the biblical texts indicates that an egalitarian relationship between the man and the woman is at least as likely to have

74

been God's design as a hierarchical one. They seem to have been created for the same purpose; although the woman may be the helper of the man, we must see this in the context of the Hebrew Bible, where help most often comes from on high.

But our study has gone beyond the biblical texts and scholarly approaches to them to engage two different generations of rewriters: the rabbis of late antiquity and modern Jewish poets. Clearly each of these groups has found the biblical stories so compelling as to warrant attention and the various individual members of these groups of rewriters have brought to the task both sensitivity to the original and perspectives shaped by their own values. The dialogue between them and the Bible moves in both directions, enabling readers to develop further insight into the Bible through these later approaches and understanding the later works better in light of how the original text makes room for their innovations.[240]

Thus, for example, the juxtaposition of Kim Chernin's "The Call" and the biblical text helps us see how voiceless the first woman is in the passages describing her creation in Genesis. Chernin helps us hear her silence, even as we hear the *adam*'s voice. We are reminded that voice plays a considerable role in assessing the relative power of people. The intelligence with which Chernin's Eve muses on her origins is missing from the biblical text, which fails to record a response from the woman to the *adam*'s well-chosen words.

The role of rib as metonym also reinforces the breadth of the various interpretative possibilities. R. Yehoshua°'s reductionist misogynistic catalogue of the ways women are Other and inferior due to their origin in the rib serves to confront us with the ways in which anatomy can be read as destiny. Linda Pastan's reading of the same anatomic structure, however, points to the way in which what we bring to a text influences our reading. For her, the choice of one rib out of many is a positive foundation for the first woman, who eventually uses the bone as a metaphor for the knock of opportunity. The choice of the rib is also significant to R. Levi, as quoted by R. Yehoshua° of Sikhnin in *Genesis Rabbah* 18:2. For him, it is explicitly God Who is doing the choosing with the goal of reining in the troublesome nature of woman. Kim Chernin's use of the rib to give strength to the newly "wakened" creature, "ribbed with mortality," is more ambiguous, linking, as it does, the strength of the rib and the weakness of mortality. These differing rewritings of the "rib" version of the creation of woman in Genesis 2:21–22 freight our choice between "rib" and "side" as the meaning of *tselaʿ* with new significance. Each of these versions of the creation of the first woman envisions differently the hierarchical relationship between women and men.

The significance of the Creation myths in Genesis is such that they can give rise to a wide variety of interpretation without loosening their grip on the creative imagination. These texts, which have in the past made room for interpretations that tend to support male dominance, have been seen in the contemporary period, in a light that opens the possibility of egalitarian readings. Genesis forecloses neither path.

As we have explored the creation of Eve in biblical, rabbinic, and modern versions, we have examined texts that ultimately define and redefine a hierarchical relationship between the man and the woman. We move to our analysis of the next stage in the development of the first woman with a heightened awareness of the way hierarchy is shaped by writers and re-writers through their playing with the polysemic biblical text. As we continue to follow the first woman's trajectory to its apogee at the beginning of Genesis 4, we are more sensitive to her expanding voice and agency, which ultimately give her the position of prominence. The story of the *adam* becomes the story of the first woman.

Chapter Two: Life in the Garden of Eden

Eve in Eden: The Test

חַוָּה

אָהַבְתִּי אֶת אָדָם. הוּא כֵאלֹהִים
חָכָם. וְהוּא עַז־לֵב, וְדָמוֹ טוֹב.
אַךְ הַנָּחָשׁ יְלַחֵשׁ דְּבָרִים תְּמוּהִים,
וְלַחֲשׁוֹ מַכְאִיב וְגַם יְלַטּוֹף.

כִּי יֵרָדֵם אָדָם הַגַּן מַשְׁמִים
וְצִפֳּרָיו שׁוֹתְקוֹת, דְּשָׁאוֹ רָטֹב, –
יִקְרָא לִי מִן הַסְּבַךְ, וּכְמְדוּרַת קְסָמִים
יַדְלִיק שִׂיחוֹ בַּלֵּב: לִקְטֹף! לִקְטֹף!

עִם שַׁחַר יַעַל, יַד אָדָם חַמָּה
לוֹטֶפֶת שׁוּב בְּשָׂרִי, וְכֹה יָרְוַח
לֵב כִּי אַאֲזִין אֶת צְלִיל דָּמָה.

אָכֵן כָּל שִׂיחַ־יוֹם, בָּאוֹר יִרְגַּע,
כָּפוּף לְצַד אַחֵר, וְכָל חֶלְקָה
בַּגַּן קְסוּמָה עַד לֵיל מוּל צֵל הַסְּבָךְ.

Eve[1]

I have loved Adam. He is like God
Wise. And he is strong of heart and his blood is good.
But the serpent will whisper puzzling things,
And his whisper hurts but also will caress.

When Adam will fall asleep, the Garden is dreary
And its birds are silent and its grass wet, —
He will call me from the thicket, and a sort of enchanted bonfire[2]
His conversation will ignite in the heart: To pluck! To pluck!

With dawn's rise,[3] Adam's warm hand
Caresses my flesh again, and it will so ease
The heart when I will listen to the sound of its blood.

Indeed every day-shrub,[4] which will be calm in the light,
Bent to another side, and every plot [of land]
In the garden is enchanted until evening *facing the thicket's shadow.*[5]

In this remarkable sonnet, the twentieth-century Hebrew writer and scholar Yaakov Fikhman (1881–1958) attempts to fill one of the many gaps in the biblical story of Eve. Fikhman, whose writings include a broad field—poetry, short stories, essays, literary criticism, elementary school textbooks—wrote a number of poems on biblical themes. In these poems he does not contradict the biblical text, but adds detail, particularly through dialogue, to "reveal the inner life" of biblical figures.[6] The biblical story of Eve progresses from the second telling of the creation of Eve, through the brief and enigmatic hint of a matrilocal society in which a man will leave his father and mother to cling to his wife, to the statement of life in Eden: "And the two of them were naked, the *adam* and his woman, and they were not ashamed" (Genesis 2:25). The biblical text is predictably silent[7] on such details as: What was life like in Eden? What were the feelings of the first man and woman? Did a moment or a long stretch of time in Eden precede the eating of the fruit?

Fikhman fills these lacunae with this sonnet, carefully crafted to incorporate significant elements from the biblical story. Afforded voice,[8] Eve expresses the internal tension between the love she professes for Adam and the nocturnal enchantments whispered by the serpent. Adam in the light of day and the serpent in night's darkness[9] vie for her allegiance.

Eve opens her monologue with a deceptively simple assertion: "I have loved Adam." The poem, although replete with contrasting forces, contains no parallel statement of Eve's feelings for the snake. But the past tense of the verb, the poem's only verb in the past, implicitly conveys her feelings. Whether translated as "I loved," "I did love," or "I have loved," it is an action that has been concluded.

The notion of love between a man and a woman is found nowhere in the early chapters of Genesis. The closest approximation is Adam's excited reaction to the creation of woman (Genesis 2:23).[10] Although one might argue that Fikhman is here providing Eve's response to that declaration, love is different from excitement. Textually, it is worth observing that the use of the root '.h.b to express love between humans lies some twenty biblical chapters and twenty generations in the future.[11]

Eve's opening assertion seizes the reader's attention both by its simplicity and forthrightness and by its form: it creates a caesura, a complete stop, midline. How we read the interruption in the flow of Eve's words depends on our analysis of the lines that follow. In a first reading the period probably functions like a colon to introduce the reasons for her love. But, reading further, one realizes that the first two lines, focusing on Adam, both include full stops. The unpredictable rhythms of the opening lines, a device we find frequently in Fikhman's work,[12] suggest Eve's conflicted state. She seems to be attempting to clarify her changing emotions, perhaps to convince herself that she does still love Adam, despite her emotional receptivity to the serpent. Yet the fitful way in which she describes Adam's good qualities makes her assertion seem forced.

The second sentence underscores the tension Eve is feeling. "He is like God / Wise." The enjambment identifying the specific way in which Adam resembles God interrupts Eve's description of Adam while extending the movement of the first line. Because the biblical text ascribes the association of knowledge with divinity to the snake, not to the woman (Genesis 3:5), the poem here subliminally links the woman with the snake. The uneven rhythm caused by the enjambment and the two caesuras in the first two lines, which describe Eve's feelings for Adam, differs markedly from the smooth flow of the following two lines in which she describes her relationship with the snake.

To present her feelings for Adam, Eve uses three static and verbless clauses.[13] First, Adam is "like God," a reminder to the reader that the *adam* was created *betselem Elohim* (in the image of God) (Genesis 1:27). Her admiration for Adam is specifically based on his having wisdom, as does God. But wisdom, the most desirable—and the least attainable—possession, ironically can be acquired only by countermanding God's command not to eat from the Tree of the Knowledge of Good and Bad.[14] Fikhman's Eve, who slides across the enjambment to define Adam's divine quality, settles on wisdom, rather than some other godly characteristic such as omnipotence.

The second and third qualities attributed by Eve to Adam are not directly connected to this moment in the primeval history. The phrase "strong of heart" neither appears in the biblical lexicon, nor resonates elsewhere in Hebrew literature. The final phrase "his blood [is] good," although apparently positive, actually pulls in two opposed directions. *Dam* (blood) first appears in Genesis in the story of Cain and Abel. This negative allusion is only partially mitigated by the word *tov* (good) that modifies it. "Good" recalls the many times God pronounces the divine handiwork "good," but it also brings to mind God's statement that it is not good for the *adam* to be alone (Genesis 2:18). In an initial reading one might mistakenly imagine that Eve is giving her approval of Adam here; but these three clauses dwindle from three words to two as Eve finds the evidence she marshals less and less convincing.

The dynamic description of the snake's activities in the third and fourth lines contrasts markedly with the static description of Adam. The active verbs[15] in these three clauses—*yilhash* (will whisper), *makh'iv* (it hurts), *yiltof* (will caress)—give the reader a sense of movement. The third line constitutes a complete thought, conveying a sense of calm after the caesuras and enjambment that complicate the preceding lines. Although the three clauses describing Adam do not allude to his effect on Eve, her description of the serpent focuses entirely on his impact on her. His whisper both pains and caresses—a clear indication of the way in which Eve is emotionally torn. The mysterious sound of the serpent echoes in the thrice repeated *hash* sound: *nahash* (serpent), *yilhash* (he will whisper), *lahasho* (his whisper). Although the first stanza, like the poem as a whole, leaves the speaker's dilemma unresolved, its implicit message is that Eve will follow the serpent.

Like the first stanza, the second is divided evenly between Adam and the serpent. By maintaining similar rhymes for the first two stanzas, Fikhman suggests parallels between some of the lines. Thus, for example, *Elohim* (God) is aurally linked not only to *temuhim* (puzzling) in the first stanza, but also to *mashmim* (dreary) and *kesamim* (enchantments) in the second. On some level God might pick up some of the resonance of the forces that seem to be working to undermine the divine order.

Adam again precedes. Here, however, he is not the focus, but located in the subordinate clause; his action, sleeping. Three simple present tense clauses follow, relating to the atmosphere or mood in the Garden when Adam is asleep. It is not clear whether the relationship is causal or merely temporal.[16] But Adam's only "action" seems to have a deleterious effect on the Garden. While we know that the silence of the birds and the dampness of the grass are natural to the night, Eve, who is awake, perceives these changes and connects them to Adam.

The second half of the stanza again contrasts with the first, presenting the serpent as actively exploiting Eve's vulnerability. His words summon her and ignite in her heart an enchanted bonfire that serves to dispel the dreariness of the night. The rhyme that repeats here echoes the *tov* (good) of the first stanza, along with the *ratov* (wet) of the second. It is technically a slant rhyme because it does not quite match up with *yiltof* (will caress) or *liktof* (to pick).[17] The quasi rhyme may suggest what is awry: the caress of the serpent's voice and its message are not quite "good." But any negative message in the rhyme is offset by the positive message of the biblical allusion to the story of the Binding of Isaac where the word *sevakh* (thicket) appears most memorably, indicating the place where Abraham sees the ram to replace Isaac as the sacrifice (Genesis 22:13). That thicket serves not to hide the ram, but to expose it for capture. Similarly, the snake does not hide in the thicket but announces its presence from it. Although the root of the word for thicket (*s.v.kh*) appears in the Hebrew Bible only in the context of plants,[18] its broadened modern meaning includes "complicated" and "complex" in the psychological sense as well— an indication of the complexity the serpent's presence introduces.

The serpent's words appear straightforward: "To pluck! To pluck!" But the serpent, insofar as his words are reported by Eve, does not explicitly indicate what is to be plucked. Given the context, the reader assumes that the serpent is urging Eve to pick the fruit of the Tree of Knowledge. Why is the message so cryptic? Perhaps Fikhman is attempting to portray the serpent as wily. After all, God admonishes the *adam* against eating the fruit, not against picking it. Eve might follow these instructions and then, unable to resist the fruit in her hand, eat it. The serpent could argue that he had not urged her to disobey God's command. The root of the Hebrew word used for "pluck" also appears together with the word used in this line for "shrub" in Job 30:4 when Job describes a desperate situation in which people are reduced to plucking the leaves of shrubs for food. Thus, the intertext here foreshadows the expulsion of the primeval couple from the lush vegetation of the Garden into the relatively barren world beyond.[19] The second stanza concludes, as does the first, with the image of an Eve torn between a passive Adam and an active serpent.

The sestet clarifies the octave: its opening at dawn contrasts with the previous dreary, nocturnal stanza. The physical caress of Adam's warm hand with the blood rushing through it relieves the tension of Eve's night.

His touch counters the caress of the serpent's whisper. Similarly, the visible enchantment of the Garden by day offsets the emotional enchanted bonfire of the night. Nevertheless, given the structure of the poem—which, to this point, has been symmetrically divided between Adam and the serpent—the reader anticipates that the action ascribed to Adam in the first tercet will leave the final one to the serpent. Unexpectedly, the closing tercet, the richest part of the poem, remains, at first glance, with Adam's time—day—rather than with the serpent's night.

This shift away from the serpent is further complicated by the ambiguity of *siaḥ*, which can mean either "shrub" or "conversation." Positing "shrub" as the primary meaning would have it echo the biblical text where we have read, "when no shrub [*siaḥ*] of the field had yet sprouted" (Genesis 2:5). Thus, the shrub would be characterized as "day" because it blooms only by day, or because it lasts but for a day, or even because it is but a day old, assuming that it had not yet been created at the time the *adam* was created. Furthermore, a shrub may be heliotropic, bending in different directions toward the light.

But *siaḥ* could just as easily mean a conversation by day, picking up on the meaning of *siaḥ* in line 8. This meaning would serve to return us to Eve's inner dialogue where the diurnal and the nocturnal are competing for her loyalty. As we read the first line it seems that the calming of the conversation by day indicates that the day, and Adam as its representative, have prevailed. But we should not forget that *tsad aḥer* ("another side" in the Hebrew) could also be read as a translation of the Aramaic term *sitra aḥra*—the other, evil or satanic side. The day's conversation is clouded by its being subject to the satanic side, the snake's side. In fact, to the night belongs the final word of the poem, bringing with it the shadow of the thicket, the source of the serpent's call. The last three words are set in type with wider spacing both for emphasis and to slow the pace of the recitation, leaving a final weighty impression that the night, the thicket, the voice of the serpent will prevail.

Fikhman not only brings to life the interlude between the creation of woman and her eating the fruit; he also proposes a plausible explanation for Eve's act. Fikhman configures the tension overwhelming Eve as a classic love triangle with three actants:[20] the attractive woman (Eve), the man (Adam), and the seducer (the serpent). God is present only in a simile; the tree, at best, in an ellipsis.[21] In Fikhman's vision the force of darkness, ultimately the most creative, dominates, enticing the woman to abandon the clarity of day.

The serpent's mysteries will prevail over Adam's certainties. Fikhman need not spell out the denouement.

Fikhman conveys this message with subtlety by exploiting the straight-forward sonnet form to express meaning at odds with the poem's logical argument. The structure of the *rime croisée* in the two quatrains of the octave pulls at the contents, which neatly devote the first two lines of each quatrain and the first tercet to Adam, who apparently comes first, while reserving the second half of each quatrain and the meaning of the second tercet for the serpent. By the sestet the form is less than classic, with a hint of terza rima, but form and content converge, indicating that resolution has taken place.

But a classic romantic triangle in which Adam and the snake vie for Eve's affection is not the only way of configuring Eve's dilemma. In his poem *"Khaveh un der eppelboym"* (Eve and the apple tree) (1942),[22] the Yiddish poet Itzik Manger (1901–1969) also presents Eve as torn between Adam and a tempter; this tempter, however, is the apple tree itself. Manger's narrator sets the scene by describing the liminal moment of sunset, a time fraught with possibilities, both positive and negative. Although Judaism often views it as a time when an appeal to God's mercy is particularly efficacious and convention sees it as a moment ripe for romance, it is also the moment before night descends, bringing all its dark terrors.

In ten quatrains, with regular meter and rhyme, Manger portrays the connection between Eve—who is yet to be named the "mother of all living" (Genesis 3:20)—and the tree, here an embodiment of death. The unyielding, regular nature of the verse strikes a contrast with the macabre scene being played out before us. Eve has here been recast as a light-hearted, but moody, young woman.[23]

חוה און דער עפּלבוים

חוה שטייט פֿאַרן עפּלבוים.
דער זונפֿאַרגאַנג איז רויט,
װאָס װיליסטו, מוטער חוה, זאָג,
װאָס װיליסטו װעגן טויט?

5 דער טויט דאָס איז דער עפּלבוים
װאָס בײגט די צװײַגן מיד.
דער אָװנט־פֿויגל אױפֿן בױם
װאָס זינגט זײַן אָװנטליד.

83

Eve and the Apple Tree[24]

Eve stands before the apple tree.
The sunset is red,
What do you know, Mother Eve, tell,
What do you know of death?

Death, that is the apple tree
Which bends its tired boughs.
It is the evening bird on the tree
That sings an evening song.

Paradoxically in the two opening stanzas of the poem, death is active, while the human being is static. Eve is stationary; the sunset seems motionless. Yet the tree bends and the bird sings. The identity of the narrating voice is hidden, as it addresses Eve in the second person, calling her Mother Eve. The voice's question, however, is a pointed one, given God's threat that immediate death would be the punishment for eating from the fruit of the tree. What does death mean to Adam and Eve, newly created and placed in Eden?

Whose voice pronounces the second stanza with its clear threat of death? None of the characters in the poem is a likely narrator. Eve, Adam, and God all speak in the course of the poem, their words set off in quotation marks. That leaves the narration in the authoritative voice of an external narrator, who, having posed the question about death, answers it. The heavy-handed warning that the tree incorporates death is reflected in the lugubrious allusions to endings: the sunset, the evening bird, and the evening song. This scene, set at the beginning of human life, is, paradoxically, all about beautiful endings, not beginnings.

The poem continues with a picture of difference, perhaps even discord, in the primal couple. Adam goes off to the wild wood each day. The forest recalls the biblical scene of the Garden filled with trees (Genesis 2:9) where God places the *adam*. Eve, fearing the forest, is drawn to the apple tree carefully planted in the center of the Garden, somehow set apart, surrounded by a clear space large enough for Eve's dance. This tree, hardly a benign presence, seems to stalk Eve, appearing in her dreams. Eve, in turn, is obsessed by the tree that has all the attraction of the forbidden. She cannot escape it.

ער רוישט און בייגט זיך איבער איר.

זי הערט דאָס וואָרט "באַשערט".

פאַרגעס וואָס "ער" דער גרויסער "דער",

וואָס ער האָט דיר פאַרווערט.   20

און חוה רײַסט אַן עפל אָפּ

און פילט זיך מאָדנע גרינג,

זי קרײַזט פאַרליבט אַרום דעם בוים,

ווי אַ גרויסער שמעטערלינג.

It [er] rustles and bends over her
She hears the word "destined [bashert]."
Forget what "He" [er] the great "That One [der],"
What He [er] has warned you.

And Eve tears an apple off
And feels strangely light,
She circles love-struck, around the tree,
Like a large butterfly.

The scene shifts from the physical world at sunset to the nocturnal realm of dreams. The tree, while not actually speaking, seems to provide clues through its rustling leaves. The adjective *bashert* (destined) is the first hint of the tree's message. Speaking of what is destined to happen, the tree entices Eve to forget the word of the nameless God. It seems to call Eve to her own destiny, long familiar to readers. But with the word *bashert*, Manger implies a mystical, romantic connection between the tree and Eve: *basherter* (the destined one) is often used in the context of love. The poem thus seems to set up a rivalry for Eve between the tree—Death—and Adam. This repeated dream seems so realistic that Eve can feel the tree's tears falling on her hair.

Bashert, however, has an additional connotation. In life, things happen because they are *bashert*, destined to happen. Does Manger suggest that Eve is destined to eat of the fruit of the forbidden tree? Is he playing off the rabbinic midrash that teaches that without the evil inclination, humans would not build homes, marry, have children[25]—provoking us, perhaps, to ask what would have happened if no one had eaten of the tree?

Manger, unlike Fikhman, introduces God into his poem as a presence, not merely a simile: the God of proscription and warning, not the God of creation and nurture. In this poem God is a weak counterpoint to the tree, an absence countering the tree's presence. Never referred to by any of the nouns that indicate divinity, God is *"Er"* (He) or the great *"Der"* (that One). The quotation marks in the original indicate the irony of a God Whose name is ineffable but Who is less compelling than the tree, which is also referred to, in the opening line of the fifth stanza, as *er,* without quotation marks.[26] On some level God is complicit in the tree's seduction of Eve; it is God who concedes that the tree is beautiful and, in a reprise of Joshua 10:12, even holds back the sunset, allowing Eve to admire the tree a bit longer.

Eve tears an apple off the tree in an action that sounds a bit like the tree's rustling in the first line of the previous stanza.[27] Touching the tree, even picking an apple, has no negative effect on Eve. Love-struck, she flits around the tree like a large butterfly. Readers, of course, may find her behavior quite strange. The image of the innocent woman fluttering her skirt or her arms like an ungainly butterfly suddenly airborne evokes a feeling of compassion. Readers know what the consequences of her action are; she does not.

Eve might be viewed as the innocent victim of the tree's pursuit were it not for her words in the penultimate stanza. Echoing God's dictum that the apple tree is beautiful, she urges it not to cry, for it is stronger than God's admonishing words. The apple tree appears nightly in Eve's dreams, crying; she can feel its tears in her heart. She addresses it:

"װיין נישט, שיינער עפלבוים,
דו רוישסט און זינגסט אין מיר
35 און דו ביסט שטאַרקער פֿונעם װאָרט,
װאָס װאָרנט מיך פֿאַר דיר."

און חוה נעמט דעם עפלבוים
מיט בײַדע הענט אַרום,
און איבער דער קרוין פֿון עפלבוים
40 ציטערן די שטערן פֿרום...

"Cry not, beautiful apple tree,
You rustle and sing in me
And you are stronger than the word,
Which warns me about you."

86

> And Eve embraces the apple tree
> With both hands
> And above the crown of the apple tree
> The pious stars tremble . . .

Hearing Eve's own voice at last, we perceive the way in which she is torn between the distant, disembodied, divine command and the real presence of the tree. The tree is a sensory presence: seen, heard, and touched;[28] God is distant, nameless. Aware as she is of God's wishes, Eve cannot heed them when presented with the countering omnipresence of the apple tree. The romantic overtones of a word like *gring* (lighthearted), persistent dreams, and the flitting of a butterfly come together in Eve's embrace of the tree.

The contrasting enticements of the diurnal Adam and the nocturnal serpent neatly divide the experience of Fikhman's Eve. The world of Manger's Eve is less clearly sectored; she does not feel the tension of two loves pulling her in opposite directions. In fact, Adam and the serpent are both absent from Manger's poem: Adam is off in his beloved wild wood and the serpent is nowhere explicitly mentioned. Manger's Eve is both constrained by the negative divine message and lured by the positive overtures of the apple tree. Her decision is never in doubt.

The closing stanza makes particularly skilled use of rhyme. By rhyming *arum* (around) and *frum* (pious) at the second and fourth lines, Manger points to the denouement he sets forth wordlessly, in the final line through the only suspension points in the poem. *Arum* is the prepositional prefix of *arumnemen* (literally, "to take around," thus "to embrace"). This word brings the relationship between Eve and the tree to its closest, most intimate, point, though short of the eating specifically banned in Genesis 2:17. However, it is also a homonym of the Hebrew *'arum* (shrewd), which, in Genesis, characterizes the serpent. Thus, through the bilingual pun, Manger brings the serpent into the picture. In embracing the tree, in touching it, Eve undertakes an action that is not actually forbidden by God's ban on eating of the fruit of the tree (Genesis 2:17). But in her biblical dialogue with the serpent, she effectively adds a ban on touching (Genesis 3:3), which she here violates. Manger's rhyme scheme links it to *frum* (pious), setting up an opposition between the piety of the distant stars that tremble at the action Eve is to take and the shrewdness of the serpent who, though absent, drives the poem. The concluding suspension points indicate that more action follows—and as Manger's poem is a reenactment of an ancient and familiar tale, there can be no doubt concerning the nature and the consequences of that action.

Manger depicts that apple tree as an ever-present source of temptation to Eve; the twentieth-century American poet, librarian, and puppeteer Helen Papell presents a tree that parallels Eve's development. Her first book of poetry, *Talking with Eve, Leah, Hagar, Miriam*,[29] opens with "Tree of Knowing." In it Papell draws upon a single verse in the biblical description of Eve's decision-making process.

Tree of Knowing

> *The woman saw that the tree was*
> *. . . a delight to the eyes"*   —Genesis 3:6

Roots curve a place to be rocked
by a mother
but Eve had none.

Bark red-brown as crust of bread
5   a mother might bless
for a daughter's journey.

A small tree
the first leaves join her shoulders
new buds open into her eyes.[30]

Eve's examination of this tree is not casual. She scrutinizes it from bottom to top before concluding, as the epigraph tells us, that it is a "delight to the eyes." Hers is not Manger's overwhelming, seductive tree but a young tree, no taller than herself. In three three-line stanzas—perhaps paralleling Eve's triple consideration of the tree in the biblical text[31]—Papell depicts a sapling, such as one might expect to find in the newly planted Garden of Eden.

Papell tells us first that the curved roots of the tree represent an absence in Eve's life: that she has no mother to rock or soothe her. The notion of being rocked in one's mother's arms: this simple observation reminds the reader that Eve had no instruction[32] other than God's, which was not communicated directly and included no embrace. The allusion to rocking implies that Eve is yet an infant or a curious young child. Deprived of a mother's care, a parentless child who has no source of moral teaching, Eve takes a solitary path.

Raising her eyes to the tree trunk, Eve sees the "bark red-brown as crust of bread." Mother, initially associated with protective care, is joined to nurture. The daughter, too, has changed before our eyes. She is in a liminal moment, older, ready, perhaps, to set out on life's journey, but fortified by the knowledge represented by the tree, rather than by physical maternal sustenance—milk or bread. This passage foreshadows the road out of Eden, away from the tree, that Eve will eventually take, after gaining the knowledge that the tree, by then mature, will offer.

The last stanza concludes the progression whereby Eve seems to have slowly disappeared from the scene. "Eve" in the first stanza, "a daughter" in the second; she becomes represented in the third as synecdoches: "her shoulders" and "her eyes" serve only as points of reference for the tree. Her shoulders are at leaf height; her eyes, at the buds. The tree, which was initially depicted as a potential surrogate for Eve's nonexistent mother, mature enough to have protruding roots, has become a metaphor for Eve herself. What delights her eyes in the tree is its potential, its buds. Familiar with Eve's story, we know that the buds will flower and fruit and that Eve will taste of that forbidden fruit; but that action lies in the future, beyond the bounds of the poem. The present holds the picture of an infant turned girl, growing into an independent woman, who sees in the tree's buds the hope of the future. Thus, Papell presents the woman alone, omitting Adam, God, and the snake from the story.

While both Fikhman and Manger depict an Eve caught between opposing forces of change and stasis, Papell omits stasis. For Fikhman and Manger these forces contend unequally for Eve's loyalty. Adam, asleep according to Fikhman, or away in the woods according to Manger, cannot prevail against the wily serpent's whispers, cannot win Eve's affection once the tree obsesses her, intruding on her dreams. In Papell's poem, no conflict appears; she envisions only the development of Eve to the threshold of womanhood, the growth of the tree about to flower.

Even as Eve is pulled apart into synecdoche in the course of this short poem, the image of the tree moves in the opposite direction. Roots in the first tercet, bark in the second, the tree as a whole appears only in the last tercet. Hardly the menacing tree of temptation or disobedience, it is apparently an uncomplicated tree, still growing. It has yet to set fruit. It is, in a sense, a prepubescent tree and, thus, a match for the prepubescent daughter whose eyes delight in it. Locating her tree—and her Eve—in the moment before the fruit sets, Papell chooses an epigraph indicative of her unsullied perspective on Eve's story. Looking at the tree is licit; eating its fruit and gaining its knowledge are not. Papell has transformed the biblical story of disobedience and expulsion into a positive statement about the motherless woman who becomes the mother of humankind.

The biblical text provides little background for the exchange between the serpent and the woman. The predictive, future-oriented verse: "Therefore a man [ish] will leave his father and his mother and cling to his woman [ishto]"(Genesis 2:24)[33] that concludes the second telling of the creation of woman is followed by a single verse that returns the reader to the Garden[34] by describing the situation of the man and woman and by half a verse introducing the serpent.

ב 25 וַיִּהְיוּ שְׁנֵיהֶם עֲרוּמִּים הָאָדָם וְאִשְׁתּוֹ וְלֹא יִתְבֹּשָׁשׁוּ: ג 1 וְהַנָּחָשׁ הָיָה עָרוּם מִכֹּל חַיַּת הַשָּׂדֶה אֲשֶׁר עָשָׂה יְ-הֹוָה אֱלֹהִים.

2:25 The two of them were naked, the *adam* and his woman, but they were not in a state of shame.[35] 3:1 But the serpent was the shrewdest of all the beasts of the field that the Lord God had made. (Genesis 2:25–3:1)

Some scholars consider Genesis 2:25 the culmination of the story of the creation of woman; others make it the opening of the Garden story.[36] Because the original biblical text flowed seamlessly with neither verse nor chapter divisions, authorial or editorial intention cannot be determined.

These verses do point to what is to come by alluding both to the serpent and to the consciousness of nakedness that are to appear in Genesis 3. Key to understanding what is to come is the use of the words *'arummim,* which here describes the humans, and *'arum,* which will characterize the serpent.[37] Bearing in mind that the vocalization of the biblical text is late, we recognize that in Genesis 2:25 *'arummim* (a plural, meaning naked) could also be read as the plural *'arumim* (meaning shrewd). Only the doubling of the *mem* sound in the plural of the word for "naked" distinguishes the two words.[38] Similarly, the singular *'arum* (shrewd) in Genesis 3:1 is separated from *'arom* (the singular of *'arummim,* naked) only by the slight distinction between the *u* and *o* vowel sounds. This sophisticated literary device makes the description of the humans and the serpent ambiguous, if not down-right misleading: Are they shrewd or naked?

The putative first-time reader[39] might posit "naked" as the first reading because the word appears in the context of *yitboshashu* (they were ashamed). Reaching the description of the serpent, one could hypothe-size that the snake was the most naked of all the animals. While the lack of significance of that information would probably rule out the reading, one could imagine that the snake's skin was seen as different from that of other animals, because snakes shed their skins.

Conversely, one might assume that both words mean "shrewd." The humans are shrewd and not ashamed of it. While the snake has the dis-tinction of being the shrewdest of the animals of the field, there is no ranking of its capacity in this area as compared to the human. The narra-tive that follows does seem to indicate that the humans, too, are no match for the serpent.

The conventional reading has the disadvantage of assigning different translations to words that are close to identical and appear in adjacent texts. The advantage of this approach is that, at this point in the history of the text, it is familiar and, partially for that very reason, it seems to make sense. If, indeed, the humans are being described as naked, it is important to give some thought to the implications of that statement. Following the eating of the fruit the issue of nakedness will be broached; what is signifi-cant here is that there is no stigma attached to the state of nakedness.

A rereading makes apparent that Genesis 2:25 provides a contrast both with the following verse about the serpent and with Genesis 3:7 where the primal couple moves to conceal their nakedness. Thus, each of the elements in this verse is in some sense proleptic, leaving us only with the information that both the man and the woman were naked and unashamed. This is all we know about life in Eden before the advent of the serpent.

Genesis 2:25 is not merely a transition from one episode, relating the creation of woman, to the next, the Garden story, including the critical act of disobedience. Before the separation of the woman described in Genesis 2:21, the *adam* was one, incorporating both man and woman. The creation of woman out of the side of the *adam* moved them irrepara-bly apart. Never again would man and woman be as close as they had been when they were really physically one—because the woman had yet to be, as it were, fleshed out. From this point on a willed act, such as a man leaving his father and mother, would be necessary to bring the two together as "one flesh" (Genesis 2:24).

But Genesis 2:25 contains an easily overlooked element referring to the couple's unity, one that will reappear in Genesis 3:7—immediately after the fruit has been eaten. The primal couple seems to be together on only one issue: the significance of their nakedness, first in innocence; later, in shame. Only in the two verses that frame the episode of the forbidden fruit (Genesis 2:25; 3:7) is the word *sheneihem* (the two of them) used. The eating itself, the punishments, the expulsion from the Garden, and life outside the Garden in no way convey the intensity of unity inherent in the verses that frame the eating of the fruit.[40]

As the text introduces the serpent, one may wonder whether it continues the preceding narrative or breaks from it. The serpent is presented as "the shrewdest of all the beasts of the field" (Genesis 3:1). The paronomastic link between *'arummim* (naked) and *'arum* (shrewd) argues for continuity, implying that the serpent's shrewdness will have an impact on the humans' nakedness. But the linking conjunction represented by the letter *vav* that opens Genesis 3 can be understood in two opposing ways. Although translated as "now" in the NJPS, as well as by Alter and Mitchell,[41] it is better seen as a *vav* contrastive, which would then be translated as "but." As such, it provides an ironic contrast between the unabashedly innocent, naked humans and the shrewd serpent.

The serpent opens a dialogue with the woman:

ג 1 וְהַנָּחָשׁ הָיָה עָרוּם מִכֹּל חַיַּת הַשָּׂדֶה אֲשֶׁר עָשָׂה יְ-הוָה אֱלֹהִים
2 ג: וַיֹּאמֶר אֶל-הָאִשָּׁה אַף כִּי-אָמַר אֱלֹהִים לֹא תֹאכְלוּ מִכֹּל עֵץ הַגָּן:
וַתֹּאמֶר הָאִשָּׁה אֶל-הַנָּחָשׁ מִפְּרִי עֵץ-הַגָּן נֹאכֵל: ג 3 וּמִפְּרִי הָעֵץ אֲשֶׁר
4 ג: בְּתוֹךְ-הַגָּן אָמַר אֱלֹהִים לֹא תֹאכְלוּ מִמֶּנּוּ וְלֹא תִגְּעוּ בּוֹ פֶּן תְּמֻתוּן:
וַיֹּאמֶר הַנָּחָשׁ אֶל-הָאִשָּׁה לֹא-מוֹת תְּמֻתוּן: ג 5 כִּי יֹדֵעַ אֱלֹהִים כִּי בְּיוֹם
6 ג: אֲכָלְכֶם מִמֶּנּוּ וְנִפְקְחוּ עֵינֵיכֶם וִהְיִיתֶם כֵּאלֹהִים יֹדְעֵי טוֹב וָרָע:
וַתֵּרֶא הָאִשָּׁה כִּי טוֹב הָעֵץ לְמַאֲכָל וְכִי תַאֲוָה-הוּא לָעֵינַיִם וְנֶחְמָד הָעֵץ
לְהַשְׂכִּיל וַתִּקַּח מִפִּרְיוֹ וַתֹּאכַל וַתִּתֵּן גַּם-לְאִישָׁהּ עִמָּהּ וַיֹּאכַל:

3:1 But the serpent was the shrewdest of all the beasts of the field that the Lord God had made. And it said to the woman, "Even so, God said that you may not eat of any tree in the Garden."

3:2 And the woman said to the serpent, "Of the fruit of the tree[s] of the Garden we may eat;   3:3 but of the fruit of the tree in the middle of the Garden God said: 'Do not eat of it and do not touch it lest you die.' "

3:4 And the serpent said to the woman, "You will not surely die;   3:5 but God knows that on the day you eat of it your eyes will be opened and you will become like divine creatures, knowing good and bad."

3:6 But the woman saw that the tree was good for eating and that it was a lust for the eyes and [that] the tree was desirable for becoming wise and she took of its fruit and ate and gave also to her man with her and he ate. (Genesis 3:1–6)

As the dialogue progresses it becomes clear that the serpent is indeed shrewd; it leads the woman to think for herself and eat the forbidden fruit. Of course the tone of the conversation, inaudible in the biblical text, might have given the listener the requisite clues as to its meaning.

E. A. Speiser proposes that the serpent's question initiating the brief dialogue with the woman is probably better read as a statement falsely indicating that God forbade eating of the fruit of all the trees in the Garden than as a question.[42] In fact, I would further suggest that the language implies that the reader is being brought into a conversation that has already started. The serpent's motivation for engaging Eve is omitted; that it[43] is wily—"the shrewdest of all the beasts"—may suggest some devious but unstated purpose.[44] In Speiser's reading, the woman interrupts the serpent, ostensibly to correct its false premise; in so doing, however, she expands the range of the prohibition in a different manner when she responds that she may not even touch the tree. Whether we assume that she does so intentionally or unintentionally or that she was misled by the *adam* depends, to a large extent, on whether or not she had been created at the time that God gave the instructions (Genesis 2:17). If she had not yet been created, then her current misrepresentation may be the product of misinformation or disinformation that the *adam* had given her, perhaps in an attempt to protect her from transgressing God's injunction. If, on the other hand, we assume that she had accurate information provided either by God or by the *adam,* we must question her motivation for adding additional strictures onto those already in place.[45]

What we do know, however, is that the woman responds fully to the serpent's first question. Faced with the serpent's claim that eating the fruit would bring not death, as God had threatened, but the divine ability to know good and bad, she deliberately and purposefully considers her course of action, independently assessing the situation. She adduces three pieces of apparently empirical evidence: "the tree was good for eating" (*tov lema'akhal*), "a lust for the eyes," and "the tree was desirable for being wise" (Genesis 3:6). Before eating she could not, of course, test the first and third propositions with certainty; at best, she could observe the tree's beauty.[46] Each of Eve's three phrases implies more than it states and harks back to Genesis 2:9, a passage that precedes the second story of the creation of woman: "And from the ground the Lord God caused to grow every tree that was desirable to the sight (*nehmad lemar'eh*) and good for food (*tov lema'akhal*), with the tree of life in the middle of the Garden, and the Tree of Knowledge of Good and Bad." Until this point God has been the sole arbiter of what constitutes goodness, as we have seen in God's daily assessments of the divine creation in Genesis 1. The woman's claim that the tree is good for eating reminds the reader of the earlier phrase, and puts the woman in the position of confirming the narrator's claim that the tree is good for food. In other words, she is judging God's work. In so doing, even before taking the fruit, she is developing wisdom, the capacity to make independent judgments—an ability that is not without risk.

But Genesis 2:9 does not foreshadow everything that Eve says on the subject of fruit trees; it is a general statement, subsequently modified to exclude the Tree of Knowledge of Good and Bad (Genesis 2:17) from the diet of the *adam*. Eve's preprandial recognition that the forbidden tree was "a lust for the eyes" implies an acceptance of the serpent's claim that "your eyes will be opened."[47] Alter's translation of *ta'avah la'einayim* (Genesis 3:6) as "a lust to the eyes" better captures the sense of the Hebrew and its distinction from the parallel phrase in Genesis 2:9, *nehmad lamar'eh* (desirable to sight), than does the NJPS "a delight to the eyes." The word *ta'avah* (lust) is stronger than "delight"; some powerful force is at work here. The third phrase, *nehmad lehaskil* (desirable for becoming wise),[48] indicates an acceptance of the serpent's perspective, as well as a rejection of God's injunction against eating from the tree. The three phrases build on one another until the woman's eagerness to partake of the fruit becomes all but palpable.

There is, of course, another perspective here. Jon D. Levenson suggests that this three-clause sequence may not be an exercise in reasoning, but rather a "process of rationalization" to which the woman "succumbed just before she engaged in humanity's first act of disobedience."[49] What is incontrovertible in Genesis 3:6 is that it progresses from the aesthetic to the gustatory to the intellectual, or from eyes, to tongue, to mind, moving ever inward. Whether one sees this as a laudable or condemnable process depends on one's sense of the outcome. No evidence internal to the verse is compelling.

The woman's slow, careful consideration of the serpent's statement, the studied construction of her argument in three three-word phrases, is set against her action in the second half of the verse. The opening of the verse had but one main verb; the closing has four, three of them with the woman as subject:[50] *"vatiqqah mipiryo vatokhal vatitten gam le'ishah 'immah vayokhal"* (and she took of its fruit and ate and gave also to her man with her and he ate). These three verbs follow in rapid succession, interrupted only by *mipiryo* (of its fruit), the object of the first verb. Once the woman has made her decision, she takes action in three steps, paralleling the three steps of her reflection. She takes the fruit, holding its beauty; eats it, verifying its appropriateness as food; and gives it to her man, an intelligent action. These acts are rapid,[51] because she need not stop again to consider each of them. His eating is separated from her actions and, as the last word in the verse, is the culmination of the action.

Assuming for the moment that Eve's words about touching the tree were her own invention, we might see her as a decisive but not rash woman who maliciously brings her man down with her. If, however, the reader assumes that either the man or God had told her that touching the tree would bring death, her actions would be differently assessed. In that case, the woman is undertaking an experiment. Taking the fruit, she tests the threat that touching the tree will bring death and demonstrates that it is false. Even eating the fruit does not bring the penalty of immediate death. Only after surviving this two-stage experiment does she give the fruit to her man. Far from deliberately misleading her man, she functions as his "royal taster."

The man's action here appears as simple as the woman's is complex. He is the subject of only one verb, "and he ate." But the simplest phrases are often the most ambiguous. Of note here, for example, is that the man is referred to as *ishah* (her man).[52] Further emphasizing the bond between them is the prepositional phrase *'immah* (with her). Cassuto, who believes that "it is the way of the world for the man to be easily swayed by the woman," cites examples of the construction used "when a person is said to associate himself in a given action with someone who leads him."[53] Cassuto notwithstanding, the import of the phrase is not clear. It is equally plausible that the phrase represents the woman's way of indicating that the man was there with her and that he was an equal partner in eating the fruit. In any case, the man's silence is striking. While the woman enters into a dialogue with the serpent and considers the attributes of the tree, the man just eats. Again, ambiguity reigns, as one may read his behavior as reflecting a lack of inquiring intelligence or a deep trust of the woman. In either case, by the end of the verse the man and the woman are both implicated in eating fruit from the forbidden tree.

There are four actants in the Garden story: God (Who prohibits and punishes), the woman (who eats and is punished), the man (who, likewise, eats and is punished), and the serpent (who tempts and is punished). They are not all present for the temptation and eating; they are, as we shall see, all present for the punishments. The woman and the serpent are present throughout; the man misses the temptation, but arrives for the eating and the punishment. God is present only for the punishment.

One of the striking gaps in the biblical narrative of the Garden story involves the role of the *adam*. Where was he during the conversation between the serpent and the woman? Was he a silent witness or was he simply not in the vicinity of the tree? *Genesis Rabbah* 19:3 offers two different possibilities for the man's absence, reflecting two different views of his role in the Garden of Eden.

ותאמר האשה אל הנחש מפרי עץ וגו' ואיכן היה אדם באותה השיחה, אבא חלפון בר קוריה אמר נתעסק בדרך הארץ וישן לו, רבנין אמרין נטלו וחיזרו בכל העולם כולו ואמר לו כן בית נטע כן בית זרע הה"ד ארץ אשר לא עבר בה איש ולא ישב אדם שם (ירמיה ב ו) לא ישב אדם הראשון שם.

"And the woman said to the serpent: Of the fruit of the tree, etc." (Genesis 3:2). And where was Adam at [the time of] this conversation?

Abba Ḥalfon bar Quriyah said: "He had been occupied with his natural functions[54] and fallen asleep."

The rabbis said: "He [God] took him and led him around the whole, entire world and said to him: 'Here is a place for planting [saplings], here is a place for sowing [seed].' As it is written, 'Through a land that no man [ish] had traversed, where no human [adam] had dwelled' (Jeremiah 2:6): [i.e.,] Adam had not dwelled there."[55]

The first explanation for the *adam*'s absence involves the man and woman alone; the second brings God into the picture. Abba Ḥalfon bar Quriyah, making clear that knowledge of sexuality itself was not the fruit's secret, presents a realistic picture of domestic tranquility, drawn from life. The man, his energy spent after intercourse, falls asleep; the woman remains awake and carries on an independent social life. The man, of course, is not culpable for following his natural instincts.[56]

A proof text from Jeremiah supports the rabbis' version. They imagine that God had taken the man on a tour of the whole world, instructing him where different crops should be planted. God becomes an accomplice before the fact, removing the man who might have prevented the woman from being tempted by the serpent. This scenario raises more issues than it resolves. It implies that God knew that Eden would fail: the expedition encompassed the whole world, not just the Garden. Also ambiguous is the proof text, drawn from Jeremiah's criticism of the people for abandoning God without even asking where the God was Who led them through the wilderness, just as the woman and the man abandon God's instruction.

These two midrashic explications are built on differing views of the relationship between the woman and the man. Abba Ḥalfon bar Quriyah keeps the man close at hand, where he can monitor the woman's actions when he is not asleep. His view also implies the *adam*'s culpability: he has been negligent in the performance of his duties. The rabbis give the woman more independence by envisioning a script in which God leads the man away, leaving the woman unsupervised. She, of course, does not rise to the occasion, but proves herself incapable of using her freedom wisely. The rabbis' perspective allows for another interpretation, which would make eating the fruit part of the divine plan. This view, scarcely hinted at in rabbinic midrash,[57] becomes more prominent in twentieth-century revisionings of the text. Both Fikhman and Manger seem to echo this midrash: Fikhman's Adam is often asleep; Manger's, away.

Questions of motivation are seldom addressed in the Hebrew Bible. In the story of the Tree of Knowledge, one question regards the serpent's choice of the woman, rather than the man, as the object of his deception. The man has been the major player to this point; the woman has neither acted nor spoken. The following midrash from *Genesis Rabbah* provides one explanation for the serpent's choice.

ולא יתבוששו, והנחש היה ערום, לא הוה צורך קרייה למימר אלא
ויעש י"י אלהים לאדם ולאשתו וגו' (בראשית ג כא), אמר ר' יהושע
בן קרחה להודיעך מאי זו חיטיה קפץ עליהם אותו הרשע, מתוך
שראם מתעסקין בדרך הארץ ונתאוה לה, אמר ר' יעקב דכפר חנן
שלא להפסיק בפרשתו שלנחש.

"But they were not in a state of shame. But the serpent was the
shrewdest" (Genesis 2:25–3:1). Should the text not have stated
nothing other than: "And the Lord God made for Adam[58] and for
his woman, etc. [garments of skin]" (Genesis 3:21) [immediately
after Genesis 2:25]?

Said R. Yehoshuaʿ ben Qarḥah: "It informs you through what
sin[59] that wicked one[60] jumped on them, because it saw them oc-
cupying themselves with their natural function,[61] it [the serpent]
lusted for her."

Said R. Yaʿakov of Kefar Ḥanan: "[It is written this way] in
order not to conclude with the passage on the serpent."[62]

A question is raised without attribution about the flow of the biblical
narrative and its structure. Would it not have been more logical to convey
the information about God's having made garments for the first man and
woman immediately after the verse stating that they were naked (Genesis
2:25) rather than after the episode about the forbidden fruit (Genesis 3:1–
20)? Most readers assume that God clothes the primal couple in garments
of skin after meting out their punishments because after eating the fruit
they recognize their nakedness and become ashamed. God provides real
garments to replace the fig leaves they had used to cover their genitalia.
The anonymous questioner of this passage suggests otherwise. The report of God's actions should directly follow the mention of their nakedness.[63] Would it not have been preferable to deal with the topic of clothing before narrating the story of the forbidden fruit?

R. Yehoshuaʿ ben Qarḥah's explanation avoids the question: the snake
caught sight of the naked couple enjoying sexual intercourse and lusted
for the woman.[64] Moshe Aryeh Mirkin, in the commentary to his edition
of *Genesis Rabbah*, reconstructs R. Yehoshuaʿ ben Qarḥah's chronology to
indicate that the couple was naked.[65] God's dressing them before they ate
the fruit logically follows the recognition that they are naked, not their
punishment, when it is inappropriate.[66] The serpent, having previously

seen them making love unclothed, decides to act on his jealousy: he tempts the woman on the assumption that eating the fruit will kill both the man and the woman. Although it will not save the woman for him, it will, at least, give her to no one. Thus the logical sequence would have them clothed by God after their intercourse and before the conversation with the serpent. The opening of the eyes of both of them and the concomitant recognition of their nakedness (Genesis 3:7) occurs only after they have been banished from the Garden.[67] The *adam*'s confession that he had hidden because he recognized his nakedness and was afraid would then be read as a confession of spiritual, not physical, nakedness; the *adam* was naked of the one commandment that God had given him.[68]

But R. Ya'akov of Kefar Ḥanan thinks otherwise. He proposes that the placement of Genesis 3:21 after the punishments is designed to prevent the passage from ending on the negative note of the verses regarding the serpent. Although this may well be extrapolated from the rabbinic reluctance to concluding texts on a negative note,[69] the explanation does not work here because the preceding verse (Genesis 3:20), in which the *adam* names the woman, would also have provided closure of a nature that is, if not positive, at least not negative. As Theodor points out in his notes,[70] the key to understanding R. Ya'akov of Kefar Ḥanan's proposal may lie in the connection between the woman's name *Ḥavvah* (Eve) and the Aramaic word for snake, *ḥivya*, which, in turn, underlies the rabbinic notion that the woman and the serpent were connected.[71] In other words, the naming of the woman itself constituted a continuation of the discussion of the serpent's story; to move beyond it and bring in a positive note, the text inserted here, out of chronological order, God's caring for the human couple who, in this reading, had yet to transgress God's order.

Curiously, there is no consideration of why, if God had clothed them earlier, the man and woman would have needed to cover themselves with leaves after eating the forbidden fruit (Genesis 3:7). There would have to have been a difference between the coverings. Perhaps they were engaged in a naked dalliance when God called. Perhaps the skin referred to is the epidermis, which needed further covering. The text is open to multiple interpretations.

While the following midrash from *Genesis Rabbah* 19:5 does not address those questions directly, it does imply that the various rabbis cited considered the issue significant.

99

ותקח מפריו ותאכל אמר ר' אייבו סחטה ענבים ונתנה לו, ר' שמלאי
אמר ביישוב בת עלה אמרה לו מה את סבור שאני מיתה וחוה
אחרת נבראת לך אין כל חדש תחת השמש (קהלת א ט), או שמא
אני מתה ואת יושב לך היטליס לא תהו בראה לשבת יצרה (ישעיה
מה יח), רבנין אמ' התחילה מיללת עליו בקולה.

"She took of its fruit, and she ate" (Genesis 3:6). R. Aibu said:
"She pressed grapes and gave [some of the juice] to him."

R. Simlai said: "She came upon him with her answers pre-
pared,[72] saying to him: 'What are you thinking? That I [will] die
and another Eve is created for you? [That will not happen because it is written:]—"There is nothing new under the sun" (Ecclesiastes 1:9). Or [do you think] that I will die while you remain
free of responsibility [hetalis]?[73] [That will not happen because it
is written:] "He [God] did not create it [the earth] nothingness,
He formed it to be inhabited" ' (Isaiah 45:18)."

The rabbis said: "She began wailing over him with her
voice."[74]

R. Aibu suggests that what the woman gave to the man was not actually a
fruit but, literally, "of the fruit," in other words, fruit juice. Once a fruit
has been squeezed and produced juice, the original fruit is no longer visually identifiable. Thus, one may assume that R. Aibu is imputing to the
woman a plot to deceive the man so that he would not know the origins
of the juice and would drink it unquestioningly. R. Aibu's assumption is
supported by the biblical text's use of the word mipiryo (of its fruit),
which he understands to mean something other than the fruit itself.[75]

R. Simlai understands the woman's strategy as overt, in contrast with
the covert operation R. Aibu visualizes. While he does not give the man
voice, he assumes that the woman comes with her argument, fueled by
jealousy, ready.[76] She demonstrates that the adam derives no advantage
from refusing to eat of the fruit. She has eaten it herself and remains very
much alive. R. Simlai has her assume first that the man may be reluctant
to share her fate because he expects God to kill her and provide him a new
woman. Citing Ecclesiastes, she demonstrates that the time for God's
creation ex nihilo has ceased. Can it be that the man assumes that she will
die and he will be free to do as he pleases? Sarcastically confronting him

once more with a biblical text, she proves that God can neither allow him to survive alone nor kill him because God intended that humans populate the world. The only way God's plan can come to fruition is by their remaining alive. In the sophisticated argument R. Simlai gives the woman, she draws persuasive inferences from timeless scripture.

Finally, the rabbis said: "She began weeping and crying over him." The woman ultimately persuades the man neither by deception nor by logic, but by emotion. Implicitly recalling and interpreting God's statement that the man had "listened to the voice" of his woman (Genesis 3:17), the rabbis assume that her voice and not her words persuaded the man. This depiction of the power of a hysterical woman is made more explicit in the retelling of this midrash in connection with the punishment of the man. The context there is the verse "And to the *adam* He said, 'Because you listened to the voice of your woman and ate of the tree about which I commanded you, "You shall not eat of it" (Genesis 3:17).'" In this version the midrash, after having explicitly rendered this articulate woman voiceless on God's authority, concludes: "It is not written, 'to the *words* of your woman,' but 'to the voice of your woman.'"[77] The anonymous opinion of the rabbis that the woman's approach to the man was wordless and hysterical may trump the argument that her power of persuasion was a function of her intelligence and reasoning, but does not erase it.

Pirqei Rabbi Eliʿezer explains the serpent's approach to the woman differently and further denigrates the woman's abilities. It sees the serpent as the instrument of "the great prince in heaven" Samma'el, who was concerned lest the humans usurp the heavenly creatures' authority. Samma'el rebels; he enlists the serpent, whom he has judged the most "skilled among them [the creatures] to do evil."[78]

דן נחש דין בינו לבין עצמו ואמר, אם אני אומר לאדם, יודע אני שאינו שומע לי, שהאיש קשה לעולם להוציאו מדעתו. אלא הריני אומר לאשה, שדעתה קלה עליה, שאני יודע שהיא שומעת לי, שהנשים נשמעות לכל הבריות, שנאמר, פתיות ובל ידעה מה (מש', ט יג).

The serpent had a discussion with itself, saying: "If I talk to the *adam*, I know that he will not listen to me, for it is always hard to get a man to change his mind [as it is said, 'For [a] man is hard and an evil-doer' (1 Samuel 25:3)][79]; but I will talk to the woman, whose thoughts are frivolous, for I know that she will listen to me[80]; for women listen to all creatures, as it is said, 'She [the stupid woman] is simple and does not know anything' (Proverbs 9:13)."[81]

This serpent has no personal interest in either the man or the women, nor is he motivated to eliminate humankind; he is simply Samma'el's tool, told what to accomplish, but not how. The serpent, who enjoys latitude regarding strategy, decides to start with the woman.

Two elements in this text bear special examination: proof texts and the essentialist argument. The text the serpent quotes from 1 Samuel does not comment on men as a group, but on a specific man: Abigail's husband Nabal. Nabal, no friend to David, "was a hard man and an evildoer" (1 Samuel 25:3). This text is a peculiar choice because Nabal's character is specifically unlike the *adam*'s: Nabal cannot be persuaded to do the right thing and help David; the *adam*, the serpent intuits, will be hard to persuade to do the wrong thing. Another oddity about this proof text: the few words from 1 Samuel are preceded in the biblical text by an evocation of David's future wife, Abigail, as "intelligent and beautiful." If the midrashist could extrapolate a single phrase to characterize all men, the corresponding phrase from the same verse referring to Abigail might describe all women. Abigail's virtues could not have corresponded either to the midrashist's view of women or to his need to explain the serpent's action.

The situation regarding the proof text for the woman is equally puzzling. Ignoring the lyrical beginning of Proverbs 9 metaphorically comparing Wisdom to a woman, this midrash singles out the simple woman who knows nothing depicted in verse 13. This ignorant woman, or class of women, also behaves like a harlot, sitting at her door and inviting wayfarers in. The characterization bears the generalized implication that a woman tempts men to sin, bringing them to *she'ol* (death). This midrash, through its proof texts, rejects the abundance of passages in praise of women while focusing instead on a justification of men. Once more it is worth observing how little unanimity is found among the rabbis concerning Eve as a figure or women as a group.

Genesis Rabbah 19:10 depicts Eve and her transgressing God's order in a manner that seems familiar to many readers because it echoes Hesiod's story of Pandora to whom Eve is occasionally compared.[82]

ויאמר את קולך שמעתי. ויאמר מי הגיד לך אמר ר' לוי לשואלת
חמץ שנכנסה אצל אשת חבר, אמרה לה מה בעליך עושה עימך,
אמרה לה הכל טוב הוא עושה עימי, חוץ מחבית זו שהיא מלאה
נחשים ועקרבים שאינו משליטני עליה, אמרה לה כל קוזמידין שלו
בתוכה הם והוא מבקש לישא אשה אחרת וליתנם לה, מה עשת,
הושיטה ידה בתוכה, התחילו מנשכות אותה, כיון שבא בעלה שמע
קולה צווחת, אמר לה שמא לאותה חבית הבית נגעת, כך המן העץ אשר
ציויתיך אתמהא.

"And he [the adam] said, 'I heard Your voice [and I hid].' And He
said, 'Who told you [that you are naked]?'" (Genesis 3:9–10a)

R. Levi said, "[A comparison] to a woman who borrows vinegar from the wife of a snake charmer.[83]

"She [borrower] asks her [the wife], 'What does your husband
do with [treat] you?'

"She [wife] said to her, 'Everything good he does with me, except that there is this jar, which is full of snakes and scorpions,
over which he does not give me control.'

"She [borrower] said, 'All of his jewels are in there. And he intends to marry another woman and give them to her.'

"What did she [wife] do? She extended her hand into it.
They began to bite her.

"When her husband came, he heard her voice screaming and
said to her, 'Perhaps you touched that jar?'

"Similarly [God said to the adam], 'Did you eat from the tree
about which I commanded you?'"[84]

Boyarin argues that, although this story presents a close parallel to Hesiod,[85] when read carefully it actually constitutes a *parodic subversion* of
the Pandora text.[86] The rabbinic tale most clearly diverges from the possible Greek sources in its application to the biblical text. As Boyarin explains, R. Levi, in applying the Greek story to the biblical text, changes it
in a radical way by having the role of the wife analogous to that of the
biblical man, not the biblical woman. In Genesis, God's rhetorical question is addressed to the man, using the masculine singular form of "you."
As Boyarin states, "By thus equating Adam and not Eve with the Pandora
figure of the parable, the text subverts the myth of essential, female demonic evil that the Pandora story projects explicitly."[87] Boyarin suggests

that the underlying attitude here is not misogynist, but rather androcentric. The role of the wife of the snake charmer is identified with that of Adam; the blame shifts from Eve to Adam, and Adam's eating the fruit becomes the "culturally significant moment."[88] In this reading, the woman becomes marginalized in the process of being exonerated. Boyarin sees in this process almost "a paradigm for rabbinic gender relations which, while generally solicitously patronizing toward women (as opposed to cultures which are violently misogynist), at the same time marginalize them utterly."[89]

But other aspects of this version of the story shed a different light on this narrative. The meddlesome woman enters a neighbor's house, ostensibly to borrow food she must need, either yeast or vinegar, depending on the reading of the Hebrew *h.m.ts.*[90] Either substance would function effectively as a metaphor for bitterness or troublemaking, introducing the latent subject of disorder or domestic upheaval; otherwise, on the literal level of the plot, the substance operates only as a pretext for the conversation between the housewife and her visitor.[91] The neighbor encourages the wife to disobey her husband, the source of authority. The husband is identified as a scholar or as a snake charmer, depending on the vocalization of the Hebrew.[92] His profession as snake charmer would explain the presence of a container of snakes and scorpions and would explicitly give the husband authority over the potential danger that needs to be contained or controlled.

The characters in the parable fulfill roles analogous to those in the biblical story. The husband's role recalls God's in the biblical story, as he is the ultimate authority who imposes the prohibition and poses the question regarding its transgression. As for the two female characters, if they correspond to the three remaining roles in Genesis—snake, woman, and man—either one character plays two roles or one role has been eliminated. The visiting woman, who roils the marital waters, parallels the serpent's role. Like the serpent, she opens with a broad and somewhat leading question: "What does your husband do with you?" Hardly a request for vinegar. As for her motive, does she perhaps see herself as the future second wife? Does she envy her neighbor's apparent marital bliss?

Casting two women in the three roles of tempter, transgressor/tempter, and transgressor does not exonerate the women. It identifies a woman with the snake, an identification that may grow out of the possible connection between the biblical woman's name and the word for snake.[93] It also provides a window into a rabbinic view of the relations among women. In the female's domain of the household, of food, women are portrayed as jealous troublemakers who would do well to honor and obey their husbands, who, in turn, have assumed a divine role. The parallel between the biblical man's role and that of the midrashic wife implied in the concluding verse marginalizes the woman more than it exonerates her. In the biblical text God's rhetorical question reinforces the biblical effacement of the role of the woman: God, Whose previous statement to the *adam* had been the command not to eat from the fruit of the Tree of Knowledge (Genesis 2:16–17), picks up the thread of dialogue with the *adam* to ask if he had indeed violated that divine command. There is no reason to address the woman, who might not even have been present to hear the original order. The midrashic tale, even more pointedly than the biblical story, places a man in the controlling frame of the action, women in its center. While Boyarin proposes this as androcentric rather than misogynist,[94] there is room for doubt. Paradoxically, by setting the women in the center, this midrash marginalizes them, leaving the last word to the man, just as the biblical story puts the power in God's domain by having the last word divine.

Eve in Eden: Trial and Punishment

Regardless of their motivation, in the biblical text both the man and the woman eat the fruit. Following fast upon their action comes the report of their recognition that they are naked, a problem they address forthwith by sewing for themselves garments made of fig leaves (Genesis 3:7).[95] Eve's story in this text portrays the experience as shared between the *adam* and the woman, a characteristic peculiar to this episode, as most of the narrative focuses on only one or the other of the characters. The *adam* and his woman were, "the two of them," naked when this story began, according to Genesis 2:25. As she converses with the serpent and as she eats from the fruit, nearly all of the action is Eve's. Mutuality returns when she gives the fruit to her man "with her" in Genesis 3:6. The following verse once more refers to the man and the woman as "the two of them." The mention of eyes in three consecutive verses (Genesis 3:5–7) subtly reinforces the prominence of the woman because the serpent had promised her the opening of the eyes (Genesis 3:5), and she had used her eyes to assess the merits of the tree. This knowledge of nakedness, previously acknowledged, can hardly be what the woman had imagined as divine knowledge when she took that risk.[96] The text emphasizes the sharing of an experience between the man and the woman, right down to the making of garments.

But once God, Whose absence from the Garden scene has been palpable, returns to ask the couple why they have suddenly clothed themselves, the couple comes apart. They hear, in the plural verb *vayishme'u*, the sound of God in the Garden; the text uses the masculine singular verb *vayithabbei* to denote that the *adam* and his woman hide (Genesis 3:8).[97] The woman, undeniably the main actor in the episode, is suddenly marginalized.

The first three verses of the subsequent conversation between God and the *adam* (Genesis 3:9–11) exclude the woman entirely. Using the masculine singular (*ayekkah*), God calls to the *adam* and asks him where he is. The *adam* responds using the masculine singular; and God confronts him in the masculine singular: "From the tree which I had commanded you [*tsivitikha*] not to eat from did you eat [*akhalta*]?" (Genesis 3:11b). The woman has been removed from the arena. If one assumes that her omission is due to her creation after God prohibited eating from the fruit of the tree, it would follow that her information came from the *adam*, who may well have misinformed her about the extent of the ban. In any case, considering that some rabbinic and other later texts assign her the burden of having brought death into the world, the woman's omission from this dialogue is striking. Although the *adam* is essentially but an accessory after the fact, God focuses on him, turning to the woman only when the *adam* lamely brings her in: "The woman whom You gave [to be] with me—she gave me of the tree, and I ate" (Genesis 3:12b). Apparently the unquestioning recipient of whatever is given to him whether the source is God or the woman, the *adam* reminds God that he did not act alone; he attempts to shift the blame first to the woman but ultimately to God.[98] The ten words of his response use first-person pronouns twice as objects of prepositions before taking responsibility in the last word: *"va'okhel"* (and I ate). The *adam*'s emphasis on the woman's role is underscored by his unnecessary insertion of "she." The first nine words throw up a verbal screen before he admits, in the tenth, to having eaten from the tree. His self-exonerating words lack integrity. God, however, is not faultless either. By overlooking the woman's role in making the choice to eat the forbidden fruit, God does neither human justice.

God's apparent lack of regard for the woman is palpable in the question to her: "What is this you have done?" (Genesis 3:13a). How simple is this question—but three Hebrew words[99]—in comparison with the specific double question addressed to the man. Cassuto observes that God does not question the woman in order to ascertain the facts; God knows. The *adam*'s statement has already implicated the woman.[100] Curiously, only the woman's role in giving the fruit to the *adam* is considered, but not her own eating. What is the tone? Has God accepted the *adam*'s claim that it was the woman's fault? Does God address her with contempt? Does God feel so betrayed by the woman that God can articulate no significant response to her action, only this simple question? Cassuto would have God's question mean: "How could you do so terrible a thing?"[101] Could God be losing patience with the situation? Is the fact that the serpent is not questioned at all, but simply punished, a further indication of God's ire, or is it another indication of God's seeing these three characters in descending order of significance? The text, typically silent on these matters, betrays a lack of interest in the woman's actions.[102]

"The serpent deceived me, and I ate [*hanahash hishi'ani va'okhel*]" (Genesis 3:13): the woman's three-word response forms a parallel to God's three-word question. The woman's first word, like the *adam*'s, shifts the blame. He invokes the woman; she, in turn, invokes the snake. Their last words, *va'okhel* (and I ate), are not merely parallel, but identical. The *adam*, however, uses a subordinate clause[103] to take God to task for having given him the woman; the woman does not blame God as creator of serpents. In fact, the woman's three-word response is concise and balanced. The snake is the first word; "and I ate," the last. The middle word, with the snake as its subject and a first-person singular suffix as its object, makes the progression clear. There is not so much as an extra syllable here. Further, the woman does not address her role in the *adam*'s transgression, the very action about which God is apparently questioning her. She admits only her own action.

But there is more to the woman's response than assigning blame. The woman's use of *hishi'ani* (he deceived me) indicates her level of understanding, of intelligence. The *adam* simply acknowledges the series of events that occurred; the woman realizes that she was the victim of the snake.[104] Her careful choice of the root *n.sh.'* further clarifies the high level of her linguistic acumen. If that verbal stem in that form conveys, as Helmer Ringgren explains, not simple deception, but giving the deceived a "false sense of security and false hope,"[105] it is a superb characterization of the snake's deed. Further, her confining her response to three words to parallel God's question involves some sophisticated syntax. The woman's intelligence is apparent in her reasoning, choice of words, and syntactical construction.

God asks no question of the serpent, but moves directly to punish it.[106] Contrary to popular opinion, God's responding statements are not curses. The word "curse" is used in connection with the snake, but neither the woman nor the *adam* is cursed. What, indeed, are these pronouncements? Are they prescriptive or descriptive? Do they indicate a change in God's original plan for the world? Two interpreters, Cassuto and Meyers, take somewhat different views. Cassuto proposes that "if the man and his wife had hearkened to the voice of the Creator and had been content with what He had given them, they could have eaten from the tree of life and lived forever."[107] Using the relatively neutral term "decrees," Cassuto goes on to explain: "The decrees pronounced by the Lord God mentioned here are not exclusively *punishments;* they are also, and chiefly, *measures taken for the good of the human species* in its new situation."[108] This line of reasoning defends God's punishing the progeny for the misdeeds of their progenitors. Understanding these verses as belonging to the wisdom literature and constituting a descriptive explanation for the sorry state of the world, Meyers uses another neutral term: oracles.[109] Both of them ultimately agree that the pronouncements are etiological, explaining the current state of things.

Reversing the order of the questioning to start with the serpent, God addresses each of the three actors in turn. Several aspects of all three punishments must be observed before analyzing more closely the verse addressed to the woman. Although God asks the serpent no question, it is dealt with first; its participation in the act is the most recently mentioned and it provokes God's immediate response.[110] The woman is dealt with next in chiastic order, opening and closing with the *adam*. She is the linchpin, mentioned in God's words to the serpent, while the man is mentioned in God's words to her.

God does not name the offense of either the serpent or the woman; their actions speak for themselves. God's first words to the serpent: "Because you did this [*Ki 'asita zot*]" (Genesis 3:14a) echo the words used in questioning the woman, "What is this you have done?" [*Mah zot 'asit*] (Genesis 3:13a). The serpent's lot is compared to that of cattle and wild beasts, setting it in a category defined as separate from that of humans.

The strangest part of the punishment of the serpent concerns its future relationship with the woman: "I will put enmity / Between you and the woman, / And between your seed and her seed; / They shall strike at your head / And you shall strike at their heel" (Genesis 3:15). One might assume that the basis for the enmity is the serpent's trickery. But why attribute eternal enmity to her descendants alone? Are not her descendants also the *adam*'s? Perhaps the simplest explanation is that the serpent had no relationship with the *adam*; it chose the woman as its prey. The biblical text does not indicate whether the serpent was present even as an onlooker when the woman offered the fruit to the *adam*.

The woman's punishment is anomalous. God's address to her is short. In the Hebrew, God addresses thirty-three words to the serpent, thirteen to the woman, and forty-six to the *adam*. Although the punishment is the penalty for eating the fruit and causing the man to do likewise, no charge is articulated—the only instance where no accusation precedes the penalty.[111] God tells the serpent: "Because you did this" (Genesis 3:14). To the *adam*, God explains: "Because you listened to the voice of your woman and ate of the tree about which I commanded you, 'You shall not eat of it' " (Genesis 3:17). These specific charges come close to accusing the *adam* of preferring the woman's word to God's.[112] Why does God omit the charges from the punishment of the woman? It is implausible that God considers the woman less capable of understanding than the serpent. Perhaps the reason is rhetorical. The woman is always hierarchically bracketed between the serpent and the *adam*. The justifications for their punishments apply to her as well. Whatever the explanation, it still leaves the woman less prominent than her deeds would lead us to expect.

But there is another reading of this text that underscores the image of Eve's capabilities that her complex reasoning has already provided. Eve, as an almost classic Aristotelian tragic hero, has gone through the requisite process. The hubris, bolstered by the serpent's duplicity, which led her to err, to replace God's command with her independent logic, has given way to her terse but informed acknowledgment of the misdeed. Does she finally accept her projected suffering? Neither the *adam* nor the serpent has reached the level of tragic hero because neither of them has fully acknowledged the misdeed.

The woman's punishment has been so often used to justify the oppression of women, particularly of wives, that it cannot be read except with a hermeneutic of suspicion. Like the punishments of the snake and the *adam,* its real purpose is to explain some of the hardships, both global and specific, in the situation of the Israelites.

ג 16 אֶל־הָאִשָּׁה אָמַר הַרְבָּה אַרְבֶּה עִצְּבוֹנֵךְ וְהֵרֹנֵךְ בְּעֶצֶב תֵּלְדִי בָנִים
וְאֶל־אִישֵׁךְ תְּשׁוּקָתֵךְ וְהוּא יִמְשָׁל־בָּךְ׃

> And to the woman He said, "I will greatly multiply
> Your toil and your pregnancies;
> In travail shall you give birth to children.
> Yet your desire shall be for your man
> And he shall control you [in this area]."
>
> (Genesis 3:16)

To the casual reader of the standard English translations this verse seems to justify labor pain and the subjugation of wives to their husbands. Thus, for example, the NJPS reads as follows:

> And to the woman He said, "I will make most severe
> Your pangs in childbearing;
> In pain shall you bear children.
> Yet your urge shall be for your husband
> And he shall rule over you."
>
> (Genesis 3:16)

But a closer look at the text reveals that there are many ways in which it may be read, some of them much less restrictive of the woman.

The punishment of the woman can readily be divided into two pairs of statements of varying complexity and ambiguity.[113] Before presenting a coherent interpretation of the punishment as a whole, it is necessary to examine each of its elements.

The first clause is often read as referring to labor pains, but the Hebrew does not yield that as the only possible interpretation. In her analysis of this verse in light of the context of Israelite society, Carol Meyers indicates that the first verb in the verse, *r.b.y* (to increase or make great), usually has a quantifiable object like people or animals.[114] The verbal construction *harbah arbeh* intensifies the action of the verb by setting the infinitive absolute before the conjugated verb.[115] It appears in but two other verses in the story of the first man and woman (Genesis 1:1–5:5), both in connection with God's threat to punish the *adam* with death for eating the fruit of the Tree of Knowledge (Genesis 2:17; 3:4). God's first-person intense verb is in sharp contrast to the punishment of the man where there is no first-person verb and in distinction from the curse of the serpent where the first-person *ashit* (I will put) is in midsentence without intensifier. It seems that God's involvement in the woman's future situation, or God's commitment to its configuration, is greater than it is in the other two cases.

The object of the verb *arbeh* (I will increase) *'itsevonekh veheronekh* (your pain and your childbearing) appears to be compound but is often treated as hendiadys, a figure of speech common in the Hebrew Bible.[116] The assumption of hendiadys yields translations like the NJPS "your pangs in childbearing." Arguing that the word *heronekh* is better translated as "your conceptions" than "your childbearing," Meyers denies a linkage between pain and conception.[117] Examining the other uses of the word *'itsavon*, she suggests that in parallel verses its meaning is closer to "toil" than to "pain."[118] She concludes that the correct translation: "I will greatly increase your toil and your pregnancies," is drawn from the situation of the early Israelites who depended on many conceptions to produce the children they needed to subsist in the difficult conditions of their agrarian society. I prefer "multiply" to "increase" because "multiply" has a more quantifiable aspect to it.

While this fate of many pregnancies is generally viewed as a punishment, and is better seen as an etiology, particularly given the high rate of death in childbirth, it is significant that God, Whom Genesis portrays as responsible for conception and pregnancy,[119] promises involvement. Given the importance of repeated pregnancies, there is a promise here, as well as a threat. Further, in this context, God is also providing the antidote to the death that comes with eating the forbidden fruit. Through the birth of subsequent generations, death will take on a different meaning.

The second clause in this verse, while paralleling the first, is not identical to it but an intensification.[120] It refers specifically to childbirth, rather than to conception and pregnancy.[121] In addition, the word *'etsev*, which appears in the introductory prepositional phrase, is well translated as "travail," implying both "pain" and "toil."[122] Thus the first half of the pronouncement would translate as: "I will greatly multiply / Your toil and your pregnancies; / In travail shall you give birth to children."

The second pair of clauses opens with an affirmation of female sexual desire, in contrast to the focus on male sexuality that we find more often in the Hebrew Bible:[123] *el ishekh teshukatekh* (to your man is your desire).[124] The possessive ending indicates that it is for *her* man that she will have this feeling. While limiting, it also reinforces the pair bonding that is referred to in Genesis 2:24. This desire leads the woman repeatedly to undergo the pain, burden, and risks inherent in her role.[125]

The final clause of the verse—*Vehu yimshol bakh* (and he will overrule you)—presents the greatest challenge to an egalitarian reading.[126] Although it is often cited as the proof text for male domination of women, or for husbands' control over their wives, it may be read as limited to the arena of sexual relations described in the preceding clause.[127] As Meyers states, it is no more a blanket sentencing of all women for all time to a life of subordination than is the punishment of the man a sentencing of all men for all time to work thorny fields.[128] As demonstrated in God's parallel admonition to Cain, the biblical text implies the man's capacity for controlling the woman's apparently unbridled sexual desire.[129] To make the verse clear, I propose translating the second half as: "Yet your desire shall be for your man / And he shall control you [in this area]."

One more aspect of the punishment warrants attention: the relevance of God's pronouncement to the misdeed. Does the punishment fit the crime? Unless one posits that the knowledge of good and bad was specifically connected to sexuality, which Meyers and many other commentators and scholars do not, there seems to be no connection between the two. As we have seen, both the serpent and the *adam* have been charged with eating, but not the woman. The woman has been charged with giving the man something forbidden to eat. The linkages in form and content among the punishments and between the punishments and the misdeeds cannot be overlooked.[130] The justification of the words to the man starts with God's telling him: "Because you listened to the voice of your woman" (Genesis 3:17). Paraphrased in context, God says, "Because you let your woman dominate you." Her punishment for weakening her man is that he will "control" her, at least in the limited area of sexuality.

The most striking aspect of this series of punishments is their lack of connection to the original warning: "on the day that you eat of it you shall die" (Genesis 2:17). However, while death is explicit in the punishment of the *adam* and peripheral to the other two, it is not the focus of any of them. Thus, it is the consequence of the eternal hatred that God will put between humans and snakes that they will attack each other. Similarly, childbearing, a common cause of female mortality until the modern period, is mentioned; but its link to death is omitted in the words to the first eater of the fruit of the tree, the woman. It is the *adam* who is told: "Until you return to the ground— / For from it you were taken. / For dust you are, / And to dust you shall return" (Genesis 3:19). As suspicious readers of the text we see that the woman's culpability in connection with the eating of the fruit is diminished. This de-emphasis of the woman's role can be understood in two divergent ways. She may be viewed here as incapable of independent reasoning, as less intelligent, but that is not consonant with the process she used to decide to take action. Alternatively it may be a lowering of the woman's status. She may be viewed as a mere accessory before the fact of the *adam*'s eating; *he* was the one who was initially instructed by God not to eat of the tree.

In conclusion, Genesis 3:14–19 is a series of divine pronouncements presented as the consequences of serpentine and human misdeeds. Although couched as punishments, they serve to explain the etiology of the difficulties of human existence. They may also be viewed as a stage in the maturation of the primal couple. Those who would see a progression here from childlike innocence to maturity read these verses as setting the stage for adult life outside the Garden of Eden.[131]

Eve in Eden: The Final Moments

The five verses that close Genesis 3 report a series of actions culminating in the eternal banishment of the *adam* from Eden. Although the first of these, the *adam*'s second naming of the woman, discussed below, concerns both humans, the others involve God and the *adam*. The woman is gradually marginalized as this section of the story moves toward its conclusion. As previously discussed, at the opening of the story of the forbidden fruit the *adam* and the woman are twice referred to as *sheneihem* (the two of them). *Sheneihem* reflects their mutuality without compromising their individuality. From the moment God enters the scene they are separated. God's opening question, *Ayekkah?* (Where are you?) (Genesis 3:9) is addressed to a masculine singular "you." From this point on, God, with one striking exception, deals with the *adam* and the woman separately. Where we might assume that God is addressing or referring to both humans, the text uses the masculine singular *adam*. The woman disappears from the text, unless one turns back to the definition of *adam* as including "male and female" (Genesis 1:27).[132]

The exception to the masculine singular focus of the end of this section of the narrative is the single verse in which God is described as making "garments of skin" for Adam and his woman.[133] God's clothing the humans whom God has just punished and is about to banish is well characterized as a parental gesture. Sarna suggests that the clothing serves two purposes: restoring human dignity and providing protection requisite for life beyond the Garden.[134] God's action closes the section of the divine punishments (Genesis 3:21), even as their clothing themselves opens it (Genesis 3:7).[135] Levenson asserts that this act serves to indicate that the divine human relationship has survived the eating of the forbidden fruit and the subsequent punishment.[136]

The passages dealing with nakedness and clothing necessarily address both the *adam* and the woman, as nakedness, problematic largely in the eyes of the beholder, is necessarily an issue for each of them. Clothing thus serves as an inner inclusio for the section of the tale of the first humans that involves God's investigation of their behavior and the punishments for it. The emphasis on the need for clothing underscores the unclothed state of the first humans while reinforcing the importance of gender difference—a topic critical to the punishment of the woman, which is at the center of the punishments.

A dance of togetherness and separation is bracketed by the *sheneihem* (the two of them) in Genesis 2:25 and the reference to Adam and the woman in 3:24. The unity of their being "one flesh," focusing on the woman (Genesis 2:21), is nuanced by the use of "the two of them" in the following verse. The *adam* who had once more become one flesh is now differentiated into two individuals, naked and unashamed, who function together. The woman's prominence in the eating of the fruit is followed by the repetition of "the two of them," as they recognize their nakedness and set about remedying it. God interrupts by separating them in the interrogation and punishments, but, in dressing them for their new life, restores their mutuality. They are reduced to the one figure of the *adam* once more, to be banished as one person.[137] One way to understand this is as an inclusio bracketing off the text from the creation of the *adam* in Genesis 1:27 to its exit from the Garden. The return to the use of *adam* as a proper noun accentuates its subsequent use as a

common noun. Subsuming the female within the male is more pronounced here—after the woman has been portrayed as a speaking, acting, intelligent human being—than it is in the initial Creation story. One
way to understand her apparently diminished stature is to see it as part
of the punishment of the woman, as demonstrating the result of the
woman's desire for her man; she chooses to follow him once he is banished. Another perspective would see it as part of the woman's marginalization. In either case, this frame leaves the woman out.

Finally, even as the larger story of the Garden opens with the placement of the *adam*, still alone, in the Garden (Genesis 2:15), so does it end
with his banishment (Genesis 3:24–25). The symmetry created by this
structuring of the narrative may mitigate the apparent marginalization of
the woman, but it does not erase it from the text. The somewhat dismissive attitude taken toward the woman throughout the process remains
unchallenged.

Eve in Eden: An Assessment

Seeing the story of the forbidden fruit as the tale of God's testing the primal couple provides another instructive frame. In her book *The Tested
Woman Plot*, Lois E. Bueler focuses on the many plots, particularly in Eliz-
abethan drama, that are driven by testing women. Her first example is, of
course, Eve.[138] Reading the biblical story through this lens adds yet another dimension and sharpens some of the issues.

Bueler defines the components of the plot as a test, generally a moral
choice, a trial and a judgment. The roles that the major characters play include tested woman and four male roles: tempter, accuser, defender, and
judge. As Bueler describes this plot, a character may play more than one
role.[139] Providing a fairly conventional reading of the biblical story, Bueler
finds that it fits the failed test paradigm. God, Who sets the challenge of
not eating of the fruit of the tree, also serves as accuser and judge. The
tempter is, of course, the serpent. Adam seems peripheral to the action.
Most tellingly, there is no defender to speak for the woman.[140] In the face
of Bueler's contention that the "tested woman plot" is all about reconciliation "among the males who have claimed her [the tested woman's] allegiance,"[141] there is no reconciliation in Eve's story.

A closer look at the biblical text renders the roles normally assigned to
the males less clear. In many ways, God places the challenge before the
man and, perhaps, the woman as well. It is a clear temptation, in many

ways irresistible.[142] The serpent is not really tempting the woman but testing God—probing the limits of God's ban by seeing how far one can go without incurring divine retribution.

Seeing the serpent as testing the woman makes the serpent God's accomplice. Carefully considering the two good choices she has before her—(1) obeying God's order by not eating or (2) gaining moral knowledge, knowledge of good and bad—the woman opts for knowledge.[143] In terms of the surface meaning of the biblical text, she cannot have both obedience to God's words and the moral knowledge that makes us human. Her ability to make a moral choice is thus developed. If the purpose of the tested woman plot is to reconcile the various males who have or desire power over the woman, this story is about an internal conflict in which God is tempter, accuser, and judge. But if the woman has any defender, God, to a small degree, plays that role as well, clothing the humans as a gesture of post-judgment sympathy.

Further, if the test is really about settling hierarchy among males, then God's seeing the only issue as the *adam*'s eating the forbidden fruit returns the reader to God's having originally set the test by speaking to the *adam* before the woman has been differentiated. It becomes simple symmetry.

Does she fail the test? The charge and the punishment imply that she does not pass. But readings of biblical tests often reach behind the text to seek out a moral core and contemporary moral standards do not always follow God's expressed desires. Thus, for example, Abraham, who is explicitly tested (Genesis 22:1) in the story of the Binding of Isaac, may not have passed the test through his willingness to follow God's order to sacrifice his son Isaac. Similarly, the woman may not actually have failed the test through her willingness to eat the forbidden fruit. She develops the ability to make independent moral judgments through her rational choices.

Whatever positive gloss may be inherent in the biblical texts or applicable to them, one must bear in mind that, despite some ambiguities attending the rabbinic understanding of the creation of woman, there is nearly universal condemnation of her behavior in the Garden. One point in the biblical text that puzzled the rabbis is that God addresses the woman directly. For a group of men who theoretically limited their own conversations with women in order not to be distracted from sacred study,[144] God's wasting time by speaking with a woman was inconceivable. The following midrash distorts the plain meaning of the text to preclude such a possibility.

ר' יוחנן בשם ר' לעזר ביר' שמעון. (שלא) [לא מצינו ש] דיבר
(הכת') [המקום] עם אשה אלא עם שרה בלבד. והא כת' "אל האשה
אמר הרבה ארבה" וגו'. אמ' ר' יעקב דכפר-חנין. על ידי התורגמן.

R. Yoḥanan [said] in the name of R. Leʿazar son of R. Shimʿon:
"[We have not found that the Place][145] spoke with a woman, except with Sarah alone."

"[But] it is written: 'And to the woman He said, "I will make
most severe, etc.?" ' " (Genesis 3:16).[146]

R. Yaʿakov of Kefar Ḥanan said: "Through an interpreter."[147]

While modern readers are sensitive to the nuanced differences between
God's dialogue with the adam and with the woman, which may marginalize the woman, the privileged male rabbis of the world of the study
house could not envision God's interacting directly with a woman at all,
particularly with one who had just contravened God's orders.

Another midrash explains some social conventions, including the
three mitsvot (commandments) specifically connected with women, as
the punishment of all Jewish women for Eve's misdeed. Unlike Genesis, the midrash goes to some length to relate the punishment to the
offense. The first section of this midrash, as we have seen in the discussion of the creation of woman, focuses on physical differences
between men and women, ascribing most of them to the disparity in
their creation as portrayed in Genesis 2.[148] This, the second section,
addresses issues that moderns might perceive as social conventions,
but that the discussants probably saw as immutable and eternal norms
of behavior.

מפני מה האיש יוצא וראשו מגולה והאשה יוצאה וראשה מכוסה,
אמר להם לאחד שעבר עבירה והוא מתבייש מבני אדם לפיכך היא
יוצאת מכוסה, מפני מה הן מהלכות אצל המת תחילה, אמר להן על
ידי שגרמו מיתה לעולם לפיכך מהלכות הן אצל המת תחילה, ואחריו
כל אדם ימשוך (איוב כא לג), ומפני מה ניתן לה מצות נידה, על ידי
ששפכה דמו שלאדם הראשון לפיכך ניתן לה מצות נידה, מפני מה
ניתן לה מצות חלה אמר להן מפני שקילקלה את אדם הראשון
שהיה חלתו שלעולם לפיכך ניתן לה מצות חלה, ומפני מה ניתן לה
מצות נר שלשבת, אמר להן על ידי שכיבת נשמתו שלאדם הראשון
לפיכך ניתן לה מצות נר שבת.

117

"Why does the man go out and his head is revealed and the woman goes out and her head is covered?"

He [R. Yehoshua'] said to them, "[It is] like one who has committed a sin, and he is ashamed in front of people, therefore she goes out covered."

"Why do they [women] precede alongside[149] the dead [on the way to a burial]?"

He said, "Since they caused death [to come into] the world, therefore they precede alongside the dead [on the way to a burial] and after them [the men follow, as it is written,] 'and after him every person will draw' (Job 21:33)."

"And why was she given the commandment of [menstrual] separation?"

"Because she spilled the blood of first *adam*, therefore she was given the commandment of [menstrual] separation."

"And why was she given the commandment of *ḥallah* [to sacrifice the first portion of the dough]?"

He said to them, "Because she spoiled the first *adam*, who was the *ḥallah* (first portion) of the world, therefore she was given the commandment [to sacrifice the first portion] of the dough."

"And why was she given the commandment of [lighting] the Sabbath lamp?"

He said to them, "Because she extinguished the soul of the first *adam*, therefore she was given the commandment of [lighting] the Shabbat lamp."[150]

This passage is clearly and unequivocally misogynistic. Even Boyarin, who draws a fine distinction between misogyny and androcentrism, concedes that this midrashic text belongs on the misogynistic side of the line.[151] The contempt of women expressed here is overwhelming.

The string of questions and answers that precedes this section underscores a rabbinic view of woman as the unfamiliar Other and essentializes woman as a series of mostly negative qualities, most of them physical. The one glimpse of a positive image involves woman's reliability as a container for the developing fetus—hardly a ringing endorsement. In looking at the structure of this midrash, one might have expected to see that sixth exchange as the transition from negative to positive qualities.

But the shift is rather from physical difference to societal norms. Women are no longer defined by the purported osseous origin of the first woman, but by societal norms or customs.

That men walked around bareheaded while women covered their heads is a widespread societal norm with no basis in the Hebrew Bible.[152] Seeing this custom as the result of women's shame for the first woman's having committed a sin has no basis in Jewish law. But this text links the societal norm to Eve's misdeed in eating the fruit from the Tree of Knowledge. Yet there is more to this text than meets the eye: it posits that women do indeed "go out" and there seems to be no criticism of that, as long as they know their place. While this admission might not merit comment today, it stands in sharp contrast to the suggestion that Dinah's misdeed, "going out," was what got her into trouble.[153] Further, there is no mention of woman as seductress or of woman's hair as temptation, which might also have been factors in this discussion.[154]

Similarly, regarding mourning customs, it was the women, who customarily preceded the deceased in the funeral procession, probably in the role of keeners or professional mourners.[155] These women appeared to be drawing or leading the deceased toward death, hence the proof text from Job. Despite the absence of any reference to death in God's words to the woman (Genesis 3:16), R. Yehoshua' would have this custom derived from a woman's role in bringing death into the world. Once more, what is missing here is also interesting in light of subsequent developments. These women appeared in public and their voices were heard. Indeed, they had a ritual function as official mourners.

But the part of this series that is most negative toward women—and most remarkable in terms of what it reveals about rabbinic attitudes toward Eve and the connection between her and the subsequent development of Jewish practice regarding women—is yet to come. Looking at the final three exchanges in terms of their function discloses their vital connection to the three *mitsvot* that have long been associated with women. Although they are used today, often in an apologetic manner, to indicate the high esteem in which Judaism holds women, they are here associated with the evil deed of the first woman.[156] They elide any distinction between the first woman and those to come. All women, at least all Jewish women, bear responsibility for the misdeeds of the first.

The first of these constitutes the rules governing the sexual relationships between women and men during a woman's menstrual cycle and for a number of "clean" days thereafter. In this passage, these rituals, biblical in origin,[157] are presented as the consequence of the woman's having shed the *adam*'s blood.[158] A number of logical leaps must precede such a conclusion. Not only does the woman not shed the *adam*'s blood in any direct way, but he survives to the age of 930 years (Genesis 5:3–5) despite God's threat that eating the fruit from the Tree of Knowledge of Good and Bad would entail immediate death. Further, death comes equally for men and for women, not for men only. Thus the need for women to observe these blood-related taboos would necessarily be tied to the introduction of death into humanity or into the world as a whole. It is, as Baskin claims, actually to prevent her husband from entering into a state of ritual impurity that the woman observes these strictures.[159]

The last two examples are even more telling as they are the commandments tied specifically to women, but also are, under some circumstances, required of men.[160] When baking large quantities of bread, a small portion of the dough must be burned as a sacrifice.[161] This obligation, the only vestige of the Israelite sacrificial system to obtain after the destruction of the Second Temple, falls upon women when they are the bakers. While one might have pointed to the fact that women have retained this function, almost priestly in nature, as an indication of the high esteem in which they are held, the argument here blames the woman for having spoiled the first Adam, who is now seen as the "first portion of the dough" of the world. For that reason women are commanded thereafter to sacrifice the "first portion of the dough." Similarly, her extinguishing the "soul of first Adam" requires women to light the Shabbat lamp, because the soul is often metaphorically referred to as a flame or light.

This midrash, taken as a whole, first deconstructs woman and then condemns her for societally imposed restrictions on her actions. The final three questions and responses turn those rites and customs, perceived as belonging to women, into punishments for all Jewish women, in response to the damage the first woman's action purportedly did to first Adam. In so doing it leaves little for women to take pride in or to claim as their rightful portion.

For R. Yehoshua᷾ and his questioners, who encourage this flight of misogyny, woman is without a doubt responsible for much that is wrong in the world. Woman is quintessentially Other, different from man from the moment of her birth. The ambiguous biblical text has been embellished and constrained, construed to have a meaning far different from the range of possible interpretations of the Genesis story. For this rabbi, the first woman represents all women for all time and her misdeeds require perpetual atonement.

While the rabbis saw the first woman as unalterably Other, modern writers have often reinterpreted her story. Looking at the relationship between the *adam* and the woman or at the issue of the woman's culpability through twentieth-century perspectives, they often present Eve in a more nuanced way than do the rabbis, or in a way diametrically opposed to the traditional reading.

The nature of the relationship between the first man and the first woman intrigued the twentieth-century Hebrew poet Yokheved Bat-Miriam (1901–1979). Her dense and difficult poetry bears the hallmarks of both Russian poetry and Hebrew piety. In a pair of poems entitled, respectively, *"Adam"* and *"Ḥavvah"* (Eve),[162] she portrays each of these first humans separately before describing how each appeared to the other. While the poems are almost symmetrical and have the same number of lines, it is significant that Eve sees Adam later in her poem than he sees her in his. In his analysis of the poems, David C. Jacobson points out that in the first biblical Creation story, neither Adam nor Eve was ever alone, whereas in the second, "Adam was alone until the creation of Eve, but Eve was never alone."[163] Echoing the biblical text (Genesis 2:18), Yokheved Bat-Miriam, in *"Adam,"* twice uses the word *levaddo* (by himself) to describe him. *Levaddo,* which opens both the second and the fourth stanzas (lines 5 and 13), is strikingly set off from the following line: in the first instance, by a comma; in the second, by a period. In consonance with the biblical text, Bat-Miriam makes no explicit statement of Eve's aloneness in her poem.[164] This omission may indicate that being alone was not a problem for Eve. Bat-Miriam does give each of them ample time alone: half the poem for Adam, two-thirds for Eve. In so doing she reads the biblical text a bit differently, assuming that significant time elapsed between the woman's creation and God's bringing her to the *adam* (Genesis 2:21–22).

In *"Havvah,"* Yokheved Bat-Miriam describes Eve as writ large across the universe. Her images are rich and her language, replete with biblical, rabbinic, and liturgical references, as well as uncommon words and forms, adds texture to her portrayal. Bat-Miriam's timeline is independent of biblical chronology, her central figure named only in the title. Yet she conveys, particularly through the use of active verbs, an Eve who is strong, independent, and powerful. This Eve does not need a relationship with Adam in order to rise to her full potential.

חַוָּה

נוֹשְׁמָה עָלְטַת פָּנֶיהָ
כַּלְּהָבָה נִפְרַחַת מֵרָחוֹק,
זָעָה בְּזָוִיּוֹת שְׂפָתֶיהָ
וְנוֹשְׁבָה וְנוֹשְׁבָה בְּבַת־צְחוֹק.

5 נוֹגְעָה בְּשׁוּלֵי הַיֶּרֶק,
בְּעֵץ־פְּרִי וְחַיַּת־הַשָּׂדֶה,
בְּמוֹעֲדֵי שַׁחַר וָעֶרֶב,
בְּחֶזְיוֹנֹת, עָנָן וּמַרְאֶה.

שָׁתְקָה. וּכְאֵד וּכְהֶבֶל,
10 כְּעַיִן בְּרִסִיסֵי הַדִּמְעָה,
תָּעֲתָה שְׁתִיקָתָהּ מוּל מַחְשֶׁבֶת
דְּבָרִים וְחֵרוּתָם הַגֵּאָה.

מֵחֶסֶד צְלוּלָה וּמֵרֶגֶשׁ
בִּכִי־זֶמֶר פָּעֲתָה הַיָּד,
15 אוֹסְפָה וּמְלַטְּפָה כָּל רֶגַע –
גָּמוּל, מִתְחַטֵּא וְנִמְלָט.

מִנֶּגֶד, כְּמַיִם מוּל סַהַר,
הִצְטַיֵּר אָדָם וְצָעַד.
וַתִּנָּהַר מֵאֵימָה וּמִדַּעַת
20 וַתִּגְאֶה הַגּוּיָה לָעַד, –

פּוֹרֶשֶׂת מֵעֵבֶר לָעֵדֶן,
עַל קוֹץ וְדַרְדַּר, שַׁבָּתוֹן
מִתְהַדֵּד מֵחַיִּים וּמֶהְדָּר
מָוֶת, סוֹד וְדִמְיוֹן.

122

Eve

The darkness of her face breathes
Like a flame flowering from a distance,
It moves in the corners of her lips
And blows and blows with a smile.

5 She touches the margins of the verdure
A fruit tree and the beasts[165] of the field,
At fixed times of dawn and of evening,
A vision, a cloud, and an image

She was silent. And like mist[166] and like vapor,[167]
10 Like an eye with shards of tears,
Her silence wandered facing contemplation
Of words and their proud freedom.

Clearer than grace and than feeling
The hand sobbed a crying-song,
15 Collecting and caressing each moment—
Weaned, wheedling, and escaping.

From a distance, like water facing the moon,
Adam was imagined and strode.
And she glowed with terror and knowledge
20 And she rose eternally expressed,—

Spreading out beyond Eden,
Over thorn and thistle, a sabbath
Echoing with life and glory
[Of] death, mystery, and imagination.[168]

Bat-Miriam's language is the formal, elevated language of early twentieth-century Hebrew poetry, a language that had been superseded by a more colloquial idiom by 1940. Bat-Miriam chooses not only a dated vocabulary, but rare and antiquated grammatical forms as well.[169] The allusive nature of Bat-Miriam's language in this poem and her elliptical style[170] are in tension with the constraints of the poetic structure.[171] The six four-line stanzas with their regular rhyme scheme[172] and meter[173] contain a poetic vision of great complexity.

Like Pastan's "Aspects of Eve," Bat-Miriam's poem names Eve only in the title. In five of its six stanzas, the subject of the third-person singular, feminine verbs is not stated, although it is Eve; the fifth stanza, where the subject of those verbs is "the hand," presents an example of synecdoche where the hand represents Eve. Unnamed, represented by neither a noun nor a pronoun, Eve nonetheless dominates the landscape of the poem— and of the world.

In her poem, Bat-Miriam includes references, explicit and oblique, to many parts of the story of Adam and Eve. She modifies the time frame of Genesis by implying that Eve existed before creation, because she is present throughout, whether or not she had already been created according to the biblical chronology.[174] Further, the very markers of sacred biblical days, *'erev* and *boqer* (evening and morning), are here reversed and *shahar* (dawn) replaces *boqer* (morning), indicating a more specific and limited moment, the one when light daily separates from the darkness (line 7). The opening stanza, with its mention of flaming darkness, takes the reader to the primal chaos presented in the opening of Genesis 1, before the separation of dark and light on the first day. But it is Eve who embodies the chaos, making her metonymically the primal matter out of which the world was shaped. The references to the "fruit tree" (*'ets-peri*) and the "verdure" (*hayereq*) in the second stanza recall the third day of Creation when God commands into existence the fruit tree (*'ets-peri*) (Genesis 1:11), as well as the sixth when God tells the newly created *adam* that the "fruit of tree" (*peri-'ets*) and the "vegetation" (*yereq 'esev*) are proper food (Genesis 1:29–30).[175] The prehuman state of the earth as described in Genesis 2:6 where the "flow" (*'ed*) rises to water the Garden is recalled by Bat-Miriam's use of the same Hebrew word to describe Eve's silence in the third stanza. The Sabbath that God creates by ceasing from work on the seventh day (Genesis 2:1–3) is recalled in the last stanza in the *shabbaton* Eve extends over the world beyond Eden. Godlike, Eve acts in six stanzas that culminate in the silence of rest.

The primacy of sight among the senses of the biblical Eve is reflected in Bat-Miriam's poem as well. The first woman's decision to eat the forbidden fruit is based on sight.[176] Bat-Miriam's Eve synesthetically touches *ḥazut* (vision) and *mar'eh* (image), both nouns with roots connected with sight (line 8).[177] Her silence is compared to a tear explicitly located in the eye (line 10). The location of Adam's tear in his poem is not mentioned (line 11), nor does any word associated with sight appear in "Adam." Her perception of Adam is visual, rather than auditory; further, although her hand caresses each moment (line 15), she never seems to move from sight to concrete, physical touch. The only sounds in her poem are the sounds of silence (lines 9 and 11) and of the "crying-song" (line 14). Most of what is presented in the poem is there for the reader to see, adding to the dreamlike quality of the movement from one image to the next.[178]

Eve is the sole character from the early chapters of Genesis who is actually present in the poem; Adam is described at a distance (lines 17–18). But there is an oblique reference to the snake. The "beasts of the field" (*ḥayyat hasadeh*) that appear in the second stanza are also referred to in two different contexts in the biblical text. The first time is when they are named by the *adam* (Genesis 2:19, 20) and might be read here as an additional point at which we catch a glimpse of Adam. They also appear in the biblical text as reference points for the snake (Genesis 3:1, 14), who is both more shrewd and more cursed than the other "beasts of the field." Although Cain is absent from the poem, *hevel,* the word used here for vapor, is also the Hebrew word that is rendered as Abel. God is altogether absent.

If Eve is implicitly identified with the primeval chaos, she is also, by allusion, the "mother of all living," as Adam explains the name he gives her after God metes out the punishments (Genesis 3:20).[179] The first half of this poem is rich in suggestions of pregnancy and birthing. Most striking, the very first word of the poem, *noshemah* (breathes) and the word *pa'atah* (sobbed) (line 14) appear together in a verse from Isaiah (42:14) in which the image of God as a "warrior" in the previous verse is supplemented, even superseded, by a God Who says, "I will sob (*eph'eh*),[180] I will breathe (*eshom*), I will gasp like a woman birthing." Similarly, the word *ḥazut* (vision) (line 8) connects with the "harsh vision" (*ḥazut qashah*) that Isaiah reports (21:2) has so traumatized him that he is "gripped by pangs like the pangs of a birthing woman" (Isaiah 21:3). Further, the word *gamul* (weaned) (line 16) is birth-connected;[181] the word *ta'atah* (wandered), less so, but, when used in Psalm 58:4, the root is linked to

125

the womb.[182] In the center of the poem the accumulation of somewhat unconventional evidence presents a picture of Eve for whom the appellation "mother of all living" is appropriate.

Jacobson points to a significant difference between the ways Bat-Miriam's Adam and Eve relate to the world in their respective poems.[183] Adam, upon seeing Eve and touching her hand, remembers the names he gave to the trees and the animals; Eve, prior to meeting Adam, has touched the world, the very parts of the world that Adam has named. She has carefully collected and caressed each moment, whatever its status, in a bittersweet manner with her crying-song.[184] Indeed, time is as significant as a child for Bat-Miriam's Eve. Each moment is described as *gamul* (weaned)—an explicit reference to a child. But the word *mithattei* (wheedled) also appears in the context of childhood, notably in a fairly well-known rabbinic tale about a first-century B.C.E. wonder-working rainmaker, Honi the Circle-Drawer.[185] Eve treasures each moment, knowing that it will, like a child maturing into adulthood, eventually slip through her fingers. Like life itself, in light of the death that opens the poem's closing line, each moment is evanescent. Eve has not named, categorized, or filed creation; she has reached out to draw it to her soul.

Curiously, the one part of creation she does not touch is Adam. On the contrary, she only observes him, keeping her distance. Although we are told that Adam "strode," an indication of strength, he is also seen as self-imagined, perhaps an indication of weakness.[186] Bat-Miriam's metaphoric description of Adam as "water facing the moon" bespeaks a reversal of the somewhat facile association of women with the moon, men with the sun.[187] As the moon is but a pale reflection of the sun, so woman is perceived as a being less powerful than man. In this poem, however, the man is not even the moon, but a mere reflection of the moon—and certainly not the solar source of its light. The reflection of the moon in the water is twice removed from the conventional source of light, heat, and life that is embodied in the sun.

Seeing Adam, Eve reacts with "terror" and with "knowledge." The latter connects to the Tree of Knowledge; the former, Bat-Miriam's reading of the scene, is not congruent with the biblical text before the punishments are enunciated, but may well be a response to the male domination projected in them. Although the fifth stanza of the poem is the only one that does not end with some final punctuation, flowing instead into the final stanza, the content of these two stanzas is disjunctive. Having perceived the other human, Eve turns away and sets about preparing the desolate post-Edenic world for the complexities of the human condition. While Adam's poem concludes with the "fiery path of God," Eve's ends with complexity and contradiction: "death, mystery, and imagination."

Eve's role in the world is large, even Godlike. She takes on a divine dimension as, in the sixth stanza, she completes her task—as God finishes Creation—by spreading beyond Eden a Sabbath. Her Sabbath explicitly encompasses the "thorn and thistle" that the earth gives forth as described in God's punishment of Adam (Genesis 3:18). Although resounding with life, it will also embrace "death, mystery, and imagination." As Zierler notes, this line makes Eve the source of poetry,[188] which can readily be expanded to include all the arts. But there is an even more powerful message lurking behind these words. *Sod* (mystery) is a word used by Jewish mystics and kabbalists to indicate the deepest layers of the mystery of the knowledge of God. While Eve creates a Sabbath echoing with profound religious mystery, she also takes on some of that divine mystery; she is eternally *haguyah* (expressed, or pronounced). The word leads the reader to a well-known poem attributed to the seventh-century Hebrew poet Yannai that is part of the High Holy Day liturgy.[189] One of the epithets Yannai uses for God is *haguy* (expressed as) "I will be what I will be," incorporating God's response to Moses' request to know the name of the God Who has sent him (Exodus 3:14). In traditional Judaism, God's name is ineffable, never expressed; in this poem, Eve's name is absent. God's self-description in the future tense implies eternity, as does the use of "forever" in this poem. Eve, who opened the poem in primeval chaos, incorporating light and darkness, has grown at its end to divine proportions.

While the rabbis tend to read the biblical text as a condemnation of transgressing God's command, the argument has been made by some moderns that good emerged from the encounter between the woman and the serpent. The contemporary American Jewish poet Sandy Supowit, like other modern poets, has catalogued some of the benefits the woman derives from that meeting. Supowit's poem is as transparent as Bat-Miriam's is obscure.

Things Eve Learned from the Serpent[190]

that skin can be shed,
and revision is always
possible; that each choice
has its own taste
5   and some are sharp
and biting, but palates
can be trained; that in a perfect
garden there is order,
but in wild places
10   there is growth, that one whole
woman is more wonderful
than half of any couple;
that even underfoot,
belly to the ground, even
15   with the bitterness of cold soil
in the stopped mouth,
there can be power;
that what you don't know
may not kill you, but it also
20   may not be worth
living for; that this world is bigger
than one garden, humanity
than one man, the future
than the past; that if you find yourself
25   in a story they will never stop
retelling, you might as well
have your name in the title.

    Supowit utilizes the form of her poem to highlight the message. In twenty-seven lines, ranging from four to seven words, without capitalization and with but one terminal punctuation mark, she lets her reader know that the surface meaning often proves false and that order is not requisite. Supowit's lines tumble over each other; there are more run-on lines than end-stopped ones, many more lines with caesuras than with final punctuation. This gives a breathless quality to the poem.

The title of the poem intentionally catches the reader's attention because it runs counter to the notion that the interaction between Eve and the serpent yielded nothing positive. Reading the biblical text with a hermeneutic of suspicion, Supowit's woman garners from the serpent practical, life-affirming wisdom. The informal way she presents her reading gives the impression of an acceptance of life's complexities—but life is not smooth for the woman after she eats the fruit.

Some of what Eve learns is based on the serpent's experience. The serpent's ability to shed its skin becomes a metaphor for revising in general, be it text or life itself. The permutability of power is another lesson from the life of the serpent. Depicting the serpent in its contemporary state, as an earth-bound, crawling creature, Supowit would have it suggest that, despite its lowly appearance and difficult life, it retains the power to effect change. Supowit is arguing that the trappings of power ought not to be mistaken for de facto power, which is ultimately more significant than de jure. It is significant that these lessons come directly from the nonhuman in the narrative, the serpent.

But not all of the wisdom needed for life can be acquired from the experience of others; much has to come from one's own experience. Most of Eve's knowledge is self-derived. She is the one who takes the fruit, the symbol of her freedom to choose, into her mouth and realizes that its taste, although good in anticipation, is, in reality, neither entirely pleasant, nor completely unpalatable either. Taste is the product of the interaction between food and palate, between the consequences of a choice and the human psyche. While the difficulty of training a palate is not to be dismissed, it is no more impossible than adapting to life, however unpleasant.

Supowit also makes some claims about the relationship between men and women. Her emphasis on the worth of the individual drives her to propose that a woman has intrinsic value, whether or not she is part of a couple. She asserts that a woman should not see one man as the whole of humanity. Although some view the story of Adam and Eve as an endorsement of marriage,[191] Supowit glosses it as a lesson on the significance of women as individuals.

The quality of life outside the Garden of Eden is also a major theme in this poem. While the biblical narrative depicts life outside Eden as requiring hard labor, Supowit sees its possibilities. What Adam and Eve face outside the Garden is a world full of choices, where the future calls them away from dwelling in the past. It is precisely the order of the Garden that makes it limiting and inhibiting; the wildness of the rest of the world, mirrored in the lack of order in the poem, opens opportunities for growth, for developing in unforeseeable directions.

Supowit is not entirely comfortable with Eve's choice. While some ignorance can be dangerous, plenty of areas exist where "what you don't know" is "not worth living for," and, in the case of Eve, may not have been worth dying for either. Nonetheless, Supowit's Eve manages to taste the sweet behind the bitter.

By titling her poem "Things Eve Learned from the Serpent," Supowit leaps ahead of the biblical chronology according to which the woman is named Eve after the encounter with the serpent. The rationale for so doing is stated in the poem's final fillip, a kind of envoi to the female reader who identifies with Eve: "if you find yourself / in a story they will never stop / retelling, you might as well / have your name in the title." Putting Eve's name triumphantly in the title of this creative retelling of the story, Supowit manages to rewrite the lessons of the serpent, omitting God and leaving Adam nameless. Thus she suggests that the biblical narrative—narrative in general—can be reclaimed by the compatible techniques of revision and suspicious reading.

Naming the Woman

The power to designate objects in nature and animate beings—and to exercise authority by the very act of controlling their identity—is formidable in both primitive and sophisticated societies. Names have tremendous significance in texts, particularly in Genesis.

Often cited as an indication of the male's power over the female, the two namings of the woman in Genesis 2 and 3 serve as an inclusio for the Tree of Knowledge story in which the woman is the dominant character. Viewing these namings in the context of the preceding namings in Genesis further illuminates their significance.[192]

The first Creation story sets the context for all the subsequent acts of naming. God divides the primordial chaos into separate components, sometimes explicitly assigning a name to them. Thus, "day" and "night" (Genesis 1:5), "heavens" (Genesis 1:8), "land"[193] and "seas" (Genesis 1:10) are all named with a formula that will recur as the core of the formula for naming people. At some point in the third day, after the primordial chaos has been sorted into its components and its various divisions named, God starts to create new objects in nature and animate beings, including trees, plants, cattle, creeping things, and wild beasts. They are all identified without being formulaically, specifically, named. God does, however, often, although not consistently, indicate something about their function. Thus, for example, trees are described as "making fruit [that contains] its seed within it" (Genesis 1:11–12); cattle, on the other hand, do not have a functional definition (Genesis 1:24–25). Likewise, the *adam*, is created and given the function of ruling over the earth, but not named.

It remains puzzling that some entities are formally named in this primary poetic text, while others are not. Cassuto suggests that the "three parts of the universe we designate by these names are precisely those that God organized in the period of creation. He made none other than the *heavens* that we know; the pool into which the waters were gathered is our *sea;* and the dry land that appeared there is our *earth.*"[194] This line of reasoning explains the namings that appear in the text, but it does not address those that are absent. Likewise, it offers no explanation for the omission of a formal naming speech for the *adam*, who will play the major role in the unfolding drama.

Indeed, when God turns to the creation of the *adam*, as we have seen, God says not, "Let us make a creature," but "Let us make an *adam*" (Genesis 1:26). Although the *adam* appears to be morphous, its contours, number, and gender are not initially clear, perhaps not yet determined. Stranger still is the way that the word *adam* appears to slip seamlessly between serving as a common noun, indicating, depending on context and reader's perspective, either human or man, and appearing as a proper noun, as in the name Adam. Robert Alter claims: "The term *'adam*, afterward consistently with a definite article, which is used both here [Genesis 1:26] and in the second account of the origins of humankind, is a generic term for human beings, not a proper noun."[195] In most cases where there is no definite article Alter translates *adam* as a proper noun, but there are exceptions. The verse cited here, Genesis 1:26, in which the term first appears, could just as easily be rendered "Let us make Adam in our image." There are also places where the masoretic vocalization would appear to be without a definite article, but the context might have included one, for example, Genesis 3:21.[196] In any case, the name *adam* is never formally given to the creature, leaving him, in some sense, nameless.[197] Paradoxically, this first human namer is himself essentially unnamed.

As has been discussed, at the very end of the second Creation story, when the *adam*'s voice is first heard, he excitedly announces that this new creature will be called *ishah,* woman. For many readers, this passage, coming after the *adam* has named the animals, indicates that the *adam*'s power over the woman is similar to his power over the animals. The relationship between these first two episodes of naming may be clarified by a detailed comparison. Just as God brings the animals to the *adam* to be named, so God brings the second human to the *adam.* The text uses the identical verb root *b.v.*[198] to describe this ceremonial, almost ritual, action.

But that is the sole resemblance between the two namings. The wild beasts, cattle, and birds are brought to the *adam* for the express purpose of his naming them. It is generally assumed, though not explicit in the text, that the names given here are the specific names of different kinds of animals, the broader categories having already been assigned by God.[199] The power inherent in the *adam*'s naming the animals is reinforced by the fact that the naming latitude given the *adam* was wide and that God promised to abide by the *adam*'s choices: "And the Lord God formed out of the earth all the wild beasts and all the birds of the sky and brought them to the *adam* to see what he would call them; and whatever the *adam* called each living creature, that would be its name" (Genesis 2:19). There is no indication as to whether or not these names were previously known to God nor do we hear the *adam*'s voice.

In contrast, there is no purpose ascribed to God's bringing the woman to the *adam.* In other words, she is not brought to him in order to be named. When the *adam* refers to her as *ishah,* woman, the term is not new to the reader who has encountered it in the narrator's report of God's new creation in the previous verse: "And the Lord God fashioned the rib that He had taken from him into a woman [*ishah*]" (Genesis 2:22). What is new is the proposed etymology that connects it to *ish,* man. The *adam* exclaims:

ב 23 וַיֹּאמֶר הָאָדָם זֹאת הַפַּעַם עֶצֶם מֵעֲצָמַי וּבָשָׂר מִבְּשָׂרִי לְזֹאת
יִקָּרֵא אִשָּׁה כִּי מֵאִישׁ לֻקֳחָה־זֹּאת:

> "This [*zot*] one, this time,
>   is bone from my bones
>   and flesh from my flesh.
>   This one [*zot*] shall be called woman [*ishah*],
>   for from man [*ish*] this one [*zot*] was taken."
>   (Genesis 2:23)[200]

Paradoxically, the real naming that occurs here is the *adam*'s naming himself *ish*, man, for this is the first time that the word for man appears in the biblical text.

Rabbinic embellishments of Genesis 2:23 that see God as the matchmaker or wedding attendant notwithstanding, the purpose for which God has brought the woman to the *adam* is not explicit;[201] God has already referred to this new creature as *ishah* so there is no need for the *adam* to invent a name for her. Nonetheless, in his ecstatic reception of the woman the *adam* incorporates language that suggests that he chose the name, rather than that he accepted God's choice, which he may not have known. When he explains the name, using a false, folk etymology and, in so doing, calls himself an *ish* (man), we are left with two generic terms: *ish* and *ishah*.

But the *adam* names the woman a second time, following fast upon God's original set of punishments for the serpent, the woman, and the *adam*. Although the *adam*'s own voice is not heard, his statement is a countervailing, human response to the culminating verse of God's punishment. God concludes the punishment of the *adam* by informing him:

ג 19 בְּזֵעַת אַפֶּיךָ תֹּאכַל לֶחֶם עַד שׁוּבְךָ אֶל־הָאֲדָמָה כִּי מִמֶּנָּה לֻקָּחְתָּ
כִּי־עָפָר אַתָּה וְאֶל־עָפָר תָּשׁוּב:

> "By the sweat of your brow
>   shall you eat bread,
>   until your return to the ground [*adamah*]—
>   for from it were you taken.
>   for dust you are,
>   and to dust you shall return."

(Genesis 3:19)

Basic human subsistence will now require hard work and will end in death. God, reminding the *adam* of his etymological and physical roots in the *adamah*, uses divine power to punish the *adam*. The *adam* responds by asserting the power of life over death. "The man named his wife Ḥavvah [Eve] because she was the mother of all living" (Genesis 3:20). God reminds the *adam* of his origin in the earth to which death will return him; the human challenges God by naming his woman the source of all life to come. What allows humans to triumph over death is inherent in the birth of one generation from another, not the eternal life of a single generation.

The name *Ḥavvah* or Eve is less straightforward than it seems. The sense of "mother of all living" would better be expressed by *Ḥayyah*, for which *Ḥavvah* may be, as Sarna suggests, an archaic form.[202] While this may allude to or recall cults of a mother goddess typical of some ancient Near Eastern religions, it does not link *Ḥavvah* with them in any meaningful way; *Ḥavvah* is clearly a human mortal. As the rabbis suggested, the name may also be connected to the Aramaic word *ḥivya,* a serpent.[203] It is a proper noun, while *ishah* is a common noun. Hence the double naming does not mean that the creature had two names, like Jacob/Israel, but that she was first named in a generic sense in relation to the existing creature—the man—and subsequently named Eve after the punishments.[204] God's immediate acceptance of this naming is not explicit, but implicit in the next divine action: providing the primal couple with "garments of skins" (Genesis 3:21).

The name *Ḥavvah,* whatever its true etymology, cannot be addressed apart from the *adam's* explanation for it. Strict adherence to the biblical context, reading the events sequentially, brings out the fact that, at the time of the expulsion, not only was Eve not the "mother of all living," she was the mother of nothing at all. The birth of her first child, including the only other occurrence of the name *Ḥavvah,* lies five verses ahead at the opening of Genesis 4. Is this name then an ultimate irony? Or is it a ray of hope in the future that shines through the darkness of the punishments? Given the context, it could ironically be both: on the one hand, a mocking name reminding the woman that she has no progeny; on the other, the promise of a future that subverts death.

Banishment

The possibility that humans might yet become truly immortal continues to worry God: If they remain in the Garden the *adam* may "take also of the tree of life and live forever" (Genesis 3:22). To assure that humans remain mortal they will be banished from the Garden and cherubs with flaming, rotating swords at the entrance will keep them out.[205] The banishment is less a punishment of the humans than a form of preemptive strike. It is noteworthy that at this point God again reverts to the "consultative" first-person plural: "Now that the *adam* has become like one of us, knowing good and bad" (Genesis 3:22a). This use of the plural, like the one preceding the creation of the *adam,* indicates the gravity of the decision. In each of the three verses relating to the banishment (Genesis 3:22–24), the term used for the human is *ha'adam* (the *adam*) and the verbs and pronouns referring to the *adam* are all singular. The text does not indicate that God is dealing with two separate individuals, at least one of whom has a name. The text would seem to describe a situation in which the humans, separated by their illicit eating, separate in their punishments, and separate in their having been provided clothing by God, revert to their state at Creation.

How do we read this text? One possible approach would have the woman's significance so diminished that despite God's conversation with her regarding the forbidden fruit and her subsequent punishment, she does not merit God's attention. But it is also arguable that she is not to be viewed as a prime offender. The order not to eat the fruit of the Tree of Knowledge was not given directly to her. She follows her man into the world because she desires him and, therefore, is subject to his power. By naming the woman, the man has asserted his power beyond the limits God had given him, leading God to fear further encroachment on the divine realm. The poem "The Expulsion" by the contemporary essayist and poet Katha Pollitt, while avoiding the issue of the elimination of Eve from the verses about the banishment, frames the exile from Eden in a most positive manner.

The Expulsion

Adam was happy—now he had someone to blame
for everything—shipwrecks, Troy,
the gray face in the mirror.

Eve was happy: now he would always need her.
5   She walked on boldly, swaying her beautiful hips.

The serpent admired his emerald coat,
the Angel burst into flames
(he'd never approved of them, he was right).

Even God was secretly pleased: Let
10   History Begin!

The dog had no regrets, trotting by Adam's side
self-importantly, glad to be rid

135

of the lion, the toad, the basilisk, the white-footed mouse,
who were also happy and forgot their names immediately.

15   Only the Tree of Knowledge stood forlorn,
its small hard bitter crab apples

glinting high up, in a twilight of black leaves:
how pleasant it had been, how unexpected

to have been, however briefly,
20   the center of attention.[206]

Focusing on the outcome for everyone—every creature, divine and human, sentient and plant—involved, rather than on the "banishment" itself, Pollitt in twenty lines describes something in the situation that is comforting to each participant in the drama, even though an objective observer would scarcely take comfort in them. Opening with Adam, as God had done in questioning the man and the woman, Pollitt moves through the five characters directly cited in Genesis.[207] But she does not give them equal billing: Adam gets one three-line stanza, Eve gets a couplet, God has the shortest couplet in the poem, but God's is the only voice directly heard. The serpent merits but a line; the Angel, two. The dog gets three lines, while the Tree, for all its complaining, is given six lines and the place of emphasis at the end.

The first line is incongruous: "Adam was happy." The source of the happiness is ironic. Expelled from Eden, committed to a life of hard work, Adam is pleased to recapture his innocence by blaming "everything" on Eve. The word "everything," following as it does the run-on opening line, is surprising. What is at stake here is responsibility not merely for eating of the Tree of Knowledge, but for whatever else goes wrong in life. Pollitt's examples are unexpected—accidents, war, and aging. "Shipwrecks" and "Troy" come from classical mythology and situate Adam in the realm of the epic, as the male irresistibly attracted by the charms of the female. The sirens lured sailors to wreck their ships and Helen, whose "face launched a thousand ships," allegedly caused the Trojan War. But the fault lies with Odysseus, although Greek greed and the gods' manipulation played no minor part. Likewise, Adam, to whom responsibility for avoiding the Tree's fruit was entrusted, cannot easily avoid the onus of that misdeed. Obviously, had the first humans remained in Eden, none of these unfortunate events would have transpired, rendering ironic Adam's joy at being able to escape responsibility for them.

"Eve was happy" leads us to expect a reason followed by a catalogue, like the one Pollitt presents for Adam. Her joy requires less explanation; it consists simply in being needed. What she is needed for is beside the point. One requisite role is shouldering the blame for all life's ills. Another area where she would be needed is sexual, as embodied in her bold, hip-swaying walk. Her significance as a sexual partner extends to her role in procreation. An immortal human pair, enclosed in Eden, had no need for children; a mortal pair, charged with populating the world, would—and for that Adam needs a partner. As long as the humans remain in Eden, they are also poorly situated for their task: to "fill the earth."[208]

The serpent is the ultimate irresponsible narcissist. He has no interest in relationships, positive or negative; his focus is narrow—his own appearance. He does not relate at all to the apparent loss of his legs. His focus is on the trivial, the superficial. Yet green is the color of envy and the serpent's action has been explained as the result of his envy of Adam. For all the serpent's apparent lack of interest in others, he is really motivated by jealousy.

The Angel is also deceptively simple, bursting into flames to guard the Garden against an incursion by the banished couple. This is an image, however, of self-destruction, unlike the biblical one of the cherubim with rotating, flaming swords. The parenthetical comment offers a window into the Angel's mind; it neither speaks nor is spoken to in the biblical narrative. This Angel is thematically linked with those that, according to *Genesis Rabbah*,[209] objected to the creation of humans in the first place. He finds his opposition to the divine plan confirmed by the misbehavior of Adam and Eve and the consequent impetus to banish them to prevent further misdeeds. One can imagine his self-satisfaction at the turn things have taken, vindicating his original argument. Linked by jealousy to the serpent, with which he shares the stanza, the Angel is self-destructive in his self-congratulatory self-righteousness.

Even God's reaction is not what we might have anticipated. God is not the Creator disappointed in the divine handicraft, but the risk-taker, ready to let humans take over. Eden is the place of Eternity with everlasting life lurking in the Tree of Life; beyond Eden lies the realm of the human, the mortal, the realm of History. Just as God has magisterially brought the elements of the universe into being by declaiming: "Let there be . . . ," so does God call: "Let History Begin." The break in the line after "Let" makes the introduction of History into the biblical story all the more shocking. The Deity eagerly awaits what the humans will do with the time they have. While less than omniscient, God is "secretly pleased" with what has transpired. He knows that the alternative—the humans remaining in Eden—would have thwarted the divine plan to populate the world with humans and prolonged the threat that the humans would truly become divine immortals.

The cosmic scene of the Expulsion from Eden, so often depicted in art as well as in poetry, is reduced to human size by the two couplets that follow. Adding that all-American mainstay, the dog, makes Adam and Eve an ordinary couple moving on from one abode to another. The dog considers himself on a par with the humans and different from the other animals who, at least in Pollitt's version, remain behind in Eden. Like the others, the dog, too, appraises the situation in light of his own priorities. Far from serving as the fearless defender of the humans, ready to oppose any foe, the dog sees himself as finally relieved of the presence of rival creatures, annoying or even frightening to the dog.

The four creatures the dog identifies are diverse in their power. The lion, the reputed king of the beasts, is threatening to a dog, both physically and hierarchically. Once the reader accepts the premise that all the animals are not banished along with the humans, the lion seems a logical locus for the dog's fear. Not so the toad that, despite its reputation for warty skin, poses no threat to the dog. The basilisk is the most complex of this quartet of canine foes. It can be seen as parallel to the toad in its relatively small size, assuming that it is simply a lizard. But there are allusions that would connect it to the lion instead. A late nineteenth-century text identifies it as the "king serpent," apparently because it has a yellow spot on its head that looks like a crown.[210] The basilisk would then be similar to the lion in its regal stature. As *Harry Potter* aficionados know, in the medieval period the basilisk was reputed to be dangerous, possessing the ability to kill with a breath or with a glance.[211] In the modern period it describes a small arboreal tropical American lizard that can run on its hind legs. The basilisk is thus both a parallel to the lion and a reminder of the edenic serpent, which had legs. The white-footed mouse is a small and apparently insignificant creature, hardly threatening to a dog. These creatures constitute a group that is happy. Their happiness is signified by their forgetting their names, in other words, by their reverting to Edenic bliss without human domination.

The Tree of Knowledge, depicted as the only loser in the situation, dominates the last three couplets of the poem. Its apples are not the shining globes, "good for eating and a lust for the eyes" (Genesis 3:6), that Eve described, but "small hard bitter crab apples." The leaves of the tree are black, neither the myriad shades of green of the various stages of growth, nor the radiant colors of the harvest; the apples are inaccessible, high above normal reach. The Tree of Knowledge was unaware of its own significance. Although planted in the center of the Garden, it never expected to be the "center of attention." What it loses is something it had not anticipated possessing: a role of consequence.

The glinting apples recall the Virgilian golden bough that is Aeneas's passport—or sacrifice—to Hades and to eternal truth. It links truth and death, just as knowledge and death are linked in the biblical description of the Tree of Knowledge. Ultimately, the Tree alone embodies truth in the knowledge of Good and Bad. Truth, as contained in "small hard bitter crab apples," is hard to eat, unpleasant to face. But only the tree avoids self-delusion and faces its task honestly. That is Pollitt's message.

In her modern midrash, Pollitt asserts that the banishment from the Garden was not the cataclysmic catastrophe normally depicted, but the desirable inaugural step into history, into life within temporal boundaries. God is here portrayed as "secretly pleased" with what has happened. The woman becomes the agent of history whose quest for knowledge propels humanity out of the Garden and into life. True, Pollitt's bold, hip-swaying Eve hardly matches the stereotypical view of a seeker after knowledge, but Pollitt challenges the reader to move beyond the stereotype. Her Eve has passed the test.

Conclusion: The Test

God's order to *adam* not to eat the fruit of the Tree of Knowledge of Good and Bad precipitates the entrance of the humans into the realm of history. For many modern writers and thinkers this outcome was not necessarily negative. God, Who places the attractive tree in the center of the Garden and forbids eating its fruit, places an overwhelming temptation before the *adam*. One need not see the primal couple as children[212] to understand that the allure of the forbidden is irresistible here, despite the serious penalty for disobedience.

Ironically, it is not the *adam,* but the woman, who is tested. How one views the outcome of the test depends, of course, on one's reading of gender and hierarchy, as much as it depends on the text of Genesis itself. Genesis sets out the results of eating the fruit: punishments for all three culprits, banishment for the *adam.* Reasonably enough, however, it cannot present in any detail an alternate script. What would have happened had the humans not eaten the forbidden fruit? It is pointless to speculate as to whether or not eternal life would have been theirs. Based on God's concern that they might eat the fruit of the Tree of Life and thus become immortal, it seems that human mortality was part of the divine plan ab initio (Genesis 3:21). The fact that death enters the human world not "on the day" that they eat the fruit as threatened (Genesis 2:17), but long after, points to the possibility that God was, at the very least, ambivalent about imposing this harsh penalty. Humans had to survive to fulfill the divine aim of having them populate and steward the earth.

Moral choices are born in the face of competing claims, not in the presence of one unambiguous good. The first humans were given two orders that were in tension—to populate and rule over the world and to remain ignorant of good and bad—orders that Fikhman embodies in the competing claims of Adam and the serpent. Unlike Manger's flighty girl, the biblical woman carefully weighs her decision, determining which is paramount: obeying God's cryptic command or gaining wisdom. The three factors she weighs move hierarchically from simple physical eating through an encompassing vision to the desire for moral knowledge. Her decision, expressed in her threefold positive evaluation of the fruit, puts her in violation of one of the divine commands. Her deathless punishment, God's clothing the primal couple, and their absence from subsequent biblical descriptions of malfeasance may be read as softening some of the hard edges.

Late antique and early medieval rabbinic traditions often see Eve as culpable, as responsible for her own deed and for seducing Adam into eating the fruit. The biblical punishment is read at its harshest and, as we see in R. Yehoshuaʿs litany, even expanded well beyond the original text. The biblical passage where God examines the woman directly and informs her of the punishment is effaced as inappropriate for God. The biblical texts surrounding Eve are used to justify the position of women at the margins of the Jewish world of the time.

A number of modern Jewish writers have reassessed the more traditional view of Eve. They have revisited the biblical text and found much that is admirable in the Eve it portrays. Different as they are in form, language, and tone, Bat-Miriam's quasi-mystical projection of an Eve writ large upon the landscape and Supowit's somewhat humorous riff on the "life experience" lessons Eve might have garnered from the serpent share a vision of an Eve who is powerful, not subservient. Pollitt's Eve initiates human history. None of these Eves would recognize herself in the image of an Eve who must cover her head in shame. Contemporary writers are redeeming Eve as a character with voice and power who is the equal of Adam—if not his superior.

Chapter Three: Eve Beyond the Garden

כָּתוּב בְּעִפָּרוֹן בַּקָּרוֹן הֶחָתוּם

כָּאן בַּמִּשְׁלוֹחַ הַזֶּה
אֲנִי חַוָּה
עִם הֶבֶל בְּנִי
אִם תִּרְאוּ אֶת בְּנִי הַגָּדוֹל
קַיִן בֶּן אָדָם
תַּגִּידוּ לוֹ שֶׁאֲנִי

Written in Pencil in the Sealed Boxcar

here in this transport
i am eve
with abel my son
if you see my elder son
cain son of man [*ben adam*]
tell him that i[1]

In these six stunning lines, which with the title comprise a mere
twenty-three Hebrew words, the Israeli poet and scholar of medieval Hebrew literature Dan Pagis (1930–1986) provides a narrative for Eve's life
after the birth of her first two sons. Boldly using the Holocaust tropes of
the sealed railway car and the transport to shift the story of strife in the
primal family to the Shoah, Pagis without explanation evokes all four
family members, assigning them roles that generally parallel, but occasionally challenge, their biblical stories. God is absent. The wide gaps in
the biblical story allow ample opportunity for the creative imagination to
rove in this "dark poem full of white space, an empty space that takes
away the wend of our word."[2]

While the poem itself echoes the biblical text, the title is encoded
with language derived from the liturgy of the High Holy Days. Its four
words comprise two pairs of rhyming words with similar construction,
presented in chiastic order.[3] The framing words, *katuv* (written) and
ḥatum (sealed), are past participles drawn most memorably from the

High Holy Day prayer *Untanneh Toqef*, which metaphorically portrays God writing and sealing each person's fate for the coming year. It is also the High Holy Day greeting wishing one a "good writing and sealing" (in the Book of Life). While both of those contexts present hope that the fates have yet to be sealed, Pagis's use of the past participle indicates that hope no longer remains.[4] They provide the resonance of a divinely determined fate from which one cannot escape. Like the sealed fate of those within the boxcar, the final letter of the Hebrew word *ḥatum*, ם, provides the visual message of confinement. In fact, each of the words in the title closes with a consonant, aurally echoing the captivity experienced by those within.

The two words in the center of the title, *be'ipparon* (in pencil) and *baqaron* (in the boxcar), share both the same initial preposition, although with slightly different meanings, and the same nominal ending. What is written in pencil is not inscribed for eternity; lead fades. Further, the root of the modern Hebrew word for pencil is *'afar* (dust); here a reference both to the second biblical version of the creation of the *adam* from the dust of the earth (*'afar min ha'adamah*) (Genesis 2:7) and to the punishment of the *adam*, who is fated to return to the dust (*'afar*) from which it was created (Genesis 3:19).[5]

Pagis's Eve is the first-person central figure of this fragmentary appeal. On one level she is a woman with her child in a transport. The others necessarily present in the boxcar are beyond the lens of this poem. The reader sees only the mother and child, perhaps even a "Madonna and child," playing off the Christian view of the biblical Eve as the antithesis of the redemptive Mary.[6]

As Ḥavvah, the biblical "mother of all living," Eve is also, at this moment, the mother of all dying, defined by her presence with Abel, and the mother of all who would commit the fratricide that is the slaughter of their human brethren, as expressed in her referring to Cain as "my son." As David G. Roskies comments, Pagis "transpose[s] the end of human history back to its beginnings."[7] In so doing Pagis rewrites the biblical story by inserting Eve into the lives of her sons. The mother, who, like the father, is absent from the biblical scene of the fratricide and unable to prevent it, is here relieved of that guilt by sharing Abel's fate.

Eve is a figure of universal, not specifically Jewish, proportions.[8] Ironically challenging accepted gender roles, which marginalize women and do not give them voice, Pagis situates the woman in the middle of the story of fraternal strife, letting her function as the historian whose written voice attempts to provide readers, who represent future generations, with her truncated message. The poet's choice to speak through the mother, not the father, is a tribute to Eve's dominance in the biblical text.

Eve's unfinished note raises many questions. Why does it begin with *kan* (here)? Although together with *hazeh* (this), *kan* appears to add specificity, it actually reinforces ambiguity; the "here" of the poem could theoretically be a boxcar filled with humans being transported to their death anywhere on the face of the globe.[9] Two contradictory questions arise: Who is the narrator when she is located elsewhere? And is Eve different in other places? We do not know, for example, what she might have done in the role of "first mother" east of Eden. The absence of any conclusion from the poem suggests the possibility that it is a circular text, rather than a linear one. When one comes to the end one returns to the beginning, endlessly repeating this violent story so deeply embedded in the human experience.

Like the biblical Eve, eternally exiled from Eden, our narrator is being moved away from her home. Her verbal assertion of self is, on one level, of a piece with Eve's jubilant first-person statement on the birth of Cain. But Pagis's Eve no longer sees herself as the proud mother of Cain and the bearer of his brother Abel; she is, for better or for worse, with Abel to whom she now lays claim. Without rejecting Cain, whom she identifies as "my elder son," Eve asserts her connection to Abel, whom the biblical text identifies at birth as Cain's brother rather than as the son of one or both of his parents. Cain, whose description as *gadol* may also be rendered as "big" or "great," is just as ambiguously called *ben adam*. On the simplest level it is a standard Hebrew patronymic that is as close as Adam gets to the action.[10] Thus, in a sense, Eve loosens her bond with Cain and may further imply that, just as she is with Abel, so is Adam with Cain.[11] On another level, it could be translated as "son of man," implying universality.[12] It is the phrase with which God often addresses Ezekiel,[13] reminding the reader that, while Ezekiel envisions a valley of dry bones that will come back to life (Ezekiel 37:1–14), the bones of the Jews in this transport will, in all likelihood, be incinerated, leaving only smoke (*hevel*) and ash. The most significant Hebrew poet of the early twentieth century, Ḥ. N. Bialik, in his poem "City of Slaughter,"[14] has God repeatedly address the narrator as *ben adam*. The poem, written in response to the Kishinev pogrom of

1903, concludes with a scene that ironically recalls Ezekiel's vision of dry bones. The survivors appeal for alms to passersby who might respond to the bones of the martyred relatives that the survivors are exhibiting. Finally, most poignant, the Hebrew phrase *ben adam* also means a human being, a *mentsh,* in the finest sense of the term.

Eve's writing on the wall of the sealed boxcar or cattle car stands in stark contrast with the messages for posterity left by the biblical Eve. The biblical Eve has a strong voice; Pagis's has none. The poem contains a heartrending reminder of the human need to leave what Longfellow calls "footprints on the sands of time." But this inscription is ephemeral—written in pencil, recalling the words scratched on railway cars during the Holocaust.[15] Pagis's claim that these messages were intended to inform family and friends that the writer is still alive is tempered by our knowledge that, for the overwhelming majority of these "passengers," the passage ended in death.

To whom is the message embedded in the poem addressed? Only someone within the boxcar can read it. Despite Pagis's clarification of the purpose of the message,[16] it is more likely that the inscription, discoverable only after the car has been emptied, would be read by someone entering the car—either Jew or Nazi.[17] It cannot be read as a cry for help, as the car is already sealed. It is a double message; its readers are asked to transmit a message to Cain, if they see him; Cain is to be told "that I." Readers of the poem receive one further faint hint of the meaning in the distant echo of the syntax of a verse from the Song of Songs: "I adjure you, daughters of Jerusalem, if you find my beloved tell him this, that I am sick with love" (5:8). The overwhelming love experienced by the woman cited in the Song of Songs may be read onto the poem as the unbreakable bond of love between mother and child that no act of the child can undo. On the other hand, given the rabbinic reading of the Song of Songs as the expression of the covenantal love between God and the people Israel, it may ironically convey Pagis's sentiment that the covenant is no longer operative, that the Holocaust demonstrates that God is unable or unwilling to comply with its terms and defend the beloved people Israel.

The fragment is essentially blank, broken off after the first word of the message to Cain. The reader is provided no indication as to why the message breaks off. Is the cause internal? Is Eve, overwhelmed by emotion, perhaps by fear, perhaps by love, unable to formulate her thoughts? Does

she faint or die for lack of food and water? Is the cause of the break external? Has the boxcar arrived at its final destination? Is she murdered?[18] Was
it partially erased, inadvertently or intentionally, after she completed it?
For this riddle Pagis leaves us no clues other than the silence signifying
that the world of the Holocaust—and by extension, the universe since its
creation—are ultimately impenetrable.[19]

Leaving his readers to devise the words Eve would have written, Pagis
allows full range for supplying content. The infinite possibilities are all
completely speculative: Are we to take that silence itself for the message,
as Plank suggests?[20] Is the message that "I [am]"? Is Eve's silence part of
her bonding with Abel, who is the only character in this biblical story
who never speaks and who, in Pagis's "Autobiography,"[21] cites silence as
his invention? The white space at the end of this poem opens into fear-
some infinity.[22]

A major question concerns what Pagis achieves by inscribing the Holocaust on the Creation story. How does his reading the story against the
canonical biblical text contribute to an understanding of the story in Genesis? Pagis's poem succeeds because he exploits the gaps in the biblical
story of Eve after the Expulsion from the Garden. His primary goal is to
inspire a meditation on the Holocaust that resonates for anyone familiar
with the Bible—almost anyone who could read his poem in the original
language. In this statement what Pagis envisions as the end of mortal
human time is made to confront its beginning after the expulsion from
the Garden. He implies that from its conception the human project carried the seeds of inhumanity.

Pagis transports his Eve to another point in human history as if to
underscore her eternal nature. He builds upon the end of Eve's recorded
story, leaving her the victim, not the initiator, of human iniquity. He
shares with the rabbis of classical antiquity, as well as with all poets, an
interest in how words can resonate through generations of meaning. The
rabbis mine the sacred words of the biblical text down to their letters,
making them confront one another in amazing combinations. Poets ex-
ploit echoes and connotations acquired by a text to make their poems
into a kind of echo box.

The Biblical Text: Birth

To understand Eve's story in Genesis it is important to bear its scope in
mind. Although the biblical story of Eve is often presented as concluding

with the expulsion from the Garden of Eden at the end of Genesis 3,[23] it continues outside of Eden through the beginning of Genesis 5 after the post-Eden events narrated in the intervening chapter 4. The story, which includes conception, birth, worship of God, sibling rivalry, and murder, continues the saga of the primal pair over several generations. But, significantly, Eve is seen only at the birth of her sons.

ד 1 וְהָאָדָם יָדַע אֶת־חַוָּה אִשְׁתּוֹ וַתַּהַר וַתֵּלֶד אֶת־קַיִן וַתֹּאמֶר קָנִיתִי אִישׁ אֶת־יְ-הֹוָה: ד 2 וַתֹּסֶף לָלֶדֶת אֶת־אָחִיו אֶת־הָבֶל.

4:1 The *adam* knew Eve his woman, and she conceived and bore Cain, saying, "I have created [*qaniti*] a man [*ish*] together with the Lord."   4:2 And she continued to bear his brother Abel. (Genesis 4:1–2a)

The first verb encountered post-Eden involves "knowing," not in the earlier, broad sense of being able to distinguish between good and bad, but in the intimate context of sexual relations.[24] The use of the same linguistic root ties this act to the Tree of Knowledge; the act itself is a consequence of the punishment inflicted for violating the injunction against eating the tree's fruit.[25] The conception of Cain allows both the continuation of life in the face of the threat of death—eat of the fruit and you shall surely die—and the couple's return to following God's orders by fulfilling the commandment to be fruitful and multiply (Genesis 1:28). But the need to establish human hegemony is not merely divine; it is integrated, as we have seen, into the etymology Adam offers for the second name he gives his woman—Ḥavvah, Eve— explaining that she is *em kol ḥay* (mother of all living) (Genesis 3:20).[26]

What is striking about Genesis 4:1 is speed: conception, birth, and naming all take place in fourteen Hebrew words, five of which are verbs: *yada'* (he knew), *tahar* (she conceived), *teled* (she bore), *tomer* (she said), *qaniti* (I created). Although the *adam* is the subject of the first verb, Eve is the subject governing the remaining four. Who chooses the name "Cain" for this man/child is not completely clear. This verse truncates the two-step naming formula that will become the biblical norm and has the elder son born with a name that Eve explains concisely, but not clearly.[28] Her claim as the major actor is unchallenged; her taking the prerogative of explaining the name implies that she has also chosen it. Eve's voice and agency here are hard to miss. As we have seen, Adam has already named the woman twice, the first time, *ishah* (woman) in an energetic naming speech (Genesis 2:23); the second, *Ḥavvah* (Eve) in a speech that is reported, not heard (Genesis 3:20).[28] Adam is a man of few words. His last directly reported words are his excuse for eating the fruit: "The woman You gave at my side—she gave me of the fruit, and I ate" (Genesis 3:12). In chapter 4 Eve's voice becomes stronger;[29] Adam remains silent.

The content of the naming speech is also critical, a fact made all the more complicated by the convoluted meaning of three of Eve's four words. The verb *q.n.y*, often translated as "acquire," is unexpected; the use of *ish* (man) and *et* (with) puzzling. To this point in Genesis, four different verbs have been used for the act of creation: *b.r.'*, *'.s.y*, *y.ts.r*, and *b.n.y*—all governed by one Creator. The root *y.l.d* has signified giving birth. Eve introduces *q.n.y*, a new term, that is obscure because its most common biblical meaning, "acquire, buy," seems inappropriate here.[30] Another meaning is "create," but when that is its meaning in the Bible, its subject is invariably God; often, as Cassuto indicates, specifically as Creator of a human being.[31] Eve's hubris here, tempered perhaps by her reference to God, is striking. Before this birth there were only two humans: one created by God out of nonhuman matter and the other, either created at the same time or created by God using the human material previously created. Eve's statement here claims that she is the source of new humans; God, an assistant; and the man, out of the picture. This viewpoint leads directly to the unraveling of human domestic tranquility.

The ambiguity of the verb *q.n.y* may express the relationship between parent and child, capturing both the child as a maternal possession and the child as future independent adult. This first birth introduces a new action into the world that must be described in words. This moment constitutes a major step in Eve's development as a person of independent character.[32] The process of Eve's development continues through her final reported acts.

Although Eve's use of *ish* (man) may be more readily understood than *qaniti* (created), it, too, is problematic. As we have seen, the word *ish* enters the biblical lexicon with the second Creation story (Genesis 2:23–24) where the *adam* uses the term to define himself as "man," distinct from the new creature, *ishah* (woman); the narrator also uses it to explain the bond between a man and a woman.[33] In the Garden story, the man is *ish* when the woman clearly grammatically possesses or defines him: when she gives him the forbidden fruit (Genesis 3:6) and when God claims that her desire is for him (Genesis 3:16).[34] This usage may indicate the limited nature of Eve's understanding of the word. So far in the text only two words for humans, other than *adam*, have occurred: *ish* and *ishah*. She chooses *ish* as more appropriate. Her choice raises a host of issues, paramount among them the kind of relationship she anticipates having with this new man and how it will be different from her relationship with Adam. The obvious Hebrew word would have been *ben* (son), which she will use at the birth of Seth (Genesis 4:25). It may be the fact that Cain and Abel will not provide descendants for the human future that precludes their being called *ben*[35]—which, as a patronymic, implies human continuity.

Finally, the use of the word *et*, often merely a grammatical indicator, but here most likely a preposition meaning "with," is a challenge. It may be nothing more than a reference to God's role in human affairs, particularly in the area of procreation.[36] No real justification exists, however, for ignoring the complexity; once more, what is missing is as troubling as what is present. The verse opens with Adam's "knowing" Eve, but, once the child of that "knowing" is conceived, Adam disappears entirely from the episode. Eve seems to challenge God here with her hubristic claim of procreative power, as she had with her boldly eating the fruit.[37] At the same time, one might find here traces of humility. After all, God's creation of the *adam* and its subsequent separation into two parts, or the divine creation of the man and subsequent building of the woman, were God's alone. Eve is bold in claiming God's partnership, but does not go so far as to assert that she, like God, can create life on her own.[38]

Following fast upon the birth of Cain and Eve's excited exclamation[39] is a terse announcement of the birth of Abel, with neither emotion nor explanation (Genesis 4:2a). Cain's birth involves four separate active verbs; Abel's, one verbal phrase,[40] "she continued to bear," which allows for the possibility that Abel was Cain's twin, there being no mention of a second conception.[41] By defining Abel in relation not to his parents or to God but to his brother, the text suggests that the most significant relationship in his life will be with Cain.[42]

Abel's name, *Hevel*, means "nothing, a breath." The explanation missing here is implicit in the events that follow. The name engenders no great expectations, but a void.[43] In contrast, in Pagis's poem, *Hevel* (Abel) is a presence; *Qayin* (Cain), an absence.

The disparity in the treatment of the two sons may portend what will follow. It is useful to compare it with instances of succession in the subsequent patriarchal/matriarchal narratives. Sarah and Rebecca follow God's explicit instructions to assure the succession of a favorite son. The second son inherits his father's mantle; the elder, firstborn brother, or half-brother in the case of Ishmael, becomes an outsider to the dominant clan. Eve's case markedly differs: the mother's preference is Cain, indicated by her exclamation at his birth; God's is Abel, who sacrifices the firstborn of his flock,[44] while Cain offers up simply "of the fruit of the earth" (Genesis 4:3–5). The text does not indicate the reason for the disparity in the sacrifices. Might there be a connection to Eve's treatment of Cain, her elation at his birth and lack of emotion at Abel's? Does the son valued by his mother feel that he need not put a great deal of effort into pleasing God, that God will accept him on any terms, whereas Abel offers the best of his flock?[45] Perhaps Eve's hubris consists not only of equating her creative powers with God's but also of assuming that she knows that Cain is a preferred child. The Hebrew Bible repeatedly demonstrates that God chooses whom God will, not whom humans, for whatever reason, deem appropriate.[46] Eve's exclamation, with its expression of closeness to Cain, cannot be allowed to stand unchallenged.[47]

Radical reinterpretation of the tale of the birth of Cain and Abel is not a new phenomenon. *Pirqei Rabbi Eli'ezer* provides a reworking of the material that, while not addressing the timing of the births, explains what it assumes to be the very different qualities of the sons. Taking as its source the parallel drawn between the woman and the garden in Song of Songs (4:12), it views the Garden of Eden story as an allegory in which the Garden stands for the woman.

מה הגנה זו כל מה שנזרעה היא צומחת ומוציאה כך האשה הזאת כל מה שנזרעה הרה ויולדת מבעלה בא אליה ורוכבת נחש ועברה את קין ואח'כ עברה את הבל שנא' (בראשית ד) והאדם ידע את חוה אשתו מהו ידע שהיתה מעוברת וראתה דמותו שלא היה מן התחתונים אלא מן העליונים והביטה ואמרה (שם) קניתי איש את ה'.

Just as this garden whatever is sown in it, it grows and brings forth, so [too] this woman, whatever she is sown with, she conceives and gives birth from her husband. [Samma'el][49] came to[50] her riding on the serpent, and she conceived Cain; afterward Adam came to her, and she conceived Abel, as it is written, "And the *adam* knew Eve his woman" (Genesis 4:1). What is the meaning of "knew"? [He knew] that she had conceived [by Samma'el and nonetheless had intercourse with her]. And she saw his [Cain's] likeness that it was not of the lower [earthly beings], but of the upper [heavenly beings], and she looked[51] and said: "I have created a man with the Lord."[52]

In this version, as we saw in one of R. Yehoshua's responses in *Genesis Rabbah* 17:8, the woman becomes a vessel for propagation, rather than a full participant in the conception of the child. She contributes nothing to Cain's character. Thus, Cain's demonic qualities derive from his demonic father, who is riding the phallic snake; Abel's fine qualities are Adam's legacy. Because this text presents Cain as descended from Samma'el, rather than Adam, it must further reinterpret the meaning of "knew" in Genesis 4:1, which seems to describe Cain's conception as attributable to Adam. Thus, *Pirqei Rabbi Eli'ezer,* disregarding the biblical idiomatic expression, proposes that what Adam knew is that Eve had previously had sexual relations with Samma'el. Nonetheless, Adam had relations with her. Eve, more object than subject, is the passive, powerless recipient of males' sexual advances and repository of their seed; she has no say in the matter. Adam recognizes the source of her pregnancy, although she may not. It is hard to associate the reified, earthlike Eve, who, like a garden, is sown, with the powerful Eve that one encounters in the biblical text.

The focus on Eve should not preclude examining briefly one of the most obvious puzzles in Genesis 4 because it sheds light on the depiction of women in these passages. The women with whom Cain and his descendants have children materialize without any record of their birth (Genesis 4:17–19). While there are many more women in the Bible whose birth is not recounted, what is striking about these women is that there is no provision for their existence, assuming that the initial divine Creation yields one woman and one man. In other words, if all humanity is descended from Adam and Eve and they are recorded as having only sons, with whom did Cain have children? Who was his woman?

Rabbinic midrash provides some classic solutions for this biblical gap. *Genesis Rabbah* 22:2 offers this interpretation, among others:

ותהר ותלד את קין אמר ר' אלעזר בן עזריה ג' פלאים נעשו באותו היום, בו ביום נבראו בו ביום שימשו בו ביום הוציאו תולדות, אמר ר' יהושע בן קרחה עלו למטה שנים וירדו שבעה, קין ותאומתו הבל ושתי תאומותיו.

"And she conceived and she bore Cain" (Genesis 4:1).

Said R. El'azar ben 'Azaryah: "Three wonders were performed on that day: on that very day they were created, on that very day they cohabited, and on that very day they produced offspring."

Said R. Yehoshua' ben Qarhah: "Only two entered the bed and seven left it: Cain and his twin sister, Abel and his two twin sisters."[53]

The rabbis need to read woman into the biblical text—a hermeneutic strategy often adopted by modern feminist scholars. Parsing the word *et*—here simply a grammatical indicator—the rabbis deduce that the second, fourth, and fifth occurrences of *et* in Genesis 4:1–2a indicate the births of daughters. Because there are many unnamed women in the biblical text, the rabbis here cited do not need to explain why these three daughters are nameless; only normally meaningless markers represent them.[54]

Immediately after the tale of the birth of Cain and Abel comes the story of their falling out and the first murder. Few places in the Hebrew Bible demand interpretation so clearly as do the verses regarding their relationship. While most of the proffered rabbinic explanations are far afield of Eve's story, this one, from *Genesis Rabbah* 22:7, indirectly clarifies her situation.

יהודה בר' אמר על חוה הראשונה היו הדינין, אמר ר' איבו חוה
ראשונה חזרה לעפרה, ועל מה היו הדינין, אמר ר' הונא תאומה
יתירה נולדה עם הבל, זה א' אני נוטלה וזה אומר אני נוטלה, זה א'
אני נוטלה שאני בכור, וזה א' אני נוטלה שנולדה עימי.

Yehudah son of Rabbi said: "Their quarrel was about the first Eve."

Said R. Aibu: "The first Eve had returned to dust. Then about what was their quarrel?"

Said R. Huna: "An additional twin was born with Abel, and each claimed her. The one claimed: 'I will have her because I am the firstborn'; while the other maintained: 'I must have her because she was born with me.' "[55]

This midrash, which tries to derive the reason for the murder of Abel from the biblical text, takes as one premise a gap in the biblical narrative of Cain and Abel. After God gives a warning to Cain about the potential for sin that lies in his disappointment at not having his sacrifice accepted, the biblical text records: "Cain said to Abel his brother and it was when they were in the field and Cain arose against Abel his brother and killed him" (Genesis 4:8). The words "X said to Y" are almost always followed by a direct quotation in the Bible; here they are not.

The midrash suggests a number of topics for their probable verbal disagreement, including division of property and possession of the specific piece of land that would later become the site of the Temple. Rejecting each of them as grounds for the argument between these two men who had, in one fashion or another, to divide the world between them, it settles on women. Wealth, religion, and women are thus the three apparent grounds for disagreements between men.

Citing a woman as the cause célèbre runs into the problem that there is only one woman in the text and she is their mother. To resolve the problem, Yehudah son of Rabbi revisits the rabbinic solution to the two different versions of the story of the creation of woman: that two women were created.[56] When the first proved unacceptable to Adam, God created the second. By invoking the first Eve here, Yehudah son of Rabbi, on some level, maintains fidelity to the text while avoiding incest. R. Aibu's response, with its tacit rejection of what would become the Lilith legend, seems to close the matter. Still, pressed to find some basis for the quarrel, R. Huna relies on the story that Eve had given birth to three daughters in addition to her two sons.[57]

Biblical Text: Mother and Sons

From the most memorable part of Genesis 4, Cain's murder of Abel and subsequent punishment, Eve is entirely absent. But this is not an issue of gender like Sarah's absence from the story of the Binding of Isaac; both Eve and Adam are missing here. The only participants are the two brothers and God. The maternal qualities of the "mother of all living" are not relevant to the biblical story, which presents the occupations of Cain and Abel in the second hemistich of the verse in which Abel is born, omitting their childhoods. The glimpses of the relationships between mother and sons, unlike those in the text relating to Sarah and Isaac or Rebecca and Jacob,[58] are not relevant to the story of the First Family. The altercation between the brothers and subsequent fratricide are handled by God, rather than by the parents. In the aftermath no burial, mourning, or parental grief is portrayed until the birth of Seth seventeen verses and many years later.[59] God condemns Cain to a life of wandering in the land of Nod, east of Eden. Nod seems less a geographic location than, as indicated by the Hebrew root of its name, a place of wandering.

There is no trace of the activities of either Adam or Eve in the years that intervene until the birth of Seth. The text does include a genealogy of Cain's descendants and their creativity, but Adam and Eve are absent. A number of rabbinic traditions conclude that during the 130 years from the birth of Abel to Seth's birth, mentioned in Genesis 5:3, Adam and Eve did not have sexual relations with each other.[60] If so, that may have been an indication of their unexpressed sorrow. Again, the human saga, after the punishment of Cain, focuses in large part on population; in the absence of births, neither Eve nor Adam does anything that merits recording.

The closing verse of Genesis 4 frames the chapter with births: the first results in murder and will not yield a long line of descendants; the last, through the descendants of Noah, will populate the earth, thus fulfilling the original mission that God had given to the *adam*.

ד 25 וַיֵּדַע אָדָם עוֹד אֶת־אִשְׁתּוֹ וַתֵּלֶד בֵּן וַתִּקְרָא אֶת־שְׁמוֹ שֵׁת כִּי
שָׁת־לִי אֱלֹהִים זֶרַע אַחֵר תַּחַת הֶבֶל כִּי הֲרָגוֹ קָיִן:

4:25 Adam knew his woman [*ishto*] again, and she bore a son and called his name Seth [*Shet*], because, "God has put (*shat*) [for] me an other seed in the place of Abel for Cain had killed him."[61] (Genesis 4:25)

As a way of concluding the section[62] and heightening the contrast with its triumphant opening, the narrator states that Adam "knew" his woman, here called only *ishto* (his woman) and not named, an omission that is doubly striking because of the contrast with Genesis 4:1 and the naming of the other humans, all male, in the nuclear first family. Although the detail of conception is omitted from the narration, Eve bears a son, here properly referred to as a *ben*. Unlike Cain, this son is named in the characteristic biblical naming formula. As she had done at Cain's naming, Eve explains her choice in the first person.

The emotions that are, to the modern reader, so profoundly missing at the murder of Abel lurk just beneath the surface of this verse reporting the birth of the third son of Eve and Adam. The moment is bittersweet.[63] The birth is heralded with a formal naming, but the blank spaces, like the white space in Pagis's poem, speak louder than the words: Eve is subdued.[64] Like Genesis 4:1, Genesis 4:25 includes five verbs, but the subjects that govern them are distinctly different.[65] Only Adam's role is identical in the two verses: it is over at conception. The string of four verbs governed by Eve in Genesis 4:1 is replaced by two: *vateled* (and she gave birth; the second of her verbs in 4:1) and *vatiqra* (and she called), which replaces *vatomer* (and she said). The strongest verb in 4:1, *qaniti* (I created), is replaced by *shat* (put), with God, no longer merely Eve's partner in creation, as its subject. God is the prime source of this child.[66] The fifth verb is *harago* (he killed him), governed by Cain, whose name is the last word of Eve's naming speech. The word order reflects Eve's reluctance to acknowledge her firstborn son, turned murderer.[67] The emptiness that is *Hevel* (Abel, vapor) is a void Eve has been carrying since he was murdered. There is no explicit mention of the grief or pain,[68] but, in a sense, Abel dominates the verse because he is the only person twice mentioned.[69] In comparison to the terse account of Abel's birth, the account of Seth's birth projects a sense that the family has been reconstituted after its initial tragedy.

Eve emerges from this chapter somewhat chastened, but wiser than she was at its beginning. She remains the active human, the one who speaks and thinks. She has suffered the consequences of her hubristic stance at the beginning of the chapter and has learned from them. When she finds herself in the same position once more, she defines the "miracle of birth" differently.[70] It may be argued that by the third birth she is less awestruck; however, it is not her sense of excitement in Genesis 4:1 that brings on her downfall, but the overreaching way she envisions it. The birth of Seth also brings with it a restatement of the relationship between the woman and God. God is responsible for providing the son who is a replacement for Abel. This new child's presence is intended to offer a measure of comfort. The caring God Who, in making clothing for Eve and Adam, gave them physical comfort, has now provided a measure of emotional comfort as well. Eve, in turn, is ready to accept God's comforting.

The Biblical Text: Back to Creation

Although Eve has been, almost from the moment of her creation, more active than Adam, more powerful, and more verbal, the frame of the story of the primal couple reverts to male-dominated as it closes. The opening of Genesis 5 provides a retelling of the creation of humanity, which serves as an introduction to the patriarchal genealogy of the ten generations from Adam to Noah.

ה 1 זֶה סֵפֶר תּוֹלְדֹת אָדָם בְּיוֹם בְּרֹא אֱלֹהִים אָדָם בִּדְמוּת אֱלֹהִים
עָשָׂה אֹתוֹ: ה 2 זָכָר וּנְקֵבָה בְּרָאָם וַיְבָרֶךְ אֹתָם וַיִּקְרָא אֶת־שְׁמָם אָדָם
בְּיוֹם הִבָּרְאָם: ה 3 וַיְחִי אָדָם שְׁלֹשִׁים וּמְאַת שָׁנָה וַיּוֹלֶד בִּדְמוּתוֹ
כְּצַלְמוֹ וַיִּקְרָא אֶת־שְׁמוֹ שֵׁת: ה 4 וַיִּהְיוּ יְמֵי־אָדָם אַחֲרֵי הוֹלִידוֹ אֶת־
שֵׁת שְׁמֹנֶה מֵאֹת שָׁנָה וַיּוֹלֶד בָּנִים וּבָנוֹת: ה 5 וַיִּהְיוּ כָּל־יְמֵי אָדָם
אֲשֶׁר־חַי תְּשַׁע מֵאוֹת שָׁנָה וּשְׁלֹשִׁים שָׁנָה וַיָּמֹת:

5:1 This is the record of *adam*'s lineage: On the day God created *adam* in the likeness of God He made it.   5:2 Male and female He created them and He blessed them and called their name *adam* on the day of their creation.   5:3 And [when] *adam* [had] lived 130 years he begot a son in his likeness and image and called his name Seth [*Shet*].   5:4 And the days of *adam* after the birth of Seth were 800 years and he begot sons and daughters.   5:5 And all the days of *adam* that he lived were 900 years and 30 years and he died. (Genesis 5:1–5)

The focus is on male progeny and the lineage, which will eventually lead from Noah to Abraham. Cain and Abel are excluded, for Abel died childless and Cain's line will be eliminated in the Flood. The only hint of Eve, whose name does not reappear after the birth of Cain and who is mentioned thereafter only as Adam's *ishah* (woman), is a tantalizing phrase, almost identical to the one with which we started: *zakhar unqevah bera'am vayvarekh otam* (male and female He created them and He blessed them) (Genesis 5:2). No singular pronoun refers to what is created. It seems clear that it was a dual creation in contrast to the puzzling wording of Genesis 1:27. There is a naming, but it is by God: *vayiqra et shemam adam* (And He called their name *adam*). The creature who is now named is actually not Adam, who appears to be entirely male, but a creature including both male and female. In that sense the male is never formally named.

The report of *adam*'s begetting Seth mirrors God's creation of the first human by describing Seth as in Adam's likeness and image, the same words used for the *adam*, but in reverse order.[71] This wording represents a response to Eve's assumption of the divine role of Creator in her exclamation at the birth of Cain. On the one hand, the narrator's choice of phrase gives Adam the stature vis-à-vis Seth that God has vis-à-vis the *adam*. On the other hand, it indicates that humans henceforth have human characteristics.

Eve at this point has been subsumed in *adam* and is so completely erased from the text that the naming of the only child mentioned, Seth, is no longer attributed to the woman, as in Genesis 4:25, but to *adam*, who provides no explanation for the name. It is not surprising in a patriarchal narrative that the naming of Seth, the one son whose progeny would actually survive the Flood and provide the basis for humanity as we know it, has been taken from Eve and given to Adam. Adam's lifespan and death are recorded; Eve has all but disappeared.[72] She is marginalized but, in a sense, eternal.

The absence of information about Eve's death is all the more striking because it contrasts with the reports of the deaths and/or burials of the matriarchs.[73] It is this effacement of Eve that is truly "the final stroke in the formation of the first female character"; not, as Pardes claims, the naming of Cain.[74]

In assessing Eve's role it is significant that her power is apparent in the two arenas where there is action in the biblical text: the eating of the fruit of the forbidden tree and the birth of her three sons. These sections in Genesis 3 and 4 are drawn from the *J* tradition and are more detailed than the *P* texts from Genesis 1 and 5 that frame the story. Looking at Genesis 1:1 through 5:5 as a whole, it becomes apparent that only two characters play major roles: God and Eve. Both of them think and act independently. Of course, reading the surface meaning of the story, one might reasonably deduce that Eve's actions are wrong. As we have seen, the text is considerably more complex than it appears to be. Eve's closing verse locates all the characters, human and divine, and demonstrates that she is the wiser for her experience. In that sense she does finally demonstrate not only hubris, but also an acceptance of what she has done wrong.

Modern Rewritings

The absence of an explicit biblical closure for Eve's life gives later writers, particularly in the modern period, the opportunity to reexamine Eve's story. Perhaps in the biblical and rabbinic periods it was assumed that she predeceased Adam as, indeed, each of the matriarchs died before her respective patriarch. Certainly within the biblical text Eve is deathless.

There are, of course, as many ways of looking back at Eve as there are of viewing her in the first place.

Exploiting the indeterminacy of Eve's lifespan as reported in Genesis, Deborah Drattell and David Steven Cohen open their opera *Lilith* (2000)[75] with Adam's funeral where Eve is joined by Lilith. Their roles are clearly divided, with Lilith assigned the more glamorous, seductive persona, while Eve is left to explain Lilith's presence to the Son and Daughter. The action, in a modern, ultra-Orthodox setting complete with bearded men in black garb and piously clothed women, is driven by the pulsing recitative of the music. The Seer later tells Eve, who seems haunted by Lilith, that she must make Lilith part of her soul, binding herself inextricably to Lilith, and Lilith must reciprocate.[76] Following the Seer's directions, Eve bloodies her feet on her way back to a desolate Eden where the Serpent helps her bite into the last fruit on the Tree. Transported to Lilith's domain, Eve is seduced by Lilith in the third and final act. Feeling herself drawn by the voices of Adam and the children, Eve is torn about joining Lilith, who, challenging the narrator's avowal in Genesis 2:24, tells Eve that she is missing a part,[77] supplanting Adam. Ultimately, Eve determines that she will not be subsumed by Lilith.[78] When the opera ends, Eve is at Adam's grave again, pondering the discord she has left for future generations of women. This radical revision of the story, dependent on Adam's prior death, presents as irremediable the split between Lilith and Eve.

Itzik Manger takes quite a different approach. In his gently satiric *Book of Paradise* (1939), the Yiddish poet presents both Adam and Eve among the cast with which he has peopled the daily life of Heaven. Three young angels, including the book's narrator, Shmuel-Aba Abervo, are spending the night in the section of Heaven known as King David's Estates when they see from their hiding place "two figures approaching the Tree of Knowledge. One of them is dressed in a frock coat and a top hat. The other wears hoopskirts and a hat with a long ostrich feather."[79] As they look at the Tree, Adam accuses Eve of having given him the "cursed apple to taste."[80] The couple moves from quarreling to reminiscing about the good times in Paradise. When they try to take off their clothes to revert to that happy state of innocence, it is Eve who first discovers that her clothes have "grown fast" to her body.[81] Adam, however, is first to suggest that they repent; they do, praying that God forgive them and readmit them to Eden. When they run off, frightened by a wind in the Tree, Eve forgets her purse. The angels find in it "[a] mirror, a box of powder, and a love-letter signed, 'Your loving Max.' "[82] Adam and Eve apparently sneak into Eden nightly to repeat their repentance and will continue to do so, as the more experienced angel explains, until the Messiah comes and there is a great amnesty.[83] Though penitent, Manger's Eve is also seductive. Whatever she may have written Max, apparently he wanted her. This is a parody of the story of Adam and Eve, who apparently repeat their altercation, penitence, and reconciliation nightly. Introducing Max in the role of suitor reinforces the view of Eve as seductive temptress.

The contemporary Israeli poet Miriam Oren (1921–1928) provides a summary retrospective glimpse of Eve in her brief "Ḥavvah."[84]

חַוָּה

לֹא עַל הַלֶּחֶם לְבַדּוֹ
תִּחְיֶה חַוָּה
וְלֹא עַל כְּסוּתָהּ
עוֹנָתָהּ
וְאוֹר עֵינֶיהָ   5

שֶׁבַע תִּפּוֹל חַוָּה
וּבֵין שִׁנֶּיהָ
נְגִיסָה אַחַת קְטַנָּה
מִפְּרִי הָעֵץ הַיָּרֹק כְּלַעֲנָה
10   לֹא עֵץ הַדַּעַת
רַק עֵץ הַחַיִּים
לְבַדּוֹ.

Eve

Not by bread alone
does Eve live
    not by her garments
        her conjugal rights
5   and the light of her eyes

159

Eve will fall seven times
and between her teeth
one small bite
from the fruit of the tree which was
10   as green as wormwood
not the tree of knowledge
only the tree of life
alone.[85]

To make her Eve a survivor, situated resolutely on the side of life, Oren interprets and challenges a number of traditional texts and contexts.

Opening with a challenge to the verse from Deuteronomy: "Not by bread alone shall a man (*ha'adam*) live" (8:3),[86] and substituting Eve, the "mother of all living," for the generic *adam* of the original, Oren literally links life with Eve, while the reader familiar with the biblical source perceives that implied contrast between Eve and Adam. *Adam*—humankind—has become the generalized Everywoman. The context in Deuteronomy is still more significant: "[God] subjected you to the hardship of hunger and then gave you manna to eat, which neither you nor your ancestors had ever known, in order to make you know that the *adam* does not live on bread alone, but the *adam* may live on anything that comes forth from the mouth of the Lord" (Deuteronomy 8:3). God led the Israelites in the desert for forty years, making life hard for them while protecting them in order to teach a lesson, enabling them to live in freedom in the future. Oren's Eve has also been set a challenge that makes her life harder while ostensibly teaching her a lesson. Like the Israelites, she is human and imperfect; like them, she is a survivor who will eventually prevail. Her survival depends neither on bread, a product of divine and human collaboration, nor on those things a husband must provide his wife under the terms of the traditional Jewish *ketubah* or marriage contract.[87] By inserting "the light of her eyes" (*or 'eineha*), playing on its similarity in spelling to conjugal rights (*'onatah*), Oren intimates that the sparkle in Eve's eyes is sexually inspired. At the same time she reminds us that Eve saw the fruit of the tree as "a lust for the eyes" (Genesis 3:6). But the reader, anticipating a parallel to the deuteronomic verse's ending with the divine source of life, senses the absence of God.

Oren continues the tale of Eve's survival by echoing a verse from Proverbs: "Seven times the righteous man falls and gets up, while the wicked are tripped by one misfortune" (Proverbs 24:16), offering the possibility that Eve will prevail, if she is deserving. But is she? The number seven, a common biblical number, here subtly reminds us of Cain's punishment, which leaves him banished, but protected by God's threat that anyone who kills him will be punished sevenfold (Genesis 4:15). The small bite of the fruit of the tree "as green as the wormwood" heightens the ambiguity of Eve's status. On the one hand, green, particularly in the context of a tree, symbolizes new growth, new possibilities. Further, the green of the Tree of Knowledge may be what makes it attractive to the woman (Genesis 3:6). On the other hand, it is the strange or "forbidden woman" who is in the end "as bitter as wormwood, sharp as a two-edged sword" (Proverbs 5:4).[88] To the reader's surprise, not the Tree of Knowledge, but the Tree of Life, has yielded this bitter fruit. Oren's Eve is truly the "mother of all living" in that her goal is life itself, despite the bitterness she finds therein.

The final word of the poem, "alone" (levaddo), set off as a separate line, emphasizes that not knowledge, but life itself, is Eve's portion. The emphasis it carries is reinforced by the way that it closes the circle of the poem by repeating the last word of the first line. Not by bread alone but only by the Tree of Life alone does Eve continue. The word "alone" here alludes to Genesis 2:18 and forces us to reread the first line of the poem with the issue of human loneliness in mind. Eve's creation was intended to solve the problem of the adam being alone; her survival, with the aid of the Tree of Life alone, is her ultimate reward.

Thus, while Pagis points to an Eve whose strength, and probably whose life itself, is cut short before she can even inscribe her message, Oren envisions an Eve who tastes the bitterness of life, but keeps on going, reflecting, perhaps, her own life experience.[89] As is the case with the biblical Eve, there is no intimation of the death of Oren's Eve. She helps us see the fortitude of the Eve in Genesis; like her, she appears to be a survivor, dealing with whatever life hands her.

The Israeli poet Yaakov Shai Shavit (1932–) transposes Adam and Eve to the modern period, providing a different picture of Eve. In fact, the very title of the poem, which seems unexceptional in English, signifies that the poem takes a new direction. Both in the Bible and in modern usage,[90] Ḥavvah, Eve's name, is spelled with one vav, albeit with a dagesh mark in it to indicate that in reading it the vav sound is doubled. Shavit uses two vavs and further breaks with convention by not vocalizing the title of the poem.[91]

חווה

לְאַחַר שֶׁגֹּרַשׁ מִגַּן-עֵדֶן
הָלַךְ אָדָם לָאוּנִיבֶרְסִיטָה וְנַעֲשָׂה
מְלֻמָּד

חַוָּה חָוְתָה וְקָרְאָה סְפָרִים

כַּמָּה אַתְּ רוֹאָה יוֹתֵר מִמֶּנִּי !

Eve

After he was expelled from the Garden of Eden
Adam went to the university and became
Learned

Ḥavvah experienced [*ḥavetah*] and read books

How much more do you [fem.: *at*] see than I![92]

Although his brief poem is entitled "Eve," Shavit opens it with a description of Adam, often portrayed as the human norm. Adam follows rules.
Although his motivation is not explained, his route is clearly the traditional one of turning to the institutional structures of higher education
and becoming "learned," a word set apart in the last line of the first stanza
as though it were a title or an indication of status.

Shavit's Eve seeks knowledge outside the formal structures. She is an
essentialist Eve who incorporates the view of woman as less hierarchical
than man. Shavit uses the contemporary meaning of the root letters of
her name to present a "folk etymology" that rings true for the modern
reader and challenges the Bible. Her life is not about mothering, but
about experiencing and learning.[93] Because Eve recognizes that there are
different modalities of learning, she involves two different processes, neither of them formally structured.

Bringing this vision of Eve back to the biblical text emphasizes that
Eve's choice to eat the fruit, although based on careful consideration, involves risk. Adam stays away from the fruit because he is not a risk-taker
and remains within the accepted hierarchical structures.

The last line of the poem may be interpreted in a variety of ways. The introduction of the first-person form into what had been a third-person narration adds another voice and dimension to the text. If we assume that the voice belongs to Adam, he must be so moved by the counterexample of the woman that he breaks through the conventional frame of the poem to make an I-thou statement valuing Eve's approach over his own. But, of course, there is also another way to view it. The "I"[94] and female "you" of the poem may be the modern voices of a couple in which the male seeks a paradigm for male-female behavior in the Bible—as have people in Western society for millennia. His choice of Adam's way implicitly critiques the conventional readings of the biblical story because it leaves him diminished; his learning, narrow. A knowledge-seeker like the male, the female has followed Eve's path and therefore, in the male's estimation, sees more than he does. As is the case in Genesis 3, much of the action depends on sight and eyes. Here the more inclusive seeing is the woman's—an essentialist tribute to multiple intelligences.

The contemporary American poet Marge Piercy (1936–) provides an ample, thought-provoking view of Eve as a knowledge-seeker. Piercy's "Apple Sauce for Eve"[95] depicts an Eve who does not merely survive, but triumphs. Eve is praised not only for her accomplishments, but also for the legacy she has left for those who follow. Dismissing the facile explanation of what Eve wanted, Piercy states, at the end of the poem:

> We see Adam wagging his tail, good dog, good
> dog, while you and the snake shimmy up the tree,
> lab partners in a dance of will and hunger,
> that thirst not of the flesh but of the brain.
> Men always think of women as wanting sex,
> cock, snake, when it is the world she's after.
> The birth trauma for the first conceived kid
> of the ego, I think therefore I am, I
> kick the tree, who am I, why am I,
> going, going to die, die, die.
>
> You are indeed the mother of invention,
> the first scientist. Your name means
> life: finite, dynamic, swimming against

the current of time, tasting, testing,
eating knowledge like any other nutrient.
We are all the children of your bright hunger.
We are all the products of that first experiment,
for if death was the worm in that apple,
the seeds were freedom and the flowering of choice.

Piercy's brash language confronts the biblical text, first in the tentative second person, then in the bold first person, developing an identification between Eve and the narrator. Adam is demoted to the role of "good dog," while Eve and the snake are all movement, daring to "shimmy up the tree." Piercy's Adam is reduced to "good" by the enjambment at the end of the opening line of this, the third stanza of the poem. Adam's boring, dependable obedience contrasts with the dynamic movement of the snake and Eve.

Eve as mother gives birth first to "the first conceived kid of the ego," quietly drawing attention to her hubristic statement at the birth of Cain (Genesis 4:1), as well as to the biblical record of her being the first woman to conceive a child. What she may truly claim with a sense of well-earned pride is her interest in knowledge. Expanding on Descartes's famous dictum: "Cogito ergo sum" (I think therefore I am), Piercy's Eve moves on to claim more than thought as evidence of her existence. Kicking the tree adds specificity to the rabbis' suggestion that the snake itself may have touched the tree or pushed Eve against it to disprove her claim that touching it would bring death in its wake.[96] This Eve is not one to be pushed around, but one to take action herself, even when she knows that there are attendant risks. Her assertion of self comes in the questioning of her identity and of the reasons for death that has been threatened as the consequence for eating the fruit of the Tree of Knowledge.

Resuming her second-person voice, the narrator addresses the bold Eve of her creation as "mother of invention" and "first scientist." It is, after all, Eve who is willing empirically to test the threat of punishment God has made. The jagged dynamic edges of the enjambments in the opening verses of the last stanza help define Eve's action. "Your name means / life" surprises in that it omits "mother" from the biblical explanation. It is not birthing that defines this Eve, but challenging life. Interrupting the prepositional phrase "against / the current of time," by the enjambment, Piercy gives the reader the opportunity to feel the pull of the current and thus to imagine what the biblical Eve swims against, as well as the challenges contemporary Eves face. Eve's contribution to the future of human existence is defined through her interest in furthering knowledge in a somewhat scientific manner: "tasting, testing, / eating." She explores the world with all her senses, as a baby does, to gain wisdom.

The last four lines of the stanza are less edgy, more fully developed, calmer, indicating resolution, acceptance. Each completes a whole thought. Humans are all children of Eve's "bright hunger," implying not only luminosity, but also intelligence. Using the apple metaphor, Piercy declares that, "if death was the worm in that apple / the seeds were freedom and the flowering of choice." Unpacking that metaphor leads us to conclude, with Piercy, that the snakelike worm, death, is incidental to the future of the apple; the thought that humans have gained through Eve's action both freedom and choice dominates. Piercy's facile dismissal of death contrasts with the foreboding presence of death in Pagis's poem and its shadow in Oren's. Building on the same biblical story, Piercy points to a future in which humanity enjoys the benefit of the risks Eve was willing to take.

Conclusion: Life and Death

The period of Eve's life outside the Garden is both the longest and the richest of the three segments of her life that the biblical text presents. Like her independent thinking in eating the forbidden fruit, her bold statement about her creative powers in Genesis 4:1 results not in a generation of empowered children, but in death, in this case the murder of one of her two sons by the other. In fact, one can argue that the death threatened by God as the consequence of eating the forbidden fruit is the death of Abel, the first biblical human death.[97] Thus the richly woven nexus of death and the Holocaust and the primal family in Pagis's poem speaks to a central issue in the biblical story of Eve.

But part of Eve's riddle is embodied in her having been called "the mother of all living." Despite the temptation to see Eve's life as centering on death—and, as we have seen, many rabbinic views emphasize that reading—Eve's modern feminist rereaders have emphasized the parts of Eve's story that involve life: the births, the choice to be a responsible, moral human. They tend to see the pain and hardship as part of life, but only a part. Admiration for Eve's positive contribution to the foundation of humanity outweighs the hardship. Paradoxically, life is made fuller for its having limitations.

Thus, the fecund mother,[98] whom the rabbis often undervalue, even reify, the container for the child of Samma'el, the mother of quintuplets—has taken on new prominence as the woman who is ready to risk all for moral wisdom and is not afraid to tout her own achievements.

Conclusion

Eve Framed: Invisibility and Visibility

Eve enters the biblical narrative as a dimly perceived shadow. She is subsumed in the *adam,* the first human, the antecedent of both masculine singular and masculine plural pronouns, that governs plural verbs (Genesis 1:27). She exits in similar fashion—traceable in the plural pronouns used to refer to the *adam* in Genesis 5:2. At her first appearance and her last, her presence is also implied by the description of the *adam* as "male and female." None of this suggests that she is a memorable character.

A close comparison of these texts leaves the first woman less powerful as she exits than she was at her entrance, where she was included as the plural subject of verbs like "rule." Despite the plural pronouns, *adam* in Genesis 5:2 is different from *ha'adam* of Genesis 1:27 because he is no longer "the [generic] *adam*"; he has become a specific man named Adam. The terse genealogies of Genesis 5 are immediately interrupted by the statement that Adam begat "a son in his likeness and image and called his name Seth" (Genesis 5:3). Eve is doubly excluded from this description: by the implication that she served as a vessel with no role in shaping Seth's "likeness and image" and by the change in the attribution of the name. Although Seth, a male, may have looked more like Adam than like Eve, the sharing by Seth and Adam of "a likeness and image" echoes God's role in forming the *adam* alone. Adam's death is recorded in Genesis 5:5; the woman's death is not recorded.

Within this frame, however, Eve's story, very much the product of the J tradition, is full of energy. From the description of her being "built" from the side of the *adam* to her naming speech for Seth, she is the narrative's human focus. She speaks and acts as an independent and colorful person; her actions move the plot forward just as they move humanity from infantilized ignorance to moral judgment, from dependence on the bounties of the divinely planted and watered Garden of Eden to a more independent, albeit more painful, life outside the Garden. Only God, not Adam, rivals her as a character. The tale's frame has clouded the picture.

Eve's trajectory moves from obscurity to real power, falling precipitously after reaching its apogee in her naming speech for Cain (Genesis 4:1). She is portrayed at several points during her ascent: the silent woman who is brought to the *adam* becomes the serpent's articulate respondent, the risk-taker, and, finally, the eloquent and spirited creator of human life. Her descent is equally rapid. Eve loses power as she acknowledges the limits of her role as creator when naming Seth; she becomes effaced, replaced by the *adam* as namer, and she disappears from the scene as she becomes literally incorporated into the *adam*.

The recorded rabbinic views of Eve are considerably less equivocal than the biblical texts. Many sources see Eve—and through her, womankind as a whole—in the light of gender roles that obtained in their own societies. These texts tend to focus on the rabbinic elite, which generally excluded women from their inner circle. The few women of the late antique period whom we meet are almost exclusively charged with maintaining domestic tranquility; however responsibly or irresponsibly they may carry out that role, they do not provide challenging interpretations of biblical women. The rabbis, who on the whole envisioned biblical society in the image of their own, mapped their views and experience of women's roles onto the biblical texts they were studying. They conceived no conscious "plot" against women, no focused agenda to strip the biblical Eve of her complexity, agency, and voice; an absence of historical consciousness sufficed to achieve this. The rabbinic reading of Eve, by and large, sees only her disobedience of God's explicit order and her culpability in bringing death into the world. Their interpretations are often creative and interesting, even to those who disagree with them.

Armed with an awareness of historical change, modern writers have turned their art to re-imagining or re-visioning biblical texts. Heightened self-awareness allows them to do consciously what previous interpreters did unconsciously: apply the lessons of their own experience to the texts of the past. Twentieth-century Eves are as varied as those of the rabbis, but the balance has shifted to valuing what Eve *did* as a forerunner of today's powerful, active, and articulate women. To a confrontation with any text, a rewriter necessarily brings personal experience as a human being and as an observer of the human experience. Be it Pagis's Eve as an embodiment of tragedy or Piercy's Eve as an incarnation of life, modern

Eves, like their predecessors, occupy the space between the prototype and the exemplar, trying to wrest meaning from the past to serve as a paradigm for the present and future.

When the character under consideration is biblical, the stakes in its revisioning are particularly high: the text is widely viewed as sacred, if not divine, and as prescriptive, rather than merely descriptive. The biblical stories involving Eve have for centuries been inextricably entangled with the religious and societal construction of gender. The biblical text, modern scholarship, and classic rabbinic and modern rewritings of the story, read in dialogue with one another, serve to open it up, allowing us to see that gender hierarchy and gender roles have been encoded in diverse, often contradictory ways. Even the compelling tale of the first woman's eating the forbidden fruit summons forth various interpretations.

An examination of the biblical account and its subsequent rewritings indicates the difficulties inherent in applying literature to life. These words offer no univocal message; they bear no unequivocal divine mandates. The sanctified nature of the biblical text with its multiple ambiguities makes it a particularly rich ground for exploring the foundations of commonly held views. Seeing these Eve texts in all their polysemic, multifaceted richness, as explored by later rewriters, helps us understand the richness of the texts and their power to speak to different ages and situations. Ultimately, just as women in the past may have learned the significance of obedience and the dangers of risk-taking from this story, so do women today take away a model of autonomy and intellectual curiosity.

NOTES

INTRODUCTION: THE SIGNIFICANCE OF EVE

1. Gerda Lerner, *The Creation of Patriarchy* (New York: Oxford University Press, 1986), 182.

2. Ilana Pardes, *Countertraditions in the Bible: A Feminist Approach* (Cambridge, Mass.: Harvard University Press, 1992), 13.

3. Edward L. Greenstein, "God's Golem: The Creation of Humanity in Genesis 2," *Creation in Jewish and Christian Tradition,* ed. Henning Graf Reventflow and Yair Hoffman (London: Sheffield Academic Press, 2002), 228 and passim.

4. "It is very probable that the creation of intertextual patterns affects and enriches the evoked text (RT) as well. Even if the evoked text preceded the alluding text by several hundred years, a simultaneous activation is possible for the reader of both." Ziva Ben-Porat, "The Poetics of Literary Allusion," *PTL: A Journal for Descriptive Poetics and Theory of Literature* 1 (1976): 114 n.9. Explaining why he turns to medieval biblical commentaries to elucidate the story of the creation of humanity in Genesis, Edward L. Greenstein states: "The later interpretations of the material may shed light on its earlier understanding as well." Greenstein, "God's Golem," 229.

While Ben-Porat is considering a chronological gap of merely several hundred years and Greenstein many more, there is no reason to limit the time span or, for that matter, to see the "simultaneous activation" of both texts as anything less than probable.

5. Although a still earlier layer of Jewish biblical interpretation exists (e.g., Philo, the Dead Sea Scrolls and some of the pseudepigraphic texts), I have chosen rabbinic midrash because, unlike earlier strata, it has always been situated within the mainstream of Jewish culture.

6. "The tradition of biblical interpretation has been a constant conversation, at times an argument, among its participants; at no period has the text been interpreted in a monolithic fashion. If anything marks Jewish biblical interpretation it is the diversity of approaches employed and the multiplicity of meanings produced." Adele Berlin and Marc Zvi Brettler, "Introduction: What Is 'The Jewish Study Bible'?" in *The Jewish Study Bible,* ed. Adele Berlin and Marc Zvi Brettler (New York: Oxford University Press, 2004), ix.

7. Some other figures in Genesis, women and men, are mentioned in other biblical texts: for example, Rachel and Leah in Ruth 4:11; Seth in 1 Chronicles 1:1; Noah in Isaiah 54:4 and 1 Chronicles 1:4; Abraham, Isaac, and Jacob in Exodus 3:16 and 6:3, 1 Kings 18:36, and 1 Chronicles 29:18. It is impossible to determine how many times Adam appears after Genesis 1–5 because it is virtually impossible to determine which occurrences refer to the first human and which refer to the first male.

For a concise treatment of biblical intertextual interpretation, see Benjamin D. Sommer, "Inner-biblical Interpretation," in *The Jewish Study Bible,* ed. Adele Berlin and Marc Zvi Brettler (New York: Oxford University Press, 2004), 1829–1835.

8. As Edward W. Said claims, "Even when they [texts] appear to deny it, they are nevertheless a part of the social world, human life, and of course historical moments in which they are located and interpreted." Edward W. Said, *The World, the Text and the Critic* (Cambridge, Mass.: Harvard University Press, 1983), 2.

9. *Genesis Rabbah* 63:6; *Midrash Bereshit Rabba* (in Hebrew), ed. Yehuda Theodor and Hanokh Albeck (Jerusalem: Wahrmann Books, 1965), 2:682–683, commenting on Genesis 25:22. Citations to *Genesis Rabbah* are given both to the standard numbering of the sections and to the pages in the Theodor and Albeck critical edition.

10. Phyllis A. Bird emphasizes that one can arrive at a correct exegesis "even if it exceeds what the Priestly writer of Genesis 1:26–28 intended to say or was able to conceive." Phyllis A. Bird, " 'Male and Female He Created Them': Gen 1:27b in the Context of the Priestly Account of Creation," *Harvard Theological Review* 74, no. 2 (1981): 159.

11. "This [feminist] critique engages Jewish tradition with what it sees as a preexistent underside of halakhic development—in other words, a second and suppressed voice that careful feminist rereadings of Torah and of halakhah are gradually uncovering." Tamar Ross, "Modern Orthodoxy and the Challenge of Feminism," in *Jews and Gender: The Challenge to Hierarchy*, Studies in Contemporary Jewry 16, ed. Jonathan Frankel (New York: Oxford University Press, 2000), 20.

12. "But as Christian piety and reflection sought to probe the deeper meaning of salvation, the parallel between Christ and Adam found its counterpart in the picture of Mary as the Second Eve, who by her obedience had undone the damage wrought by the mother of mankind." Jarolslav Pelikan, *The Christian Tradition: A History of the Development of Doctrine*, Vol. 1, *The Emergence of the Catholic Tradition (100–600)* (Chicago, Ill.: University of Chicago Press, 1971), 241.

13. Gerda Lerner's skepticism about the ability of new readings to displace the old and take root is appropriately buttressed by more than two thousand years of patriarchal interpretation. Lerner, *Creation*, 278 n.15.

14. See Kimelman's translation of *oto*, referring to the *adam* in Genesis 1:27 as "it." Reuven Kimelman, "The Seduction of Eve and the Exegetical Politics of Gender," *Biblical Interpretation: A Journal of Critical Approaches* 4, no. 1 (February 1996): 12.

15. Alicia Ostriker, "A Triple Hermeneutic: Scripture and Revisionist Women's Poetry," in *Reading the Bible: Approaches, Methods and Strategies*, ed. Athalya Brenner and Carole Fontaine (Sheffield: Sheffield Academic Press, 1997), 165.

16. For a general discussion of this phenomenon in modern Hebrew literature, see Gershon Shaked, "Modern Midrash: The Biblical Canon and Modern Literature," *AJS Review* 28, no. 1 (2004): 43–62. An essay by Yaakov Fikhman, whose poem about Eve is analyzed in chapter 2, counters the argument against writing poetry based on the Bible by comparing the modern phenomenon with the rabbinic rewritings of biblical characters. Yaakov Fikhman, "The Bible as a Subject for Poetry" (in Hebrew), in Yaakov Fikhman, *Ancient Images* (in Hebrew) (Jerusalem: Bialik Foundation, 1948), 11–16.

17. Particularly helpful here are the collections by David Curzon (*Modern Poetry on the Bible* [Philadelphia: Jewish Publication Society, 1994]) and by Howard Schwartz and Anthony Rudolf (*Poems Within the Ark* [New York: Avon Books, 1980]) and the studies by David C. Jacobson (*Modern Midrash: The Retelling of Traditional Jewish Narratives by Twentieth-Century Hebrew Writers* [Albany, N.Y.: State University of New York Press,

1987] and *Does David Still Play Before You? Israeli Poetry and the Bible* [Detroit, Mich.: Wayne State University Press, 1997]), Sue Ann Wasserman ("Women's Voices: The Present Through the Past" [ordination thesis, Hebrew Union College–Jewish Institute of Religion, 1987]) and Wendy Zierler (*And Rachel Stole the Idols: The Emergence of Modern Hebrew Women's Writing* [Detroit, Mich.: Wayne State University Press, 2004]).

18. See the discussion of the ways in which the Hebrew poet H. N. Bialik (1873–1934) uses biblical material in Robert Alter, *Canon and Creativity* (New Haven, Conn.: Yale University Press, 2000), 148.

19. Ibid., 148.

20. Jon D. Levenson, *Sinai and Zion: An Entry into the Jewish Bible* (San Francisco, Calif.: HarperSanFrancisco, 1987), 4.

21. For a discussion of the significance of the written word in rabbinic Judaism, see Susan A. Handelman, *The Slayers of Moses: The Emergence of Rabbinic Interpretation in Modern Literary Theory* (Albany, N.Y.: State University of New York Press, 1982), 9 and passim.

James L. Kugel has suggested calling such an approach "omnisignificance." James L. Kugel, *Ideas of Biblical Poetry: Parallelism and Its History* (New Haven, Conn.: Yale University Press, 1981), 103–105.

22. Judith Baskin, *Midrashic Women: Formations of the Feminine in Rabbinic Literature* (Hanover, N.H.: University Press of New England/Brandeis University Press, 2002), 3.

23. "Midrash" means both a collection of this rabbinic material and an individual section thereof. The Hebrew plural of "midrash" is *midrashim*.

24. H. L. Strack and Günter Stemberger, *Introduction to the Talmud and Midrash,* trans. and ed. Markus Bockmuehl, 2d printing (Minneapolis, Minn.: Fortress, 1996), 279–280.

The text I have used, unless otherwise noted, is the critical edition edited by Yehuda Theodor and Hanokh Albeck, *Midrash Bereshit Rabba* (in Hebrew) (Jerusalem: Wahrmann Books, 1965).

25. Strack and Stemberger, *Introduction to the Talmud and Midrash,* 356–357, 328–330. In the absence of a critical edition, I use here the Eshkol edition, *Pirqei Rabbi Eli'ezer* (in Hebrew) (Jerusalem: Eshkol, n. d.), supplemented by the numerous manuscript comparisons provided by Gerald Friedlander in his English translation, *Pirkê de Rabbi Eliezer,* trans. and annotated by Gerald Friedlander (London, 1916; reissued New York: Hermon, 1965).

26. In that sense it is closer to modern poetry than to *Genesis Rabbah.* It has also been suggested that it may be the work of an individual as yet unidentified.

27. David Stern, "Midrash and Jewish Interpretation," in *The Jewish Study Bible,* ed. Adele Berlin and Marc Zvi Brettler (New York: Oxford University Press, 2004), 1873–1874. Stern's essay (pp. 1863–1875) offers a clear, concise, and searching introduction to rabbinic midrash.

28. For a comprehensive consideration of the attitudes of the rabbis of late antiquity toward women, with particular emphasis on law, see Judith Hauptman, *Rereading the Rabbis: A Woman's Voice* (Boulder, Colo.: Westview, 1998); for a comprehensive consideration of their attitudes toward women as expressed in the midrash, see Baskin, *Midrashic Women.*

29. In a few exceptional cases women are consulted while they remain marginal to the discourse. One example is the consultation with the maids about the meaning of words the rabbis no longer understood in B. Rosh Hashanah 26b.

According to Meir Bar-Ilan, who equates literacy with the ability to write more than one's name, the rate of literacy among both men and women was low, particularly among women. Writing is, of course, not requisite for reading. Meir Bar-Ilan, *Some Jewish Women in Antiquity* (Atlanta, Ga.: Scholars Press, 1998), 31–51.

30. "Rabbinic literature in the best of circumstances is characterized by a multivocal dialectical structure that preserves not only the definitive opinions of the majority, but also retains minority points of view." Baskin, *Midrashic Women*, 5.

31. David Stern, *Midrash and Theory: Ancient Jewish Exegesis and Contemporary Literary Studies* (Evanston, Ill.: Northwestern University Press, 1996), 71.

32. Handelman points out: "Rabbinic thought can also at times suspend the [Aristotelian] Law of Contradiction. The same is true of poetry, rhetoric, metaphor, and so forth, all of which play with the equivocalness and ambiguity of words." Handelman, *Slayers*, 13.

33. Stern, *Midrash and Theory*, 6.

34. "We never hear the biblical voice in stark and unpackaged purity. It is always refracted by those who have gone before us." Gary A. Anderson, *The Genesis of Perfection: Adam and Eve in Jewish and Christian Imagination* (Louisville, Ky.: Westminster, 2001), 72.

35. "[I]f anything has title to the status of 'fact' in multilayered ancient texts like the Bible, it is surely only the final completed form before us, not hypothetical strands isolated with acumen often as arbitrary as the most far-fetched literary analysis." Stephen A. Geller, "Blood Cult: Towards a Literary Theology of the Priestly Work of the Pentateuch," *Prooftexts: A Journal of Jewish Literary History* 12, no. 2 (May 1992): 98.

36. See *The Anchor Bible: Genesis,* intro., trans., and notes by E. A. Speiser, 2d ed. (Garden City, N.Y.: Doubleday, 1964), xxiv–xxvi; and Marc Zvi Brettler, "Torah: Introduction," in *The Jewish Study Bible,* ed. Adele Berlin and Marc Zvi Brettler (New York: Oxford University Press, 2004), 1–7.

37. Jon D. Levenson, *Creation and the Persistence of Evil* (Princeton, N.J.: Princeton University Press, 1988), 68.

38. Speiser, *Genesis,* xxvi–xxix.

39. Given the gendered nature of the Hebrew language, *adam* would necessarily become the antecedent of either masculine or feminine pronouns. *Adam* has the markers of a regular masculine singular noun. The parallel feminine noun, *adamah,* means "earth." This specific case of the masculine form being assumed is not at issue; the development of a language in which the masculine is the default—therefore the dominant—form is.

40. For an extensive discussion of biblical portrayals of God in roles usually associated with women, as well as the denial of God's being a male, see Phyllis Trible, "Depatriarchalizing in Biblical Interpretation," in *The Jewish Woman: New Perspectives,* ed. Elizabeth Koltun (New York: Schocken, 1976), 219–221.

41. "The idea that God might possess any form of sexuality, or any differentiation analogous to it, would have been for P an utterly foreign and repugnant notion." Bird, "Male and Female," 148.

42. Translating God raises a host of theological and gender issues. In my translations of the Bible I have used "God" for *Elohim* and "Lord" for *YHWH,* following the New Jewish Publication Society (*The Torah, [the Prophets, the Writings]: A New Translation*

of the Holy Scriptures According to the Masoretic Text [Philadelphia: Jewish Publication Society, 1962–1968], henceforth NJPS) and masculine pronouns when necessary. When translating rabbinic midrash, I have done the same. In modern literature *YHWH* does not appear, simplifying matters a bit, but still forcing the translator to choose between an accurate translation and one that is gender-neutral. In translations I have opted for the former; in my own writing, I have chosen the latter, despite the awkwardness that it occasionally produces in English.

43. Robert Alter, *The Art of Biblical Narrative* (New York: Basic Books, 1981), 12.

44. Reuven Kimelman, "Seduction," 15 n.33. Although Kimelman is referring specifically to Genesis 2:18, his comment has much wider applicability.

45. James L. Kugel claims with reference to the first century of the Common Era: "The story of Adam and Eve and their life in the Garden of Eden fascinated the Bible's earliest interpreters, since it seemed to concern the very nature of human existence. This biblical story was probably written about more than any other." James L. Kugel, *Traditions of the Bible* (Cambridge, Mass.: Harvard University Press, 1997), 94.

46. Despite the many rabbinic statements treating Eve as the prototype of women, even Jewish women, some of which we shall discuss below, it is clearly Sarah and Abraham who take on the role as progenitors of all Jews—a role so important that converts to Judaism are given the Jewish Hebrew name "X, son or daughter of Abraham and Sarah."

47. A salient example is the statement "From the Editors," which appeared in the first issue of *Lilith*, a feminist quarterly "exploring the world of the Jewish woman": "*Lilith* is named for Adam's legendary first companion and his equal. Lilith predated Eve, and was originally the embodiment of independent womanhood"; *Lilith* 1, no. 1 (fall 1976): 3. In the first article in the issue, "The Lilith Question," Aviva Cantor Zuckoff explores some of the Lilith traditions from a twentieth-century feminist perspective (5–10, 38). Zuckoff's article is accompanied by a collection of annotated Lilith sources compiled by Judy Weinberg (8, 38).

48. Trible, "Depatriarchalizing," 217–240.

49. Phyllis Trible, *God and the Rhetoric of Sexuality* (Philadelphia: Fortress, 1978), 72–143.

50. Bal, *Lethal Love: Feminist Literary Readings of Biblical Love Stories* (Bloomington, Ind.: Indiana University Press, 1987). Unlike Trible and Bal, I see no love story in Genesis 1–5.

51. Kristin E. Kvam, Linda S. Schearing, and Valerie H. Ziegler, eds., *Eve and Adam: Jewish, Christian, and Muslim Readings on Genesis and Gender* (Bloomington: Indiana University Press, 1999).

52. Carol Meyers, *Discovering Eve: Ancient Israelite Women in Context* (New York: Oxford University Press, 1988).

53. Tikva Frymer-Kensky, *In the Wake of the Goddesses: Women, Culture, and the Biblical Transformation of Pagan Myth* (New York: Fawcett Columbine, first Ballantine ed., 1993).

54. Daniel Boyarin, *Carnal Israel: Reading Sex in Rabbinic Culture* (Berkeley and Los Angeles: University of California Press, 1993).

55. Baskin, *Midrashic Women.*

56. Nehama Aschkenasy, *Eve's Journey: Feminine Images in Hebraic Literary Tradition* (Detroit, Mich.: Wayne State University Press, 1986).

57. Pamela Norris, *Eve: A Biography* (New York: New York University Press, 1999).

58. Alter, *Canon*, 45.

59. Ibid., 8.

CHAPTER 1. THE CREATION OF WOMAN

1. As discussed in the introduction, in order to preserve the original ambiguity, I shall use the Hebrew word *adam* wherever it appears in the texts, rather than translate it as "human," "man," or "Adam." Further, I use the neuter "it" as the pronoun in the biblical texts whenever appropriate in order to remind the reader that, in many of these texts, the *adam* is not necessarily only male.

When translating biblical texts, I have chosen to use the word "woman" for *ishah*, which means both "woman" and "wife," in order to avoid superimposing the template of marriage on a mythic time when it is inappropriate. Similarly, I use the word "man," rather than "husband," to translate *ish* throughout the biblical texts. In some midrashic texts, however, where the rabbis are dealing with the context of marriage, I translate *ishah* as "wife."

2. Biblical translations from Genesis 1–5 are mine; the others are drawn from the NJPS.

3. Excerpted from *Genesis Rabbah* 8:1; *Midrash Bereshit Rabba* (in Hebrew), ed. Yehudah Theodor and Ḥanokh Albeck (Jerusalem: Wahrman, 1965), 1:55. This and all other translations of postbiblical literature are my own, unless otherwise indicated.

4. A full discussion of the meaning of *tselaʿ* is found later in this chapter.

5. Kim Chernin, *The Hunger Song* (London: Menard, 1983), 40–41. This poem is the third in an eleven-poem sequence entitled "The Uncertainty of Eve," from Chernin's only collection of poetry. Her interest in Eve is also indicated in the title of her book *Reinventing Eve: Modern Woman in Search of Herself* (New York: HarperPerennial, 1994), originally published by New York Times Books in 1987.

6. Having had the opportunity to teach texts relating to Eve in many contexts in both academic and adult education settings, I have found that the "rib story" in Genesis 2 is overwhelmingly the one remembered; not the ones in Genesis 1 and 5.

7. Here is Phyllis Trible's assessment of the situation: "Over the centuries this misogynous reading has acquired a status of canonicity so that those who deplore and those who applaud the story both agree upon its meaning." I find somewhat facile the ensuing catalogue of particulars on which, she proposes, all agree, although it probably represents the view dominant at the time when it was written. Phyllis Trible, *God and the Rhetoric of Sexuality* (Philadelphia: Fortress, 1978), 73.

8. See the introduction.

9. For a summary of rabbinic views, see Judith R. Baskin, *Midrashic Women: Formations of the Feminine in Rabbinic Literature* (Hanover, N.H.: University Press of New England/Brandeis University Press, 2002), 45–46.

10. Edward L. Greenstein, "God's Golem: The Creation of Humanity in Genesis 2," in *Creation in Jewish and Christian Tradition*, ed. Henning Graf Reventflow and Yair Hoffman (London: Sheffield Academic Press, 2002), 228.

Sarna presents the case for seeing the second story as complementary to the first. "Chapter 2 is not another creation story. As such it would be singularly incomplete. In fact, it presupposes a knowledge of much of the preceding account of Creation." *The JPS Commentary: Genesis,* commentary by Nahum M. Sarna (New York: Jewish Publication Society, 1989), 16.

11. See Edward L. Greenstein, "An Equivocal Reading of the Sale of Joseph," *Literary Interpretations of Biblical Narratives,* ed. Kenneth R. R. Gros Louis (Nashville, Tenn.: Abingdon, 1982), 2:114–117.

12. Lilith's reputation has been more positively evaluated in the last few decades, largely in response to feminism. A summary of the Lilith legends can be found in Daniel Boyarin, *Carnal Israel: Reading Sex in Rabbinic Culture* (Berkeley and Los Angeles: University of California Press, 1993), 95–96.

13. Ilana Pardes, *Countertraditions in the Bible: A Feminist Approach* (Cambridge, Mass.: Harvard University Press, 1992), 22.

14. Here we get a glimpse of the process that led up to Creation, unlike Genesis 1:14–15 where the function of the sun, moon, and stars is spelled out as part of Creation itself. Similarly in Genesis 1:22 where God blesses the sea monsters, creatures, and birds, the blessing that they "fill the waters in the seas, and let the birds increase on the earth" follows their creation and does not provide a hierarchy.

15. The word *Elohim,* which is used for "God" throughout Genesis 1, has the *-im* ending characteristic of masculine plural Hebrew nouns. It can also mean "gods," as in "other gods" (Exodus 20:3). In the context of Genesis 1, the meaning is clearly singular as each of the other verbs it governs is singular. "Let us make" is one of the rare occasions in the Hebrew Bible where the verb does not conform to the meaning. As Helmer Ringgren concedes, why *Elohim* has a plural form "has not yet been explained satisfactorily." Helmer Ringgren, "*elohim,*" in *Theological Dictionary of the Old Testament,* ed. G. Johannes Botterweck and Helmer Ringgren, trans. John T. Willlis (Grand Rapids, Mich.: Eerdmans, 1977), 1:272.

16. As Phyllis Bird observes: "The Priestly account of creation is an exceedingly compressed account, marked by a repetitive structure of announcement and execution report." Phyllis A. Bird, " 'Male and Female He Created Them': Gen 1:27b in the Context of the Priestly Account of Creation," *Harvard Theological Review* 74, no. 2 (1981): 135.

17. For an exhaustive study of this phrase, see W. Randall Garr, *In His Own Image and Likeness: Humanity, Divinity and Monotheism* (Leiden: Brill, 2003).

18. *The Anchor Bible: Genesis,* intro., trans., and notes by E. A. Speiser, 2d ed. (Garden City, N.Y.: Doubleday, 1964), 4, 7.

19. Umberto Cassuto, *A Commentary on the Book of Genesis,* trans. Israel Abrahams, Part I, From Adam to Noah (Jerusalem: Magnes, 1978), 55. I have cited the translation to facilitate access for English readers.

20. Trible, *God,* 13.

21. Tikva Frymer-Kensky, *In the Wake of the Goddesses: Women, Culture, and the Biblical Transformation of Pagan Myth* (New York: Fawcett Columbine, 1st Ballantine ed., 1993), 153.

22. Ibid., 106 and passim.

23. "The extraordinary use of the first person plural evokes the image of a heavenly court in which God is surrounded by His angelic host. Such a celestial scene is depicted in several biblical passages. Two other occurrences of God's using the first person plural form of a verb are in Genesis 3:22 and 11:7." Sarna, *JPS Genesis*, 12, s.v. "Let us make." It is striking that the two additional verses Sarna cites are from *J* texts where the term used for God is most often *YHWH*.

24. F. J. Stendebach, "*tselem*," in *Theological Dictionary of the Old Testament*, ed. G. Johannes Botterweck and Helmer Ringgren, trans. Douglas W. Stott (Grand Rapids, Mich.: Eerdmans, 2003), 12:394.

25. Edward L. Greenstein, "Presenting Genesis 1, Constructively and Deconstructively," *Prooftexts: A Journal of Jewish Literary History* 21, no. 1 (winter 2001): 1–22.

26. Stephen A. Geller: "Blood Cult: Towards a Literary Theology of the Priestly Work of the Pentateuch," *Prooftexts: A Journal of Jewish Literary History* 12, no. 2 (May 1992): 116–117 and passim.

27. Ibid., 101–102, 114.

28. Garr, *In His Own Image*, 63. See, for example, Genesis 11:7.

29. Ibid., 90–91.

30. Ibid., 92.

31. In analyzing this verse, *Genesis Rabbah* 8:3 (Theodor and Albeck, 1:58–59) also compares God to a Roman emperor who seeks the advice and consent of his two consuls before embarking on a new project. The consuls in reality must consent. Citing this midrash, Burton L. Visotzky suggests that the effect of the metaphor is to indicate both that God needed no consultation and that the Roman emperors with designs on divinity were to be mocked. Burton L. Visotzky, *Reading the Book: Making the Bible a Timeless Text* (New York: Anchor, 1991), 190–191.

32. The verbs are: *yirdu*, "they shall rule" (Genesis 1:26); *peru*, "be fertile"; *revu*, "increase"; *mil'u*, "fill"; *khivshu*, "subdue"; *redu*, "rule over" (Genesis 1:28). The rabbinic exegesis does, at least in one instance, assume that *khivshuha* (Genesis 1:28) is singular. See discussion of *Genesis Rabbah* 8:12 below.

33. The plural in the previous verse: "They shall rule over the fish of the sea" and so forth is not particularly troubling as it may reasonably be considered to refer to a time in the future when there will be more than one human. One human could scarcely control so many other creatures.

34. Cassuto, *Commentary*, 1:58.

35. "Feminist critics have raised the question as to whether here and in the second account of human origins, in chapter 2, *'adam* is to be imagined as sexually undifferentiated until the fashioning of woman, though that proposal leads to certain dizzying paradoxes in following the story." Robert Alter, trans. and comm., *Genesis* (New York: Norton, 1996), 5, commentary to verse 27.

36. On the gender exclusivity of "man," I know no source more telling than Muriel Rukeyser's poem "Myth" in her *Breaking Open* (New York: Random House, 1973), 20.

37. Fritz Maass, "*adam*," in *Theological Dictionary of the Old Testament*, ed. G. Johannes Botterweck and Helmer Ringgren, trans. John T. Willis (Grand Rapids, Mich.: Eerdmans, 1977), 1:75. Bird points out that a singular collective refers to each of the

other orders of creatures created on the sixth day, except the *tanninim* or "sea creatures." Bird, "Male and Female," 146 n.45. Those collective nouns are not truly parallel to the *adam* because the *adam* becomes a character in the story, while the other creatures remain unindividuated, in the background.

38. Jon D. Levenson, "Genesis: Introduction and Annotations," in *The Jewish Study Bible,* ed. Adele Berlin and Marc Zvi Brettler (New York: Oxford University Press, 2004), 14, vv. 26–28.

39. Alter, *Genesis,* 5, commentary to verse 26.

40. "The pointed citation of the account in chapter 1 ties in the genealogical list with the initial story of human origins: creation is recapitulated, and continues." Alter, *Genesis,* 23, s.v. "in the image of God."

41. They generally read Genesis 2 as an expanded, detailed version of Genesis 1 and therefore, paradoxically, often had less trouble with it.

42. The similarity to Aristophanes' speech in Plato's *Symposium* is striking. The biblical text allows for only one creature to be divided, not the three in Plato. Plato, *Symposium,* trans., with intro. and notes by Alexander Nehamas and Paul Woodruff (Indianapolis, Ind.: Hackett, 1989), 25, citation 189E–29, citation 193A.

43. *Genesis Rabbah* 8:1; Theodor and Albeck, 1:55. This passage is here repeated from the opening of this chapter for the convenience of readers.

44. B. Berakhot 61a; B. ʿEruvin 18a; Judah Goldin, *The Fathers According to Rabbi Nathan* (New Haven, Conn.: Yale University Press, 1955), chap. 1, p. 15.

Dating *The Fathers According to Rabbi Nathan* is uncertain. Judah Goldin suggests that the composition of the contents could "not be much later than the third or following century"; see Goldin, *Fathers,* xxi.

Baskin argues that the reason for the inclusion of this midrash is "its homiletical benefits in teaching that only when the male and female are united are they truly *adam,* that is truly human." Baskin, *Midrashic Women,* 62. I would counter that there are many other possible texts that make that point, most clearly Genesis 2:24, which Baskin considers the strongest endorsement of marriage. Baskin, *Midrashic Women,* 63.

45. As Boyarin points out, "the myth of a primal androgyne was widespread in late antiquity, particularly among Platonists in the Jewish (and eventually, Christian) traditions." Boyarin, *Carnal,* 36.

46. Burton L. Visotzky suggests that R. Yirmeyah uses the verses from Genesis 5 "to tilt the balance," given their agreement with Genesis 1. Visotzky, *Reading,* 200.

47. If R. Shemuʾel bar Naḥman is arguing against R. Yirmeyah ben Leʿazar, rather than filling in the detail of his suggestion, he may be wondering not about how R. Yirmeyah ben Leʿazar's creature would be split, but about how it would reproduce.

The versions of this midrash in B. ʿEruvin 18a and B. Berakhot 61a record a difference of opinion between third-century Rav and Shemuʾel as to whether the creature had two faces or "fronts" or two backs or "tails."

48. Note that the comparison between the *adam* and the Tabernacle and between the woman and one of its sides is implicit here.

49. Baskin, *Midrashic Women,* 47. Baskin transliterates R. Shemuʾel bar Naḥman as "R. Samuel b. Naḥmani" here. I use "Naḥman" in accordance with the Theodor and Albeck text.

50. "According to the one who says it was a face, which of the two faces went ahead?—R. Naḥman ben Yitzḥak [responded]: It makes sense that the man's face went ahead, since it has been taught: 'A man should not walk behind a woman on the road'" (B. Berakhot 61a). This is not the place to discuss the modesty rules that would allow a woman to walk behind a man, but prevent him from walking behind her. Suffice it to say that here the two-faced creature is dominated by the masculine.

51. "Il [Dieu] a d'emblée voulu deux êtres séparés et égaux. Mais cela n'était pas possible; cette indépendance initiale entre des êtres égaux aurait été probablement la guerre." Emmanuel Levinas, *Du sacré au saint: cinq nouvelles lectures talmudiques* (Paris: Editions de Minuit, 1977), 142.

52. In other words, Baskin reads the rabbis as assuming that the side that is removed from the *adam* is the female; the one remaining, male. Baskin, *Midrashic Women*, 47.

53. Baskin contends that the omission of R. Yirmeyah ben Le'azar's suggestion of simultaneous creation from *Genesis Rabbah* 24:6 (should read 24:2; Theodor and Albeck, 1:230–231) where other parts of the long 8:1 section do reappear indicates that it was decidely a minority view that was suppressed. Baskin, *Misrashic Women*, 60–61.

54. Boyarin cites "[t]he more common [than the view that Eve was created second] rabbinic view that Eve and Adam (or at any rate their genitals) were both contained physically in the first human being." Boyarin, *Carnal*, 46. Daniel Boyarin, *Unheroic Conduct: The Rise of Heterosexuality and the Invention of the Jewish Man* (Berkeley and Los Angeles: University of California Press, 1997), 25 n.76.

55. Visotzky, *Reading*, 202.

56. Chernin, *Hunger*, 40–41.

57. There is also a reference here to the four elements.

58. Alicia Suskin Ostriker, *The Nakedness of the Fathers* (New Brunswick, N.J.: Rutgers University Press, 1994), 3–4.

59. Exodus 6:2. See also D. N. Freedman, "YHWH," in *Theological Dictionary of the Old Testament*, ed. G. Johannes Botterweck and Helmer Ringgren, trans. David E. Green (Grand Rapids, Mich.: Eerdmans, 1986), 5:500. Freedman further suggests that the form is actually a *hif'il*, meaning "to make come into being, to create," rather than the *qal*, "to be" (5:513–514). This suggestion is, of course, as irrelevant to Ostriker's poem as the fact that the text she uses as the basis for her rewriting refers to God as *Elohim*.

60. For example, "Created grass   herb yielding seed" (line 14).

61. Bird, "Male," 136.

62. Visotzky, *Reading*, 185.

63. Curiously, both words appear in Genesis 5:3, where they describe the way in which Seth resembled his father. This constitutes a remarkable effacement of the first woman. See below, chapter 3.

64. Stendebach, "tselem," 12:393; H. D. Preuss, "demut," in *Theological Dictionary of the Old Testament*, ed. G. Johannes Botterweck and Helmer Ringgren, trans. John T. Willis and Geoffrey W. Bromiley (Grand Rapids, Mich.: Eerdmans, 2003), 3:39.

65. Helen Schüngel-Straumann, "On the Creation of Man and Woman in Genesis 1–3: The History and Reception of the Texts Reconsidered," in *A Feminist Companion to Genesis*, ed. Athalya Brenner (Sheffield: Sheffield Academic Press, 1993), 73.

66. A midrash suggests that the reason for God's speed is that the angels could not decide whether or not creating the human would be a positive step, given the projected nature of human behavior. While they were arguing about God's proposal, God had already completed the task. *Genesis Rabbah* 8:5; Theodor and Albeck, 1:60. See also Levenson, "Genesis," 14, vv. 26–28.

67. While one could argue that there are actually thirteen words, counting the word *et*, which precedes *ha'adam* in the first clause, I maintain that when its function is solely to indicate that a specific accusative follows the verb, *et* should not be counted. This approach is supported by the hyphen connecting *et* and *ha'adam* in this verse.

68. Trible, *God*, 16.

69. Cassuto, *Commentary*, 1:57. Despite the fact that the layout of the Hebrew gives no indication of its special structure, Speiser sets only this verse in Genesis 1 as poetry in order to provide some of the same experience to the English reader. Speiser, *Genesis*, 4.

70. Trible, in her close analysis of this verse, claims that the third clause clarifies the second because the phrase "male and female" is parallel to "in the image of God" in the previous clause and "this formal parallelism indicates a semantic correspondence." The meaning of that phrase in the first and second clauses is "inaccessible" because the same words are repeated, leaving no parallel to elucidate its meaning. Trible, *God*, 16–20. I would, however, take issue with her statement that "'Male and female' is its vehicle [of the metaphor]; 'the image of God,' its tenor" (ibid., 17). God has been speaking throughout this text and therefore may be more familiar than "male and female," which appears here for the first time. I would argue that within this text the "image of God" is more familiar, or the vehicle; "male and female," the tenor.

71. Rejecting these ancient Near Eastern parallels as applicable only to royalty and not to ordinary humanity, Stendebach determines that there are two tenable theories about the significance of these terms. One would see the humans as God's earthly representatives; the other, as "God's counterparts." Stendebach, "*tselem*," 12:394.

72. "In other words, the resemblance of man to God bespeaks the infinite worth of a human being and affirms the inviolability of the human person. The killing of any other creature, even wantonly, is not murder. Only a human being may be murdered. It would seem, then, that 'in the image of God' conveys something about the nature of the human being as opposed to the animal kingdom; it also asserts human dominance over nature." Sarna, *JPS Genesis*, 12, s.v. "in our image, after our likeness."

73. Bird, "Male," 138.

74. Cassuto, *Commentary*, 1:57.

75. My reading is tenable because *adam*, rather than *Elohim*, is the antecedent of "its." This reading does not contradict Genesis 1:26, which has God use the phrase "in our image," because the step in the creation of the *adam* that gives God pause and warrants divine deliberation is the second step, the addition of the divine aspect.

76. Edward L. Greenstein has suggested to me that the latter reading may be a parallel to the creation of the "seed-bearing plants according to their kind" in Genesis 1:12.

77. This reading would be bolstered by reading the previous verse as indicating that God assumes that the *adam* is a known quantity and suggests that it be created in the divine image.

78. Michael Fishbane, *Text and Texture: Close Readings of Selected Biblical Texts* (New York: Schocken, 1979), 10–11. Fishbane, who cites as his source Cassuto, *Commentary,* 1:16–17, presents this argument more clearly than does his source.

79. For example, the sea and the skies, created on days two and three, are the source and location of the "swarms of living creatures" and "birds" of the fifth day (Genesis 1:20).

80. Cassuto would have the use of *"demut"* here and *"tselem"* in Genesis 1:27 reflect the "rhythm of the verse." Cassuto, *Commentary,* 1:275.

81. Alter, *Genesis,* 5, commentary to verse 26.

82. Von Rad and Speiser go so far as to declare that Adam is named in these verses: "Above all, *adam* ('man') is here used as a proper name ('Adam'), which was true neither in ch.1 nor in chs. 2, 3. Further, the note that God himself so named his creature has no equivalent in ch.1, 26 ff." Gerhard von Rad, *Genesis: A Commentary,* rev. ed. (Philadelphia: Westminster, 1972), 70. "This passage tells us at last of the naming of Adam." Speiser, *Genesis,* 40.

83. In fact, in Genesis 5:1–5 the word *adam* appears six times, never with the definite article.

84. The classic naming formula is "s/he named the child's name X; for s/he said . . . (the explanation of the name)." Pardes, *Countertraditions,* 43.

85. Cassuto, *Commentary,* 1:276.

86. Naming is discussed in greater detail in chapters 2 and 3.

87. Lois E. Bueler, *The Tested Woman Plot* (Columbus, Ohio: Ohio State University Press, 2001), 33.

88. R. E. Clements, *"zakhar,"* in *Theological Dictionary of the Old Testament,* ed. G. Joannes Botterweck and Helmer Ringgren, trans. David E. Green (Grand Rapids, Mich.: Eerdmans, 2003), 4:84.

89. Sarna provides parallels to the image of God as potter in ancient Egyptian, Mesopotamian, and Greek literature. *JPS Genesis,* 17. Speiser suggests a large number of divergences, including the "earthy and vividly personal approach" of J, its being "earth-centered," "differences in phraseology and references to the Deity." Speiser, *Genesis,* 18–19.

90. Mieke Bal, *Lethal Love: Feminist Literary Readings of Biblical Love Stories* (Bloomington, Ind.: Indiana University Press, 1987), 113.

91. Speiser suggests that "clods" is a translation of *'afar* preferable to "dust." Speiser, *Genesis,* 16. That meaning is clearly the one intended here both because the earth has to be capable of retaining some shape and because the water has just been mentioned in the text.

92. Speiser, *Genesis,* 16.

93. Although Speiser suggests that, in English, "earthling" would better translate *adam* while emphasizing the earth connection, he uses "man" in his own translation. David Rosenberg, in his translation of the J texts, does use "earthling," rendering the verse: "Y shaped an earthling from the clay of this earth, blew into its nostrils the wind of life. Now look: man becomes a creature of flesh." Harold Bloom, *The Book of J,* translated from the Hebrew by David Rosenberg (New York: Grove Weidenfeld, 1990), 61.

94. In his article on *tsela'* Heinz-Josef Fabry makes the point that the structural parallel between Genesis 2:7 and 2:21b–22 "suggests that these two creation statements

from *J* are more closely related." Heinz-Josef Fabry, "*tsela'*," in *Theological Dictionary of the Old Testament*, ed. G. Johannes Botterweck and Helmer Ringgren, trans. Douglass W. Stott (Grand Rapids, Mich: Eerdmans, 2003), 12:402.

95. The other relevant intervening events are discussed below because they contribute to the examination of the role that the *adam* and the woman are to play in the world.

96. Although *tsela'* and *tselem* clearly come from different roots, the two words both sound and look similar. Perhaps wordplay is at work here.

97. See Avraham Even-Shoshan, *A New Concordance* (in Hebrew) (Jerusalem: Kiryat-Sepher, 1990), s.v. *ts.l.'*, 988. Examples of the meaning "side" abound in the description of the tabernacle or *mishkan* (e.g., Exodus 26:25–27) and of the meaning "side room" in Ezekiel 41:5–11.

98. The phrase *vayiqqah ahat mitsal'otav* in Genesis 2:21 is translated in various ways. Tyndale (1530): "And then he toke out one of his rybbes"; Douay (1609): "he tooke one of his ribbes": *Woman's Bible* (1895): "and he took one of his ribs"; *In the Beginning*, trans. and commentary by Everett Fox (New York: Schocken, 1983): "he took one of his ribs"; *The Torah* (Philadelphia: Jewish Publication Society, 1962): "He took one of his ribs"; Bloom, *Book of J*: "he took a rib"; Alter, *Genesis*: "He took one of his ribs." Fox adds a note: "Or possibly 'sides,' paralleling other ancient peoples' concepts of an original being that was androgynous" (Fox, *In the Beginning*, 13, v. 21, s.v. "ribs").

99. Reuven Kimelman, "The Seduction of Eve and the Exegetical Politics of Gender," *Biblical Interpretation: A Journal of Contemporary Approaches* 4, no. 1 (February 1996): 15.

100. The standard dictionary of biblical Hebrew offers these six translations: rib of man (citing Genesis 2 examples only); rib of hill; side-chambers or cells; ribs of cedar; leaves of door; side of ark. Francis Brown, with the cooperation of S. R. Driver and Charles A. Briggs, *A Hebrew and English Dictionary of the Old Testament* (Oxford: Clarendon, 1907; reprinted and corrected, 1962), 854 s.v. *tsela'*.

101. Fabry, "*tsela'*," 12:405. *Pleuron* is also ambiguous, as in other contexts it, too, can mean "rib."

Amnon Shapira provides a brief discussion of the different meanings of *tsela'* in "On the Egalitarian Status of Women in the Bible" (in Hebrew), *Beit Mikra* 44, no. 4 (summer 1999): 314–315.

102. "This semantic singularity, of course, suggests that one seek a different solution." Fabry, "*tsela'*," 12:402.

103. Although I have not found anyone who connects the double meaning of *pleuron* in Greek and *costa* in Latin to the [mis]translation of *tsela'*, it seems to be the probable source of the confusion. "Costa" clearly has both meanings. Virgil, for example, is cited as using it with each of the different meanings. Charlton T. Lewis and Charles Short, *A New Latin Dictionary* (New York: Harper, 1879), s.v. "costa." French also maintains the ambiguity. Translation into English requires choosing one or the other of the meanings.

104. It is surprising that Cassuto did not entertain the possibility that *tsela'* means something other than rib, considering the lengths to which he goes to emphasize that it was not merely the bone of the rib that was involved: "He [God] did not take the bone alone, as the exegetes usually understand the verse; the hard bone would not have been suitable material for the fashioning of the tender and delicate body of the woman. The

meaning of the text is that the Creator took together with the bone also the flesh attached to it, and from the flesh He formed the woman's flesh, and from the bone her bones." Cassuto, *Commentary*, 1:134. There is no need to comment on the essentialist nature of Cassuto's vision of the female.

Further, Speiser does not comment on the issue and translates it as "rib." Speiser, *Genesis*, 15–18. As Jon D. Levenson pointed out to me, the translation as "side" is complicated because it is not mandated by other ancient Near Eastern languages and because there is no other Hebrew word for rib.

105. Fabry, "*tsela*ʿ," 12:402. It also explains the use of *vayiven* (and He built) to describe what God did with the *tsela*ʿ.

106. Ibid.

107. Ibid., 12:403. Fabry's further suggestion that the use of a term that recalls sacred building "suggests that human beings come to the fulfillment for which they are destined by creation only as man and wife and as 'God's temple' (cf. 1 Corinthians 3:16)," is a reading of the text that goes so far beyond its own terms as to become untenable.

108. "This passage is also a locus classicus for feminist theology insofar as it can be interpreted as an expression of a lesser, equal or higher valuation of women." Fabry, "*tsela*ʿ," 12:401. I find Fabry's essay clear and helpful; however, insofar as this biblical text refers only to the woman of Creation, it is prudent not to extend its meaning to apply to all women.

109. N. P. Bratsiotis "*ʾish*," in *Theological Dictionary of the Old Testament*, ed. G. Johannes Botterweck and Helmer Ringgren, trans. John T. Willis (Grand Rapids, Mich.: Eerdmans, 2003), 1:224.

110. Bratsiotis expatiates on the *ish* vs. *ishah* relationship in Genesis 2:23, but ignores the preceding *ishah* vs. *adam* relationship in Genesis 2:22. Bratsiotis, "*ʾish*," 224.

111. "Adam exists so that God can be known to be God, as Eve exists so that Adam can be known to be Adam." Bueler, *Tested Woman*, 18.

112. Robert Alter, referring both to the *adam*'s reported naming of the animals and to its recorded words upon being presented with the *ishah*, attributes greater significance to them, pointing out that the description of the *adam* "as passive matter is bracketed on both sides by his performance as master of language." Robert Alter, *The Art of Biblical Narrative* (New York: Basic Books, 1981), 31.

113. The more common translation of this phrase, "this one at last" (NJPS; Speiser, *Genesis*) treats these two Hebrew words as though they were linked. While it is a tenable translation, it effaces the threefold repetition of *zot* and the somewhat irregular form of the *adam*'s speech.

Another possibility to entertain, given that this is the only occurrence of the phrase *zot hapaʿam* in the Hebrew Bible, is that the two words together mean what *hapaʿam hazot* would mean: "this time."

M. Sæbø suggests that when *paʿam* is used in a temporal sense, as it is here, it means a specific point in time. While he mentions that in this verse, it "can involve implications for the theology of creation," he does not spell out those implications. M. Sæbø, "*paʿam*," in *Theological Dictionary of the Old Testament*, ed. G. Joannes Botterweck and Helmer Ringgren, trans. Douglas W. Stott (Grand Rapids, Mich.: Eerdmans, 2003), 12:49.

Everett Fox's translation, "This-time, she-is-it!" also separates the two words, but reverses them and, to my mind, reads into them a bit more than the text calls for (*Five Books*, 20).

114. The words that do not repeat are: *pa'am* (time); *yiqqarei* (shall be called); *ki* (because); and *luqoḥah* (was taken).

115. Trible presents a discussion of the ways in which the newly created female is unique (Trible, *God*, 96–98).

116. K.-M. Beysé, "'*etsem*," in *Theological Dictionary of the Old Testament*, ed. G. Johannes Botterweck and Helmer Ringgren, trans. David E. Green (Grand Rapids, Mich.: Eerdmans, 2001), 306.

117. Bratsiotis, "'*ish*," 1:222.

118. Speiser, *Genesis*, 18; Trible, *God*, 98.

119. Alter, *Art of Biblical Narrative*, 31.

120. Sarna, *JPS Genesis*, 23 on Genesis 2:23.

121. Bratsiotis, "'*ish*," 1:226.

122. Ibid.

123. Speiser, *Genesis*, xxvii.

124. Trible, *God*, 98; Bal, *Lethal Love*, 117.

125. Trible, *God*, 100. The issue of the *adam*'s naming this creature is discussed in the context of his naming her *Ḥavvah* at the end of Genesis 3; see chapter 2. Naming in general is discussed in greater detail in chapter 3.

126. Pardes, *Countertraditions*, 30.

127. This NJPS translation fits the midrash better than the literal translation "with throats bent back."

128. The meaning of the original here is complex. The proof text from Isaiah 3:16, where the verb describing the women's action is spelled slightly differently from the way it appears in the midrash, is conventionally understood to mean making flirtatious eye contact. It develops the meaning, based on an Aramaic word for eye makeup, of painting one's eyes red. The spelling used in the midrash also connotes looking at, thence looking at things she ought not be interested in, curious. The import here is clear, but the specific translation is open to some interpretation. See Michael Sokoloff, *A Dictionary of Jewish Palestinian Aramaic* (Ramat Gan, Israel: Bar Ilan University Press, 1990), 388, s.v. *s.q.r*; 572, s.v. *s.q.r.*

129. *Genesis Rabbah* 18:2; Theodor and Albeck, 1:162–163.

130. R. Yehoshua' of Sikhnin, a fourth-century *amora* living in Palestine, often relates traditions that he learned from his teacher R. Levi, a late third-century *amora* living in Palestine.

131. The biblical word *vayiven* is from the root *b.n.y*, which is connected with building; the root of *hitbonen—b.y.n*—is associated with understanding or introspection. Edward L. Greenstein has suggested to me that the four Hebrew consonants that appear in the masoretic text vocalized as *vayiven* could be vocalized as *vayaven*, which would mean, in rabbinic Hebrew, "he considered" and provide a stronger textual basis for this reading.

132. Baskin, *Midrashic Women*, 53.

133. Leila Leah Bronner, *From Eve to Esther: Rabbinic Reconstructions of Biblical Women* (Louisville, Ky.: Westminster John Knox, 1994), 32.

134. For a considered feminist analysis of Proverbs 1–8, see Frymer-Kensky, *In the Wake*, 179–183.

135. It is worth noting that the horror of the coming subjugation of Zion is ascribed but a few verses earlier to its being ruled by women (Isaiah 3:12).

136. The modern, Western sensitivity to blaming the victim, particularly in the case of this probable rape, has yet to be developed.

137. This is not the place to explore each of these examples in depth; suffice it to recognize that Sarah's and Rachel's behaviors are not condemned in the biblical text. Dinah's going out "to visit the daughters of the land" was, however, often condemned by the rabbis who saw it as the reason she was raped. See Tikva Frymer-Kensky, "The Dinah Affair," in *Reading the Women of the Bible* (New York: Schocken, 2000), 179–198.

138. It would not be the eating that is at fault, but improper speech, cited as "gossip." Gluttony was not particularly associated with women. But Eve's entering into a conversation with the snake is clearly the beginning of her downfall.

139. The word *qol* means both "voice" and "sound."

140. The Hebrew phrase *noah lehitpattot* is hard to translate in this passage. The root of the infinitive *lehitpattot* is *p.t.y,* which belongs to the domain of seduction, not appeasement. Thus, in the reflexive mode, the verb should be literally translated as "easy to seduce oneself," but the context in which this is a positive quality in a man argues otherwise. "Easily appeased," the English rendering used by both Baskin (*Midrashic Women,* 66) and the Soncino translation (*Midrash Rabbah: Genesis,* trans. H. Freedman [London: Soncino, 1983], 138), is no closer to the original word than "pacify," which Boyarin uses (Boyarin, *Carnal Israel,* 90). None of these translators suggests that the rendering is irregular, as was suggested to me by my colleague Avraham Holtz.

The *Concordance to the Babylonian Talmud* suggests that in the reflexive mode this verb means "to come to terms and be appeased" and cites four references: B. ʿEruvin 19a and 55a, B. Yevamot 61b, and B. Sanhedrin 100b. Benjamin Kasowski, *Thesaurus Talmudis Concordantiae Verborum* (in Hebrew) (Jerusalem, 1975), 32:600, s.v. *l'hitpattot.* Kasowski's translation notwithstanding, most of these references are to sexual seduction. Conversely, the *Even-Shoshan Dictionary* (in Hebrew), ed. Avraham Even-Shoshan and staff (Jerusalem: Evan-Shoshan, 2003), 1557, s.v. *p.t.h,*[1] defines the word in this conjugation as meaning "was seduced," citing this passage as an example.

The Babylonian Talmud (B. Niddah 31b) presents a different version of this dialogue, which includes four of the questions in this passage from *Genesis Rabbah* 17:8; but in that context they refer to sexual relations between men and women. The questions involve man's pursuit of woman, the male superior position in intercourse, the ready male acceptance of conciliation (*piyyus*), and the attractive sweetness of a woman's voice. I assume that this passage has influenced the reading of its parallel in *Genesis Rabbah* 17:8.

141. Excerpted from *Genesis Rabbah* 17:8; Theodor and Albeck, 1:158–159. This passage, which deals with the nature of the woman, is the first section of the midrash; the second, final section, which responds to the eating of the fruit, will be discussed in chapter 2.

142. Boyarin, *Carnal,* 90.

143. Ibid., 90–91 n.23.

144. Another discussion of this passage may be found in Baskin, *Midrashic Women*, 65–68.

145. A discussion of woman's alterity as conveyed in rabbinic texts may be found in Judith Hauptman, *Rereading the Rabbis: A Woman's Voice* (Boulder, Colo.: Westview, 1998), 30–31 and passim and in Baskin, *Midrashic Women*, 141–164, and passim.

146. This anomaly is explained in one contemporary commentary as follows: "And that was the nature of this thing [birth] in their days, and the thing has changed so that both a son and a daughter come out at times [facing] one way and at times another way." *The Annotated Midrash Rabbah* (in Hebrew), ed. members of the "Annotated Midrash Institute" (Jerusalem, 1984), 264.

147. While Theodor and Albeck cite no variant that has this strange question and answer referring to anything other than birth, an examination of parallel texts elsewhere in rabbinic literature yields another intriguing possibility. Both *Avot deRabbi Natan B* 9 and B. Niddah 31b set this distinction in the context of male and female positions for intercourse, which traditionally place the man on top. This makes more sense than the odd obstetrics of *Genesis Rabbah* 17:8, for it would have the woman looking up at the man's front, perhaps, specifically his chest, while the man would look down at the ground. Notice that this text would have the man look right past the woman.

148. B. Shabbat 62a. In its original context, R. Yosef uses this statement to explain 'Ulla's position on what men and women can carry in restricted areas on Shabbat. The context does not require a generalization as sweeping as the one we have here. For a study of this expression, see Baskin, *Midrashic Women*, 167–168 n.2.

149. See Joel Roth, "On the Ordination of Women as Rabbis," in *The Ordination of Women as Rabbis*, ed. Simon Greenberg (New York: Jewish Theological Seminary, 1988), 176–177 n.43.

150. We hear echoes of the biblical "Bone of my bones, flesh [meat] of my flesh [meat]" (Genesis 2:23) here. Strikingly, while the shared bone and meat are parallel markers of mutuality in the biblical verse, they are here divisively gender-based.

151. Baskin, *Midrashic Women*, 67.

152. The midrash does not link the loss of the "rib" with the later verse: "Therefore a man [*ish*] will leave his father and mother and cling to his woman [*ishto*] and they become one flesh" (Genesis 2:24). It is helpful to compare this passage with one in B. 'Eruvin 100b that similarly discusses the way in which women and men indicate their interest in sexual activity. Surprisingly, the passage opens with R. Shemu'el bar Naḥman citing R. Yoḥanan's opinion that when a woman solicits her husband to fulfill a commandment (understood in context, to mean to have intercourse), they will produce sons of outstanding quality. But, as the discussion continues, the rabbis evince a great deal of discomfort about encouraging women openly to make demands of their husbands. The resolution is that a woman's solicitation should be unvoiced, silent, interior, while a man may solicit his wife openly. For a further discussion of this passage, see Hauptman, *Rereading*, 153.

153. Another midrash that spells out this view in greater detail is *Genesis Rabbah* 18:3, where the woman is described as having more storage spaces than a man, broad at the bottom and narrow on top so that she might better hold the fetus (Theodor and Albeck,

1:163). Baskin sees in this text "the most apt expression of rabbinic Judaism's understanding of appropriate female functions and of women's essential alterity from men." Baskin, *Midrashic Women*, 1.

154. "[T]he ovum is a very recent discovery, and biology, until early modern times, considered the male sperm to be the sole agent in engendering the child." Frymer-Kensky, *In the Wake*, 48.

155. Boyarin, for example, goes so far as to use this as the proof of his argument that the rabbis essentialize women "owing to their desire to ensure that their procreative role not be compromised." Boyarin, *Carnal*, 90. Baskin sees this as yet another instance where sexual liberty comes into play. Woman's reliability is grounded in the restrictions on her sexual relations. Because she is limited to her husband, she is more reliable than her husband. Baskin, *Midrashic Women*, 67–68.

156. The only clause in which *p.q.d* does not appear is "he [R. Yehoshuaʿ] said to them."

157. See M. Bava Metziʿa 4:1. The specific word *mafqid* that opens the chapter is the present participle of the word *hifqid*, deposited, which appears in our text.

158. Linda Pastan, *Aspects of Eve* (New York: Liveright, 1975), 16–17.

159. Alicia Suskin Ostriker, *Stealing the Language: The Emergence of Women's Poetry in America* (Boston: Beacon, 1986), 210–211. Claudine Herrmann's book, *Les Voleuses de langue* (Paris: des Femmes. 1976), appeared in English with the title *The Tongue Snatchers*, trans. with intro. and notes by Nancy Kline (Lincoln: University of Nebraska, 1989).

160. Often, Eve's name does not appear in the title. Examples from the same collection include: "To Consider a House" (16–17), "Eclipse" (54), and "A Symposium: Apples" (55). Pastan, *Aspects*.

161. Sanford Pinsker, "Family Values and the Jewishness of Linda Pastan's Poetic Vision," in *Women Poets of the Americas: Toward a Pan-American Gathering*, ed. Jacqueline Vaught Brogan and Cordelia Chávez Candelaria (Notre Dame, Ind.: University of Notre Dame Press, 1999), 206.

162. There are many potential parallels between the bone and the Jewish people as chosen by God for a particular relationship and/or task and the divine choice of the rib. Pastan does not suggest a specific analogy but leaves that to the reader.

163. This ending of the poem, diverging from the biblical story, is so surprising that it forces the reader to stop and reconsider the meaning of the poem. Cf. Barbara Hernstein Smith's dictum: "The surprise ending is one which forces and *rewards* a readjustment of the reader's expectations; it justifies itself retrospectively." *Poetic Closure: A Study of How Poems End* (Chicago: University of Chicago Press, 1968), 213.

164. One example is "Fruit of the Tree," from Linda Pastan, *Imperfect Paradise* (New York: Norton, 1988), 73, which includes: "Eve would be the mother / of Newton and Bohr." These lines express a view of knowledge as positive and thus make eating the forbidden fruit positive, as well.

165. Matthew 7:7 (*New English Bible*, 1971).

166. Harold Wentworth and Stuart Berg Flexner, comps. and eds., *Dictionary of American Slang*, second supp. ed. (New York: Crowell, 1975), 426, s.v. "rib." See also the 1949 American film *Adam's Rib*.

167. J. E. Lighter, ed., *Random House Historical Dictionary of American Slang* (New York: Random House, 1994), 1:227, s.v. "bone."

168. Lighter, *American Slang*, 2:372, s.v. "knock." The expression "knocked up" clearly derives from this usage.

169. Art Spiegelman, *In the Shadow of No Towers* (New York: Pantheon, 2004), comic supplement and plate III.

170. Excerpted from *Genesis Rabbah* 18:1; Theodor and Albeck, 1:160–161.

171. As demonstrated by Yitzhak D. Gilat, in the mishnaic period there were many different ages at which children took on legal responsibilities in various areas. Some of these depended on the developmental age of the individual child. Over time, the individualized standards, like this one that requires testing intellectual and moral development, were supplanted by uniform standards. As Gilat claims, in the intellectual arena women were generally considered to mature earlier than men. Yitzhak D. Gilat, "Thirteen Years Old [and Subject] to the Commandments?" (in Hebrew), in *Meḥqerei Talmud: Talmudic Studies,* ed. Yaacov Sussman and David Rosenthal (Jerusalem: Magnes Press, 1990), 1:39–53. Others, such as Judith Hauptman, assess the situation differently. She believes that there were two forces at work: one was genuine disagreement among the rabbis; the other, the development of different standards to suit different situations (Hauptman, *Rereading,* 241 n.20.)

The same is true of the biological sphere where girls and boys were initially individually checked for physical signs of puberty, generally two pubic hairs, before they were considered adults. Here too, fixed ages (in this case the same as for vows) became standard. Because the biological and the intellectual ages are the same, and because the discussion of vows in M. Niddah appears in a context where much of the deliberation centers on puberty, they are often assumed to be linked, although no link is explicit. Thus, for example, Tirzah Meacham claims, based on the mishnah cited in this midrash, that "puberty signs become absolute criteria to determine understanding (*binah*) at a given age." Tirzah Meacham, "Woman More Intelligent than Man: Creation Gone Awry," *Approaches to Ancient Judaism,* n.s., 5 (1993): 57.

In the final analysis, however, it seems that intellectual and biological development are separable. As Judith Romney Wegner claims, M. Niddah 5:6, which forms the basis of the midrash we are discussing, while "reflecting the earlier onset of puberty in girls, also demonstrates the sages' belief that girls mature mentally—as well as physically—earlier than boys. Because intelligence is an important part of personhood, the sages are saying that a girl *intrinsically* becomes a person earlier than a boy." Judith Romney Wegner, *Chattel or Person? The Status of Women in the Mishnah* (New York: Oxford University Press, 1988), 36–37. Thus, the halakhic principle, predicated on a woman's earlier intellectual development, stands. If this were not true, then a girl in her eleventh year who had reached puberty, or a boy in his twelfth, would not have to be tested to determine whether or not her or his vows were valid.

172. Meacham maintains that this discussion may be a piece of talmudic argumentation that was originally in the Palestinian Talmud, but has since been lost. ("Woman," 64 n.8).

173. Boyarin sees "Eve's ornaments [as] a positive gift of God," but does not mention that this positive valuation implies that there was something negative about her that warranted amelioration. Boyarin, *Carnal,* 103.

174. See the discussion of Isaiah 3:16 in the context of *Genesis Rabbah* 18:2.

175. Cassuto, *Commentary*, 1:135.

176. B. Bava Batra 58a. This comparison is one of a series.

177. Trible, *Genesis*, 95.

178. Gerhard von Rad sees God as "father of the bride" (*Genesis*, 84). Trible calls her chapter on Genesis 2–3 "A Love Story Gone Awry" (Trible, *God*, 72); Bal refers to Genesis 1–3 as the "first love story of the Bible, the first love story of our culture" (Bal, *Lethal*, 104). Fabry, too, seems to fall into the same trap: "Theologically the Yahwist suggests that human beings come to the fulfillment for which they are destined by creation only as man and wife and as 'God's temple'" (Fabry, "*tselaʿ*," 402). Levenson's interpretation is more nuanced: "The Lord's creation of woman from man emphasizes the close connection between them and lays the groundwork for the understanding of marriage (and its association with procreation) in v. 24" (Levenson, "Genesis," 16, vv. 2:18–24).

179. Sarna, *JPS Genesis*, 23, s.v. "He brought her to the man."

180. It is no accident that five of the "Seven Blessings" at a Jewish wedding refer in some way to Adam, Creation, or the Garden of Eden.

181. Bratsiotis, "*ʾish*," 227–228.

182. Chernin, *Hunger Song*, 40–41.

183. "We would retain the translation of 'man,' however, because 'husband' conjures up the image of marriage, which does not fit the archetypal literary setting of the Eden story." Carol Meyers, *Discovering Eve: Ancient Israelite Women in Context* (New York: Oxford University Press, 1988), 110.

184. Bird, "Male," 155.

185. "Isaac then brought her [Rebekah] into the tent of his mother Sarah, and he took Rebekah as his woman [or wife]. Isaac loved her, and thus found comfort after his mother's death" (Genesis 24:67).

186. Sarna, *JPS Genesis*, 23, s.v. "Hence."

187. Cassuto denies the notion that this is "an echo of the system of matriarchy, in which the woman was the head of the family. But in the epoch of the Torah this system had long disappeared." Cassuto, *Commentary*, 1:137.

188. Both Abraham and Jacob leave home—at God's command and to escape his brother's wrath, respectively. Jacob actually does take up residence in his wives' home, which had been his mother's home as well, for as many as twenty-one years, but leaves at the first prudent opportunity. For a discussion of kinship systems in Genesis 12–36, with particular emphasis on the competing avuncular and patrilocal systems, see Robert A. Oden, Jr., "Jacob as Father, Husband and Nephew: Kinship Studies and the Patriarchal Narratives," *Journal of Biblical Literature* 102, no. 2 (1983), 189–205.

189. Bird points out that divine blessing plays a significant role in the P texts. Bird, "Male," 152.

190. Ostriker, *Nakedness*, 4.

191. Given the fact that the fish, fowl, and crawling things are all located in a part of the previously created universe, it seems reasonable that "the earth," which is anomalous in the list, is intended as the location of the cattle, rather than as an independent entity. Cassuto reads it as broadening the scope of the statement to avoid the repetition of the list of all living things that had been previously created. Cassuto, *Commentary*, 1:57.

192. "While post-biblical Jews and Christians frequently asserted the superiority of the male over the female in their interpretation of Genesis 1:28, the Bible makes no such distinction here. Man and woman share equally in the various aspects of the divine charge." Jeremy Cohen, *"Be Fertile and Increase, Fill the Earth and Master It": The Ancient and Medieval Career of a Biblical Text* (Ithaca, N.Y.: Cornell University Press, 1989), 13.

193. The other difference is the relatively trivial conflation of "the cattle, the whole earth, and all the creeping things that creep on the earth" (Genesis 1:26) into "all the living things that creep on earth" (Genesis 1:28).

194. The text of the Torah originally had no vowels. At some point now generally assumed to be between the sixth and the ninth centuries C.E., the Masoretes wrote down the traditional vocalization. To this day Torah scrolls, which are scribed by hand, do not include vowels.

195. Amnon Shapira points out that there are seven uses of the plural referring to the *adam* in Genesis 1:27–28, including *vekhivshuha*. Shapira, "On the Egalitarian," 316. This usage further bolsters the argument that *vekhivshuha* is a plural if one accepts Cassuto's theory about the large number of sevens in Genesis 1. Cassuto, *Commentary*, 1:12–17. On Cassuto's theory, see Jon D. Levenson, *Creation and the Persistence of Evil* (Princeton, N.J.: Princeton University Press, 1988), 67–69.

196. In Hebrew when a group is plural and includes at least one masculine noun, it is treated as a masculine plural. Thus, there is no significance attached to the fact that all four imperative verbs in this sequence are masculine.

197. Excerpted from *Genesis Rabbah* 8:12; Theodor and Albeck, 1:66.

198. These are not the only two possible readings of the consonants *v.kh.v.sh.h.*

199. There is an extensive discussion of this midrash in Baskin, *Midrashic Women*, 51–52 and 121. She explains the logic a bit differently, assuming that R. Yose bar Zimra also reads the three previous verbs as singular, based on his reading of the fourth one in the series (51). I consider unlikely his reading clear plurals as singular and therefore assume that he is seeing all the verbs as connected, part of the larger task of procreation.

200. R. Ḥanina is quoted as having said: "A person who is commanded [by God] to do something and does it is greater than someone who is not commanded and does it" (B. Kiddushin 31a et al.).

201. Baskin, *Midrashic Women*, 51.

202. For an extensive discussion of the obligation to have children, see Cohen, *"Be Fertile."*

203. Visotzky, *Reading*, 202.

204. Some of the disparity between this verse and the one in Genesis 1 results from the different order of the steps in Creation. The task of multiplying and filling the earth would seem to require a procreative partner. The animals and the other orders of beings are not created in this version until Genesis 2:9.

205. Genesis 1:3, 10, 12, 18, 21, 25, 31; 2:9, 12, 17.

206. Cassuto, *Commentary*, 1:92.

207. Often, there is a connection between helplessness and solitude. Von Rad makes the point that "[s]olitude is therefore defined here very realistically as helplessness." Von Rad, *Genesis*, 82.

208. Greenstein, "God's Golem," 237.

209. Similarly, although in a different context, when Gideon tries to separate a band of true loyalists from the many volunteers, God asks him to take them down to drink at the water and that anyone who laps at the water like a dog *tatsig oto levad,* "set him apart," literally, "set him alone" (Judges 7:5).

210. *Genesis Rabbah* 17:2; Theodor and Albeck, 1:151–152.

211. Note that two of these proof texts cite God's blessing of Noah after the flood (Genesis 9:6–7) in which the language strongly echoes that of Genesis 1:27–28. Using these verses, instead of the more familiar ones from Genesis 1, signals that these blessings were meant for all time, not just for some mythic, prehistoric, idyllic age.

212. "Therefore will an *adam* leave his father and mother and cling to his woman" (Genesis 2:24).

213. M. Yoma 1:1. I am grateful to Michael Sokoloff for drawing my attention to this text. This practice may have been linked to the use of the term *debeithu* (literally, of his house) to mean "wife" in Aramaic.

214. "R. Yose said: 'Never in my life did I call my wife "my wife" or my ox "my ox." Rather, I called my wife "my house" and my ox "my field" ' " (B. Shabbat 118b, translation mine). The context here is a series of stories featuring R. Yose. This story is sandwiched between one about the five instances of intercourse that had resulted in his fathering five outstanding sons and one that indicates that he never looked at his place of circumcision. Were it not for the involvement of the ox, one might have assumed that it was about his reluctance to refer to his wife as such for fear of overstepping the rabbinic guidelines for modesty about sexual matters. The same story is told in both B. Gittin 52b and *Ruth Rabbah* 2:8 in different contexts. For an extensive exploration of this phenomenon see Gail Labovitz, "My Wife I Called 'My House': Marriage, Metaphor, and Discourses of Gender in Rabbinic Literature," Ph.D. diss., Jewish Theological Seminary, 2002.

215. For a discussion of Abigail see Frymer-Kensky, *Reading,* 315–323.

216. For example: "It is I, the Lord, who made everything, / Who alone [*levaddi*] stretched out the heavens / And unaided spread out the earth" (Isaiah 44:24). "Blessed is the Lord who alone [*levaddo*] does wondrous things" (Psalms 72:18).

217. Abraham Joshua Heschel, *God in Search of Man* (New York: Farrar, Straus and Cudahy, 1955).

218. Although the only English translation of this text renders both uses of the word *yaḥid* as "alone," its meaning here, and generally, is better "unique." *Pirkê de Rabbi Eliezer,* trans. and annotated by Gerald Friedlander (London, 1916; reissued, New York: Hermon, 1965), 85–86 (chap. 2). Friedlander points out many variants in different manuscripts. There is no critical edition of the original.

219. As Friedlander notes, some of the manuscripts read "My" instead of "his," clearly an error.

220. The "creatures [*haberiyyot*]" referred to here are probably, as Friedlander suggests, the animals that were assumed to have the power of speech in Eden (*Pirkê de Rabbi Eliezer,* 85 n.9). The snake's ability to speak persuasively (Genesis 3:1, 4–5) must have been a contributing factor to this view.

221. Excerpted from *Pirkei Rabbi Eli'ezer* (in Hebrew) (Jerusalem: Eshkol, s.d.), chap. 12, 38–39.

222. Greenstein cites both parallels in other mythologies and the actions of biblical humans. Greenstein, "God's Golem," 238–239.

223. *Pirkei Rabbi Eliʿezer,* chap. 11, 36.

224. For further discussion of the meaning of "good" both in this context and in the rest of the primeval history in Genesis, see Greenstein, "Presenting," 13–14.

225. Greenstein cites another possibility, coming from a Semitic root meaning "strong." Greenstein, "God's Golem," 237.

226. Those referring to God are Exodus 18:4; Deuteronomy 33:7, 26, 29; Hosea 13:9; Psalms 20:3; Psalms 33:20; Psalms 70:6; Psalms 89:20; Psalms 115:9, 10, 11; Psalms 121:1, 2; Psalms 124:8; Psalms 146:5. Those referring to humans, usually in a context in which their help proves futile, are Isaiah 30:5; Ezekiel 12:14; Daniel 11:34.

227. For a discussion of the different understandings of the word ʿezer see Judy Weiss, "An Analysis of the Story of the Creation of Woman in the Palestinian Targumim," M.A. essay in Jewish Women's Studies at Jewish Theological Seminary, May 2000, 26–36.

228. Even-Shoshan lists 151 uses of *neged* in various forms that fall into four categories of meaning. The two occurrences in the Creation story (Genesis 2:18, 20) are a category unto themselves and explained as leʿummato, "facing him." Even-Shoshan, *Concordance,* 738–739, s.v. *neged.*

229. Cassuto, in fact, claims that the naming of the animals had the additional agenda of having the *adam* realize that, although "some of them were indeed suited to serve him and help him to some extent, but yet there was not one among them that was his *like* [. . . kᵉneghdō], he would become conscious of his loneliness and would yearn for one who could be his life companion and a helper fit to be his soul-mate [. . . ʿēzer kᵉneghdō] in the full sense of the words, and, in consequence, he would be ready to appreciate and cherish the gift that the Lord God was to give him" (Cassuto, *Commentary,* 128).

230. Speiser, *Genesis,* 17, s. v. "an aid for him."

231. Greenstein, "God's Golem," 237.

232. See Trible, *God,* 96–97. Trible's otherwise strong analysis of this section is undercut by her use of wedding metaphors. As mentioned above, referring to God as "the divine matchmaker" charges the text with an inappropriate layer of meaning.

233. Naming is discussed in greater detail in chapter 3.

234. Pardes does make the interesting point that, if we consider differentiation as creation, semiotically speaking, woman is created first. "Although man is the first to speak and differentiate, woman is the first to be differentiated." Pardes, *Countertraditions,* 30.

235. For example, Deuteronomy 21:17.

236. Other examples of God's preferred who are not firstborn include Isaac, Jacob, Joseph, Moses, and David. The exception may be Abram/Abraham, who, assuming that Teraḥ's sons are listed in birth order, would be the first (Genesis 11:27).

237. "2:11 A woman must be a learner, listening quietly and with due submission. 2:12 I do not permit a woman to be a teacher, nor must woman domineer over man; she should be quiet. 2:13 For Adam was created first, and Eve afterwards; 2:14 and it was not Adam who was deceived; it was the woman who,

yielding to deception, fell into sin. 2:15 Yet she will be saved through mother-hood—if only women continue in faith, love, and holiness, with a sober mind." (NEB 1 Timothy 2:11–15).

238. Phyllis Trible, "Depatriarchalizing in Biblical Interpretation," in *The Jewish Woman: New Perspectives,* ed. Elizabeth Koltun (New York: Schocken, 1976), 222.

239. There are those who opine that humanity represents the high point of Creation. Sarna, for example, claims: "Man is indeed the pinnacle of Creation." Sarna, *JPS Genesis,* 14. See also von Rad, *Genesis,* 77. It is really the Sabbath that occupies that position. See Fishbane, *Text,* 11; and Greenstein, "Presenting," 4.

240. It is to be noted that the rabbis were, as a group, less self-conscious of their in-novativeness than are the contemporary poets.

CHAPTER 2. LIFE IN THE GARDEN OF EDEN

1. Hebrew original is published in Yaakov Fikhman, *A Corner of a Field: Poems* (in He-brew) (Tel Aviv: Schocken, 1944), 140. An English translation of this poem appears in Howard Schwartz and Anthony Rudolf, *Voices within the Ark* (New York: Avon Books, 1980), 78–79. While I have consulted it, I have translated the poem more literally in order to maintain a greater degree of faithfulness to the original.

In my translation I have attempted to reflect the tenses of the Hebrew verbs Fikhman uses. The Hebrew future can be used, as it is here, to indicate action that continues from the present into the future. Although I have put the verbs in the simple English future to distinguish them from verbs in the present, it should be understood that they are actually better construed as indicating repeated action that will continue into the future. Thus, for example, "the serpent will whisper" really means "the serpent will continue to whisper."

2. Although the words *medurat kesamim* might be literally translated as "a bonfire of enchantments," they constitute a hendiadys and thus would better read as "an en-chanted bonfire."

3. Literally "with the dawn [that] will rise."

4. The Hebrew here, *siah-yom,* is ambiguous, as discussed below.

5. In the Hebrew text these words are printed with extra space between the letters, an indication of emphasis. Italics have the same effect in English.

6. Ya'aqov Bahat, "The Bible in the Works of Yaakov Fikhman" (in Hebrew), in *Yaakov Fikhman: A Collection of Critical Essays on His Writings* (in Hebrew), ed. Nurit Govrin (Tel Aviv: Am Oved, 1971), 134–135.

7. Erich Auerbach, *Mimesis,* trans. Willard Trask (Garden City, N.Y.: Doubleday An-chor Books, 1953), 1–20.

8. In an essay focusing on women's writing, particularly in Hebrew, Fikhman makes the case that throughout history women have de facto, if not de jure, had a major influence, despite the discrimination against them. He supports the entrance of women into the field of Hebrew letters. Yaakov Fikhman, "On Women's Creativity," in Yaakov Fikhman, *The Concept of Modern Poetry and Other Essays* (in Hebrew) (Israel: He-brew Writers Association and Eked, 1982), 355–363.

9. See Dan Miron, "About the Lyric Poetry of Yaakov Fikhman" (in Hebrew), in *Yaakov Fikhman: A Collection of Critical Essays on His Writings* (in Hebrew), ed. Nurit Govrin (Tel Aviv: Am Oved, 1971), 153, for a discussion of Fikhman's connection to the dark.

10. See the discussion of love and marriage in chapter 1.

11. The root *’.h.b* first appears in the story of the Binding of Isaac (Genesis 22) where it refers to Abraham's love for Isaac. In its one nominal and fourteen verbal appearances in Genesis, the root refers six times to the love of a parent for a child (Genesis 22:2; 25:8, 28; 37:3, 4; 44:20); six times to the love of a man for a woman (Genesis 24:67; 29:18, 20, 30, 32; 34:30); and three times to the love of a food (Genesis 27:4, 9, 14). It never refers to the love of a woman for a man.

12. Miron sees breaks in meter as characteristic of Fikhman's work (Miron, "Lyric Poetry," 152).

13. In Hebrew the present tense of the verb "to be" is not used, but understood from the ellipsis.

14. Note that the Hebrew Bible uses the noun *da‘at* for knowledge or wisdom in reference to the tree; Fikhman uses the adjective *hakham* (wise), derived from the same root as the noun *hokhmah* (wisdom). Although the words are often used to define each other, they are not identical. *Hokhmah* connotes wisdom as in Proverbs 8; *da‘at*, knowledge. *Da‘at*, with its root *y.d.‘*, has sexual overtones, as in Genesis 4:1. Because *y.d.‘* is transitive, Fikhman would have been hard-pressed to use its adjectival or participial form here.

15. Technically the serpent is the subject of only the first of these verbs; the serpent's whisper is the subject of the other two.

16. *Ki,* translated here as "when," can also mean "because."

17. Final "v" and "f" sounds are often close to indistinguishable in Hebrew, particularly as pronounced by former Yiddish speakers like Fikhman. Despite their aural proximity, however, they are orthographically distinct. Fikhman does use them as rhymes in other poems as well. See, for example, *"Helqah shekhuhah"* and *"Le’ahar sharav"* in Fikhman, *A Corner,* 14, 55, respectively.

18. Other appearances in the Hebrew Bible are Isaiah 9:17 and 10:34, Jeremiah 4:7, Nahum 1:10, Psalms 74:5, and Job 8:17.

19. Interestingly, this verse is read by R. Levi as indicating that scholars who interrupt their study will be reduced to eating saltwort and wormwood (B. Hagigah 12b).

20. Ruth Kartun-Blum, *Profane Scriptures: Reflections in Dialogue with the Bible in Modern Hebrew Poetry* (Cincinnati, Ohio: Hebrew Union College, 1999), 19.

21. Assuming that the fruit of the tree is the unexpressed object of "to pluck."

22. Itzik Manger, *Itzik's Midrash* (in Yiddish), ed. Chone Shmeruk (Jerusalem: Hebrew University, 1969), 9–10. As Shmeruk's note at the opening of the book indicates, this poem was not originally included in *Pentateuch Poems* (in Yiddish) in 1935 or in the 1951 edition of *Itzik's Midrash* (in Yiddish) but in Itzik Manger, *Clouds over the Roof* (in Yiddish) (London: Alenenyu, 1942), xi. The Yiddish text and an English translation by Leonard Wolf may be found in *The Penguin Book of Modern Yiddish Verse,* ed. Irving Howe, Ruth R. Wisse, and Chone Shmeruk (New York: Viking, 1987), 562–565. I have provided a more literal translation. with the help of Rabbi Ben-Zion Gold, who has most generously shared with me his knowledge of Yiddish poetry, as well as his love for it.

23. Dov Sadan cites Shlomo Bickel and Avraham Blatt as emphasizing the way Manger transposes scenes from the biblical landscape to his own. Dov Sadan, *Controversy and*

Its Resolution, in Itzik Manger, *Itzik's Midrash,* ed. Chone Shmeruk (Jerusalem: Hebrew University, 1969), xvii–xviii. "Manger's biblical folk, by having their ordinariness intensified, manage to become extraordinary"; David Roskies, introduction to Itzik Manger, *The World According to Itzik: Selected Poetry and Prose* (New Haven, Conn.: Yale University Press, 2002), xxix.

24. Note that Manger, like many other twentieth-century Jewish writers, follows the Christian assumption that the tree in question was an apple tree.

25. *Genesis Rabbah* 9:7; Theodor and Albeck, 1:71–72.

26. Because there are no capital letters in Yiddish, all the appearances of *"er"* in Yiddish are identical except for the quotation marks.

27. *Roysht* (rustles) is close to *rayst* (tears), particularly in the Yiddish of those who tend to efface the distinction between "s" and "sh."

28. Note that nowhere in this poem does Eve eat the fruit of the tree. She does, however, pick an apple and embrace the tree. Her actions remind the reader that, in the biblical text, Eve erroneously claims that the divine prohibition includes both eating the fruit of the tree and touching it (Genesis 3:4).

29. Helen Papell, *Talking with Eve, Leah, Hagar, Miriam* (New York: Jewish Women's Resource Center, 1996).

30. Ibid., 9.

31. Three parallel clauses in Genesis 3:6 describe what Eve sees in the tree. See below, this chapter.

32. Another poem that emphasizes the absence of role models in Eve's life is Lynn Gottlieb's "Eve's Song in the Garden," in Schwartz and Rudolf, *Voices,* 476.

33. See chapter 1 above.

34. Robert Alter suggests that the relationship between Genesis 2:24 and the story that follows is that Genesis 2:25 ff. "unsettles the neatness of the etiological certainty" of Genesis 2:24. Robert Alter, trans. and comm., *Genesis* (New York: Norton, 1996), 10, commentary to 2:25.

35. In this translation I have been persuaded by Horst Seebass, who maintains that "this root is in no way oriented to sexual shame—Gen.2:25 (hithpael) seems to mean, 'they (the man and his wife) were not found in a state of shame as far as their nakedness was concerned.'" Horst Seebass, *"bosh,"* in *Theological Dictionary of the Old Testament,* ed. G. Johannes Botterweck and Helmer Ringgren, trans. John T. Willis (Grand Rapids, Mich.: Eerdmans, 1977), 2:52.

36. Speiser, in *The Anchor Bible: Genesis,* intro., trans., and notes by E. A. Speiser (Garden City, N.Y.: Doubleday, 1964) 2d edition, 9th printing, 21, includes Genesis 2:25 in the section entitled "The Fall of Man." Cassuto, however, sees "The Story of the Garden of Eden" extending from Genesis 2:4 to 3:24 and includes 2:25 in the "paragraph" dealing with the creation of woman (1:137), as does Stephen Mitchell, who includes it in a paragraph with the preceding verse; *Genesis: A New Translation of the Classic Biblical Stories* (New York: HarperCollins, 1996), 6. NJPS puts it with chapter 3.

37. See Cassuto, 1:143–144, for a fuller discussion of the various linguistic options and the consequences of this choice.

38. The letter *mem* has a dot in it that indicates that the letter is doubled, although it does not appear twice in the text. The apparent difference between the *u* vowels is insignificant in biblical Hebrew.

39. It is hard to imagine a first-time reader of these biblical passages who is not familiar with the contours of the story.

40. An exploration of the parallel use of the word *sheneihem* (the two of them) with reference to Abraham and Isaac in the story of the Binding of Isaac (Genesis 22:6, 8) lies beyond the scope of this research.

41. Robert Alter, *Genesis: Translation and Commentary* (New York: Norton, 1996), 11; Mitchell, *Genesis*, 6.

42. Speiser, *Genesis*, 23. The uncertain nature of the opening words *af ki* (even so) is discussed by Cassuto (1:144) at length; like Alter (*Genesis*, 11), I find Speiser's resolution of the difficulties preferable to Cassuto's.

43. I have treated the serpent as a neuter noun in English in order to reduce the tendency to ascribe human qualities to the speaking serpent.

44. One of the more fanciful explanations of the serpent's words is, surprisingly, provided by Cassuto, who, ruling out the possibility of a talking serpent, declares the conversation to have taken place "in the woman's mind, between her wiliness and her innocence, clothed in the garb of a parable" (*Commentary*, 1:142). In taking this point of view, Cassuto tacitly supports the strand of rabbinic tradition that would identify the serpent with the woman. See below, this chapter.

See also *Genesis Rabbah* (Theodor and Albeck, 1:195) where the woman is referred to as the serpent of the man.

45. I find Cassuto's suggestion that this is not an amplification, but a restatement, less than convincing (*Commentary*, 1:145). Alter, following most commentators, assumes that Eve has enlarged on God's prohibition (*Genesis*, 11). Assuming that this represents an expansion of God's orders, Levenson explains the possibilities (Levenson, "Genesis," 16–17, vv.3:1b–3).

46. Cassuto suggests that she might have determined the flavor by means of the scent, but that is often difficult to do without piercing the skin of the fruit (*Commentary*, 1:147).

47. Alter, *Genesis*, 12. However, Alter translates the phrase in Genesis 2:9 as "lovely to look at" (*Genesis*, 8). Fox retains the repetition of *nehmad* by translating it as "desirable" in both verses. Everett Fox, trans., intro., commentary, and notes, *The Five Books of Moses* (New York: Schocken, 1995), 19, 21.

48. Alter explains his translation of *nehmad lehaskil*, "lovely to look at," as a variant meaning of the verb *lehaskil*. His reasoning is less than convincing: while it would produce a parallel to the opening phrase, the sequence of the phrases requires not a parallel but an intensification. Using the same words to translate a different phrase in Genesis 2:9 (*Genesis*, 8) further obfuscates the text.

49. Levenson, "Genesis," 17, v. 6.

50. The traditional Jewish cantillation of this verse would have the break fall after the verb "and she ate." The effect is to separate the action of her taking of the fruit and eating it from her giving it to her man and his eating it.

51. Cassuto, *Commentary*, 1:147.

52. See below for the complementary wording in the punishment verse (Genesis 3:16).

53. Cassuto, *Commentary*, 1:148. The examples Cassuto cites are all of a man, a pater-familias, leading his family.

54. A rabbinic euphemism for sexual intercourse.

55. Excerpted from *Genesis Rabbah* 19:3; Theodor and Albeck, 1:171–172.

56. See B. Sanhedrin 38b for an outline of how the *adam* and the woman spent the twelve hours of their first day.

57. See, for example, *Genesis Rabbah* 9:7 (Theodor and Albeck, 1:71–72) where the desire for evil is credited with moving humans to marry, establish homes, and bear children, but is not linked to eating the forbidden fruit.

58. Because the masoretic vocalization does not indicate a definite article here, this *adam* is conventionally seen as a proper noun. It could, of course, be an error in vocalization and really mean "the *adam*."

59. There is some confusion as to the meaning of this word in the original and a number of manuscript variants. This choice makes the most sense.

60. The serpent.

61. Sexual intercourse. See note 43 to this chapter.

62. Excerpted from *Genesis Rabbah* 18:6; Theodor and Albeck, 1:168–169.

63. *"Ein muqdam um'uhar batorah"* (There is nothing early or late in the Torah) is a rabbinic principle indicating that the biblical order is not always chronological. B. Pesaḥim 6b.

64. The serpent's phallic shape seems to be lurking behind this interpretation.

65. Moshe Aryeh Mirkin, ed., *Midrash Rabbah* (Tel Aviv: Yavneh, 1956), 1:133.

66. This reading, following Mirkin, eliminates the nuancing of God's wrath provided by God's dressing Adam and Eve after the punishments (Mirkin, *Midrash Rabbah*, 1:133).

67. Mirkin relies on *Genesis Rabbah* 15:7 (Theodor and Albeck, 1:140–141) in reconstructing this chronology (Mirkin, *Midrash Rabbah*, 1:133).

68. Mirkin, *Midrash Rabbah*, 1:133 points to this opinion as expressed in *Genesis Rabbah* 19:6 (Theodor and Albeck, 1:175).

69. One clear example is the modification of the public liturgical reading of Lamentations to repeat the penultimate verse (5:21) after the completion of the book in order to avoid concluding with the expression of God's rejection in 5:22.

70. Theodor and Albeck, 1:169.

71. See below.

72. R. Simlai's words are repeated in *Genesis Rabbah* 20:8 (Theodor and Albeck, 1:191) where the text is clearer. I am incorporating that text in this translation.

73. The precise meaning of this word is a matter of some dispute. I am following Mirkin, who suggests that it means free from the burden of natural reproduction. Mirkin, *Midrash Rabbah*, 1:137.

74. Excerpted from *Genesis Rabbah* 19:5; Theodor and Albeck, 1:174.

75. The identification of the fruit with the apple so prevalent in Western culture apparently has its origin in the Latin homonyms *malus* (evil) and *malum* (an apple). The rabbis discuss various possibilities, including the grape, which is explained as linked to the verse from Deuteronomy 32:32: "Their grapes are grapes of gall, they have clusters of bitterness." See *Genesis Rabbah* 15:7; Theodor and Albeck, 1:140.

76. The *Even-Shoshan Dictionary* uses this passage in *Genesis Rabbah* as the example of the meaning of the phrase *beyishuv hada'at*, here translated as "with argument ready" (2:723 s.v. *yishuv hada'at*).

77. *Genesis Rabbah* 20:8; Theodor and Albeck, 1:191.

78. *Pirqei Rabbi Eli'ezer*, chapter 13.

79. The Friedlander translation, based on the Epstein manuscript, cites here as a proof text for the stereotyping of men as unyielding in 1 Samuel 25:3, which he notes does not appear in the printed editions (Friedlander, *Pirkê*, 94, especially n.1). Because I do not have the Hebrew, I have bracketed this text in the translation, but not omitted it from consideration because it seems logical that the text would provide a proof text for this assertion.

Abigail and Nabal are also cited in *Genesis Rabbah* 17:2, which is discussed in chapter 1.

80. Dina Stein comments that the Hebrew words "listen to" in this context suggest responding favorably to sexual advances. If that is the case here, it links this midrash with *Genesis Rabbah* 18:6, discussed earlier in this chapter, where the snake is depicted as lusting for the woman and jealous of the man. Dina Stein, *Maxim, Magic and Myth: Pirqei Rabbi Eli'ezer in Light of Research in Folk Literature* (in Hebrew) (Jerusalem: Magnes Press of Hebrew University, 2004), 81. Unfortunately, this book appeared at a point when I could no longer incorporate it fully in my research.

81. *Pirqei Rabbi Eli'ezer*, chapter 13; Friedlander, 94.

82. Another version of this midrash appears in *Pirqei Rabbi Eli'ezer*, chapter 13.

83. Although the word may also mean "colleague" (which, in turn, refers to a scholar), "snake charmer" better fits the context because it would explain the husband's professional interest in snakes and scorpions.

84. *Genesis Rabbah* 19:10; Theodor and Albeck, 1:179–180.

85. Hesiod, *Works and Days*, trans. R. M. Frazer (Norman, Okla.: University of Oklahoma Press, 1983), 98–99. See also Samuel T. Lachs, "The Pandora-Eve Motif in Rabbinic Literature," *Harvard Theological Review* 67 (1974): 341–345.

86. Daniel Boyarin, *Carnal Israel: Reading Sex in Talmudic Culture* (Berkeley and Los Angeles: University of California Press), 86; italics in the original.

87. Ibid., 87.

88. Ibid.

89. Ibid.

90. The Hebrew noun *h.m.ts* could be vocalized either *hamets* (yeast) or *homets* (vinegar). Both Boyarin and Freedman and Simon translate it as "vinegar." Boyarin, *Carnal*, 86; Freedman and Simon, *Midrash Rabbah*, 1:156.

91. This quest for vinegar or yeast is not necessarily as innocent as Freedman and Simon suppose when they assume that she is a poor woman who has come for some vinegar into which she intends to dip her bread. Freedman and Simon, *Midrash Rabbah*, 1:156 n.2. Mirkin's proposal that she is a woman who uses her quest as an excuse to enter another woman's home to make trouble there is more than likely correct (Mirkin, *Midrash Rabbah*, 1:142). The woman professes no ongoing interest in vinegar, but seems more interested in acidic gossip.

92. The Hebrew noun *h.b* [or *v*].*r* can be vocalized either *haver* (literally a colleague, but in rabbinic circles, a scholar) or *habbar* (snake charmer). The former would connect the husband

with R. Levi's world, but, Boyarin and Freedman notwithstanding, I agree with Mirkin that the proper translation is "snake charmer."

93. See below, this chapter.

94. "On the other hand, this text provides a powerful example of androcentrism at the same time that it subverts misogyny, for it emphasizes that the culturally significant moment is Adam's eating of the fruit not Eve's" (Boyarin, *Carnal*, 87). Like Boyarin, I have focused on the *Genesis Rabbah* text, rather than the one in *Avot deRabbi Natan,* which forms the basis of Aschkenasy's argument. Nehama Aschkenasy, *Eve's Journey* (Philadelphia: University of Pennsylvania Press, 1986), 43–45.

95. The presence of fig trees in the Garden leads some rabbis to speculate that the forbidden fruit itself was actually a fig. *Genesis Rabbah* 15:7, Theodor and Albeck, 1:140.

96. I agree in part with Cassuto that "the cognition that had seemed so desirable to them as to warrant transgression, for its sake, of the Creator's precept, appeared to them, once they had received it, vastly different from what they had originally imagined." He does, unfortunately from my perspective, make the assumption that the man's eating of the fruit was as intentional as the woman's. His further statement: "The first knowledge they acquired was the wretched and grieving realization that they were naked" (*Commentary*, 1:148) is not warranted by the text, which contains no indication that the knowledge itself was in any way upsetting to the primal couple. They seem to go about remedying their situation in a rather straightforward manner.

97. Another place where a singular verb has a compound subject is Numbers 12:1, where the compound subject, Miriam and Aaron, governs the feminine singular verb, "spoke." The argument that in both these cases the verb agrees with the proximate subject simply moves the question to the order of the elements in the compound subject.

98. R. Shim'on ben Lakish suggests that the blasphemy implicit in the *adam's* trying to implicate God causes his banishment from the Garden (*Genesis Rabbah* 19:12 [Theodor and Albeck, 1:182]).

99. *Mah zot 'asit.*

100. Cassuto, *Commentary,* 1:158.

101. Ibid.

102. Another possible explanation for the silence might be that the woman is less culpable because she did not hear the command directly from God.

103. God's second question to the *adam* contains a similar subordinate clause.

104. Aschkenasy asserts that the woman's ability to reason and articulate her response to God's question and the complexity of her language set her apart as a thinking individual. Her suggestion that the woman is really saying, "therefore I ate," while the *adam,* using the same words, is saying simply, "and I ate" is, however, less than compelling. Aschkenasy, *Woman*, 128–129.

105. Helmer Ringgren, *"n.sh.'*,*"* in *Theological Dictionary of the Old Testament,* ed. G. Johannes Botterweck, Helmer Ringgren, and Heinz-Josef Fabry, trans., Douglas W. Stott (Grand Rapids, Mich.: Eerdmans, 1999), 10:54.

106. Cassuto claims that the reason for this is to avoid giving any credence to the "ancient mythologies" in which the serpent and monsters are "sovereign entities that rise in revolt against the Creator and oppose His will." Cassuto, *Commentary,* 1:158.

107. Ibid., 162.

108. Ibid., 163; italics in original.

109. Carol Meyers, *Discovering Eve: Ancient Israelite Women in Context* (New York: Oxford University Press, 1988), 99, 118.

110. Cassuto points out that the questioning is done in reverse order of the actual actions; the punishments in the same order (*Commentary*, 1:158–159). Cf. *Genesis Rabbah* 20:3 (Theodor and Albeck, 1:183) in which R. Ḥiyya is cited as explaining that "when discussing misconduct one starts with the least important [literally, smallest]."

111. Cassuto correctly points out that the punishments of both the serpent and the *adam* involved eating because their misdeeds involved eating. He neither notes nor explains why the woman, as prime eater, is spared (*Commentary*, 1:160). He points to the five times God uses the verb *'.kh.l* (to eat) while speaking to the *adam* (*Commentary*, 1:168).

112. Interestingly, along these lines there is a passage in *Genesis Rabbah* 20:2 (Theodor and Albeck, 1:183) that explains that God did not discuss the malfeasance with the serpent because it could retort: "You commanded them and I commanded them. Why did they abandon Your commands and go along with mine?"

113. Meyers, *Discovering*, 98.

114. Ibid., 100.

115. Meyers points out that it serves the function of an adverb in English (ibid., 99). It is one of the devices through which Hebrew compensates for its paucity of adverbs.

116. Speiser, who goes so far as to consider this "a parade example of hendiadys," would translate it "your pangs that result from your pregnancy." Speiser, *Genesis*, 24.

117. Meyers, *Discovering*, 101–103. Cassuto would also see the terms as separate, rather than as a hendiadys. He sees the suffering as general, rather than specific to childbearing (*Commentary*, 1:165).

118. Meyers, *Discovering*, 104–106.

119. See, for example, Genesis 29:31, 30:22.

120. For a description of biblical parallelism used this way see Robert Alter, *The Art of Biblical Poetry* (New York: Basic Books, 1985), 3–26.

121. I differ with Meyers who argues that *teledi,* ordinarily translated as "give birth," here refers instead to the complex process of having children and raising them. While there are examples in the Bible that support her argument, it seems to me that the preponderant situation when the verb is used as it is here (in the feminine *qal* form as a transitive verb) is to give birth. Meyers, *Discovering*, 106.

122. Ibid., 106–109. Cassuto suggests that the words *'itsavon* and *'etsev* are used here instead of the normal lexical markers of birth to help the reader keep in mind that it was all connected with the *'ets* or tree (*Commentary*, 1:165).

123. The Song of Songs, with its parallel roles, is an exception.

124. Meyers's observation that the absence of a verb in this clause indicates the continuation of an existing situation rather than a change implies that the future tense of the verbs in the other three clauses represents a change (Meyers, *Discovering*, 110). I am reluctant to take this route.

125. Meyers suggests that it specifically counteracts the negative aspects of the burden of increased toil, childbearing, and child-rearing described in the first half of the verse (ibid., 113).

126. Meyers characterizes it as "perhaps the most problematic in all the Hebrew Bible from a feminist perspective" (ibid., 113).

127. "Rather, in light of an understandable reluctance on the part of women to enter into the risks of pregnancy and birth, and because of the social and economic necessity that she do so frequently, the male's will within the realm of sexuality is to be imposed on the will of the female." Meyers proposes the translations "And he shall overrule you" or "And he shall predominate over you" (ibid., 116–117).

128. Ibid., 121.

129. In words describing sin that are somewhat obscure, God admonishes Cain that if he does not do the right thing, "*lapetaḥ ḥattat rovets ve'elekha teshuqato ve'attah timshol bo*" (sin lies in wait at the opening and its desire is to you and you will overrule it) (Genesis 4:7). This is usually read as indicating Cain's capacity for controlling sin's desire for him. The parallel syntactic position of sin and woman in these verses could give rise to further negative valuations of the woman.

130. Cassuto points to the fact that the woman is mentioned at the end of the words to the serpent, indicating that the speaker is about to focus on her; similarly, the man comes up at the end of the words to the woman (*Commentary*, 1:66).

131. "The primal couple have left the magical garden of their childhood and their innocence and entered into the harsh world of adulthood with its painful realities." Levenson, "Genesis," 17–18, vv. 14–19.

132. It is facile to explain this problem by turning to the gendered nature of Hebrew. On the one hand, the development of a language as neuter-free necessarily reflects something of the worldview of its speakers; on the other hand, the use of the plural, "the two of them," would also have served to resolve these issues.

133. The Talmud sees this as a paradigmatic act of lovingkindness on God's part, one that humans would do well to emulate (B. Sotah 14a).

134. Sarna, *JPS Genesis*, 29, s.v. "garments."

135. Cassuto points to the triple mention of nakedness: the closing of the verses dealing with the creation of woman (Genesis 2:25), as well as the framing of this section (Genesis 3:7 and 3:21) (*Commentary*, 1:148–149).

136. Levenson, "Genesis," 18, vv. 20–21.

137. Of particular interest is the play between the shifting use of *adam* as a common and a proper noun. When God metes out the punishments, *adam* has no definite article (Genesis 3:17), leading the reader to assume that it is actually a proper noun; in the subsequent naming of the woman, it reverts to the common noun it has been throughout the narrative (Genesis 3:20). The cycle repeats with the proper noun in Genesis 3:21 and the common noun in verses 22 and 24.

138. Lois E. Bueler, *The Tested Woman Plot* (Columbus, Ohio: Ohio State University Press, 2001), 11–21 and passim.

139. Ibid., 15.

140. Ibid., 16.

141. Ibid., 11.

142. Jung accuses God of "double-faced behavior" in this instance because he points out the tree, and then forbids eating its fruit. Carl Gustav Jung, *Answer to Job*, 375, as cited in Bueler, *Tested Woman*, 255 n.21.

143. Bueler sees Eve caught between "two incompatible moral arguments" (ibid., 195).

144. A well-known rabbinic dictum is *al tarbeh siḥah 'im ha'ishah* ("Do not speak a great deal with the woman") (M. Avot 1:5).

145. A term for God, Who is viewed as omnipresent.

146. The aforementioned dictum from M. Avot 1:5 is linguistically linked to the punishment of the woman in Genesis 3:16 through the use of the word *tarbeh* (you will multiply), which is the second-person form of the verb *arbeh* (I will multiply) that God uses in Genesis 3:16.

147. Although this midrash appears in *Genesis Rabbah* 20:6 (Theodor and Albeck, 1:188), I have cited the version that appears in J. Sotah because it is clearer (J. Sotah 7:1; Academy for Hebrew Language edition, 2001, col. 933).

148. For a full discussion of the first section of this midrash, see above, chapter 1.

149. The syntax is not completely clear in this text. Parallel texts in J. Sanhedrin 2:3 (Academy for Hebrew Language edition, 2001, col. 1277) and B. Sanhedrin 20a indicate that there was some disagreement about whether men or women walk first in a funeral procession. J. Sanhedrin does suggest that those who say that the women precede base their opinion on Eve's connection to death; however, it also explains that those who claim that the men precede do so to protect "the honor of the daughters of Israel, so that the men not be looking at the women." The discussion in B. Sanhedrin 20a regarding whether the women mourners walk before or after the deceased in a funeral procession raises the possibility of varying local custom but seems to come down on the side of women preceding based on the behavior of King David at the funeral of Avner (2 Samuel 3:31).

150. *Genesis Rabbah* 17:8; Theodor and Albeck, 1:159–160.

151. Boyarin, *Carnal*, 90–91, esp. n.23. See the discussion of the first part of *Genesis Rabbah* 17:8 in chapter 1.

152. Women commonly covered their heads in the ancient Near East and in the Greco-Roman world. Baskin, *Midrashic Women*, 68. For more information on women's headcovering in the ancient Mediterranean basin see Molly Myerowitz Levine, "The Gendered Grammar of Ancient Mediterranean Hair," in *Off with Her Head! The Denial of Women's Identity in Myth, Religion and Culture,* ed. Howard Eilberg Schwartz and Wendy Doniger (Berkeley: University of California Press, 1995), 76–130.

153. See discussion of *Genesis Rabbah* 18:2 in chapter 1, above.

154. Although Baskin discusses the requirement that a married woman's hair be covered in the context of this passage (*Midrashic Women*, 68), this text in *Genesis Rabbah* does not focus on women's hair as a sexual enticement and its consequent covering. It would have been an obvious way to elaborate the first woman's negative legacy. For that reason it is striking that it is omitted.

155. Nissan Rubin indicates that there were two different customs regarding the funeral procession. The custom in Jerusalem had the men who performed the eulogy precede the deceased and the women keeners follow, whereas in Judea the women keeners preceded and the male eulogists followed. See Nissan Rubin, *The End of Life: Rites of Burial and Mourning in the Talmud and Midrash* (in Hebrew) (Tel Aviv: Kibutz Me'uchad, 1997), 193–194 and 307 n.10.

156. The notes to the Soncino translation of *Genesis Rabbah* present a reversal of the plain sense of this misogynistic passage. "The attitude of Judaism towards woman is

shown in these replies. In accordance with scripture, she is charged with having brought death into the world through her disobedience, yet her punishment is not to be accursed, but on the contrary, hers is the privilege to emphasize the inviolate character of woman, to sanctify the bread one eats and spread the cheer of the Sabbath as symbolised by light" (*Midrash Rabbah: Genesis,* 139 n.7).

157. See Leviticus 15:19–33, 18:19, and 20:18.

158. For a discussion of the variety of midrashic explanations for the rules limiting sexual contact during a woman's menstrual cycle and requiring ritual bathing thereafter, see Charlotte Fonrobert, *Menstrual Purity: Rabbinic and Christian Reconstructions of Biblical Gender* (Stanford, Calif.: Stanford University Press, 2000), 29–37 and passim.

159. Baskin, *Midrashic Women,* 71.

160. A man who bakes must separate a portion of the dough; a man may light Shabbat lamps and, indeed, should do so if no one else is performing the ritual on his behalf. As Boyarin notes, these three commandments are linked to women because "they belong particularly to the woman's sphere as understood by the rabbinic culture" (*Carnal,* 92).

161. Numbers 15:20.

162. Yokheved Bat-Miriam, *Poems* (Merḥavyah: Sifriyat Poaʿlim, 1963), 183–186. First published in *Maḥbarot lesifrut* 1:1 (*Shevat* 1940).

163. David C. Jacobson, *Modern Midrash: The Retelling of Traditional Jewish Narratives by Twentieth-Century Hebrew Writers* (Albany, N.Y.: State University of New York Press, 1987), 125.

164. Compare with Miriam in Bat-Miriam's "Miriam," as discussed by Ilana Pardes. In "Miriam," the title figure is found in "resplendent isolation" (Ilana Pardes, "Yocheved Bat-Miriam: The Poetic Strength of a Matronym," in *Gender and Text in Modern Hebrew and Yiddish Literature,* ed. Naomi B. Sokoloff, Anne Lapidus Lerner, and Anita Norich (New York: Jewish Theological Seminary, 1992), 53.

165. The NJPS translation of *ḥayyat-hasadeh* (Genesis 2:19), the term Bat-Miriam uses, is "wild beasts."

166. Although the word *ed* is translated as "flow" in Genesis 2:6, it is used here in the sense of "mist," parallel to "vapor."

167. The word *hevel,* used here as a parallel to "mist," is also the Hebrew name rendered as Abel in English.

168. Yokheved Bat-Miriam, *Poems* (in Hebrew) (Merḥavyah: Sifriyat Poʿalim, 1972), 185–186. While the translation is mine, I have consulted the translation provided by Wendy Zierler, *And Rachel Stole the Idols: The Emergence of Modern Hebrew Women's Writing* (Detroit, Mich.: Wayne State University Press, 2004), 64–65 and the phrases translated by David C. Jacobson in *Modern Midrash: The Retelling of Traditional Jewish Narratives by Twentieth-Century Hebrew Writers* (Albany, N.Y.: State University of New York Press, 1987), 124–129.

169. An example is her use of the unusual present *qal* forms *noshemah* (line 1), *noshevah* (line 4), *nogeʿah* (line 5), *osefah* (line 15), instead of the common *noshemet, noshevet, nogaʿat,* and *osefet* forms. Ruth Kartun-Blum suggests that Bat-Miriam uses unusual verb forms for aural effect. Kartun-Blum, *Receding Horizons: Studies in the Poetry of Yokheved Bat-Miriam* (in Hebrew) (Ramat-Gan: Massada, 1977), 70 n.21.

170. Ibid., 54. Kartun-Blum considers her the most Proustian of modern Hebrew writers.

171. Kartun-Blum sees the conservative strophic form as key to the tension in the poems of Bat-Miriam's *Figures on the Horizon* (in Hebrew) (1942) collection. Kartun-Blum, *Receding*, 22, 34.

172. Second and fourth lines rhyme throughout, although the rhymes are less rich in the second, fourth, and sixth stanzas than in the first, third, and fifth. There is generally assonance in the first and third lines.

173. The poem is written in dactylic trimeter; the first and third lines in each stanza end in "feminine" rhymes.

174. Zierler discusses Bat-Miriam's presentation of time as flexible and fluid in her discussion of "The Darkness of the Void" (in Hebrew), an earlier poem about Eve. Wendy I. Zierler, *And Rachel Stole the Idols: The Emergence of Modern Hebrew Women's Writing* (Detroit, Mich.: Wayne State University Press, 2004), 61.

175. Bat-Miriam's use of *yereq*, a noun that means "greenery," conforms to Kartun-Blum's observation that green in Bat-Miriam's poetry is linked to growth and life as distinct from death; *Receding*, 134.

176. See Genesis 3:5–3:7 and the discussion earlier in this chapter.

177. Kartun-Blum comments on the prevalence of synesthetic connections in Bat-Miriam's poetry; *Receding*, 47.

178. Kartun-Blum sees this as part of Bat-Miriam's vision of the world as a boundless unity; *Receding*, 33.

179. For a full discussion of this naming, see below, "Naming the Woman."

180. This is the only appearance of this verb root in the Hebrew Bible.

181. See the biblical use in Isaiah 11:8.

182. "The wicked are defiant from birth; the liars go astray [*ta'u*] from the womb."

183. Jacobson, *Modern*, 124–127.

184. I take issue with Jacobson's translation and interpretation that would have Eve happier, or perhaps more at peace, than Adam (Jacobson, *Modern*, 126).

185. As related in the Mishnah, Honi would draw a circle and stand in its center until God fulfilled his request, most often for rain. Once, when the rain had lasted too long, causing flooding, he was taken to task by the head of the Sanhedrin, Shim'on ben Shetah, who, noting that Honi's actions merited excommunication, said: "But what can I do to you, for you implore [*mithattei*] the Place [God] and He does what you will, like a son who implores his father and he does his will" (M. Ta'anit 3:8).

Bat-Miriam's use of *mithattei* is difficult to translate, as it could come from either of two roots with the same letters but different meanings. Jacobson uses "forgiving," probably basing his translation on the more common meaning derived from *h.t.'* ("sin," but here meaning "purified") (Jacobson, *Modern*, 126). Zierler, while acknowledging the closeness to that root, chooses "preening," extrapolating from the rarer root, which generally means "beg" or "cajole" (Zierler, *And Rachel*, 61). I have chosen "wheedle," derived from the second root, because it conveys the image of a spoiled child implicit in Honi's tale and appropriate to this context.

186. Zierler sees in this word an oblique allusion to the word *vayitser*, used to describe God's creation of the *adam* (Genesis 2:7) (*And Rachel*, 67).

187. See, for example, Joseph's dream in which the father is the sun; the mother, the moon (Genesis 37:9–10).

188. Zierler, *And Rachel*, 67.

189. "Who Holds in Hand," in *High Holy Day Prayer Book* (in Hebrew), ed. Daniel Goldschmidt (Jerusalem: Koren, 1970), 1:225.

190. *Jewish Women's Literary Annual* 4 (2000–2001): 21.

191. For example, Sarna, *JPS Genesis*, 23.

192. The namings of Eve and Adam's children will be discussed in chapter 3.

193. The NJPS translation "earth" is misleading here: one might assume that the Hebrew was *adamah*, later to be connected to *adam*, rather than *erets*.

194. Cassuto, *Commentary*, 1:27; italics in original.

195. Alter, *Genesis*, 5.

196. Conceding that most scholars think that these are simply errors in the masoretic vocalization, Cassuto presents a complicated theory to explain the lack of definite article vocalization for the prepositions preceding *adam* in Genesis 2:20, 3:17, and 3:21. He compares *adam* to *Elohim*, which can mean either the specific, proper noun, God of Israel, or the generic "gods." In the case of *Elohim*, he claims that the vocalization of the prepositions does not follow the definite article formula. (*Commentary*, 1:166–167).

197. This provides an intriguing parallel to the way that most women in the Hebrew Bible remain nameless; see Nehama Aschkenasy, *Woman at the Window* (Detroit, Mich.: Wayne State University Press, 1998), 120.

198. Regarding the "wild beasts and the birds of the sky," the text says: *vayavei* (and he brought) (Genesis 2:19); regarding the second human, the text says *vayivi'eha* (and he brought her) (Genesis 2:22).

199. See Genesis 1:21, 24; 2:19. The facile assumption that the names are of species and not of individual animals is challenged by the American poet Anthony Hecht, who proposes that the names the *adam* bestows upon the animals are proper names. Thus, for example, he concludes his sonnet "Naming the Animals" with Adam's looking at the cow and saying: "Thou shalt be called Fred." Reprinted in David Curzon, ed. and trans., *Modern Poems on the Bible: An Anthology* (Philadelphia: Jewish Publication Society, 1994), 61.

200. A full treatment of the rest of this passage can be found in chapter 1.

201. See above, chapter 1. While the text does imply that the woman is created to be a help for the *adam*, to alleviate his loneliness, it says nothing about the institution of marriage.

202. In this context Ḥayyah might mean "living thing, i. e., life personified, or propagator of life." Sarna, *JPS Genesis*, 29, s.v. "Eve."

203. The rabbis occasionally refer to Eve as Adam's serpent. See *Genesis Rabbah* 20:11 (Theodor and Albeck, 1:195); 22:2 (Theodor and Albeck, 1:205).

204. An interesting parallel with Jacob, whose new name does not seem to stick consistently, is that each of them receives a second name after having challenged God (or in Jacob's case, a divine being). Each of them receives the second name at a literally liminal point: Eve as she exits Eden to enter the "real" world; Jacob, as he crosses the Jabbok (Genesis 32:28–29).

205. God's concern that humans may yet become immortal gives the lie to those who argue that humans were designed to be immortal, incurring death only because of the eating of the fruit of the forbidden tree. Levenson, "Genesis," 18, vv. 22–24.

206. *New Yorker,* November 12, 2001, 78.

207. Genesis 3:11–24.

208. Genesis 1:28.

209. See *Genesis Rabbah* 8:5; Theodor and Albeck, 1:60.

210. "A fabulous serpent said to be three spans long, with a spot on its head like a crown." M. G. Easton, *Illustrated Bible Dictionary* (New York: Harper and Brothers, 1895), 84, s.v. "basilisk." The word, which appears in many Bible translations, comes from the Greek *basileus* (king).

211. Barbara G. Walker, *The Woman's Dictionary of Symbols and Sacred Objects* (Edison, N.J.: Castle, 1988), 235, s.v. "basilisk."

212. Sally Frank, in her article using Eve's story as an example of the importance of narrative in legal work, presents youth as one of a number of possible legal defenses Eve might have used. Sally Frank, "Eve Was Right to Eat the 'Apple': The Importance of Narrative in the Art of Lawyering," *Yale Journal of Law and Feminism* 8, no. 1 (1996): 101–104.

CHAPTER 3. EVE BEYOND THE GARDEN

1. Dan Pagis, *Metamorphosis* (in Hebrew) (Ramat-Gan: Makor, 1970), 22. Although Hebrew has no upper-case letters, I have used them in the title to convey a sense of its formal, structured language. The informal idiom of the poem itself is conveyed through the use of lower-case letters in the text of the poem. Stephen Mitchell does the same in his translation in Dan Pagis, *Points of Departure* (Philadelphia: Jewish Publication Society, 1981), 22.

2. Karl A. Plank, "Scripture in a Sealed Railway-Car: A Poem of Dan Pagis," *Journal of Literature and Theology* 7, no. 4 (December 1993), 356. He finds in Pagis's recasting of the Genesis narrative an example of Primo Levi's assertion that the stories of Holocaust victims and survivors are "the stories of a new Bible," affirming "both continuity and discontinuity" (355).

3. A detailed analysis of the "deliberate artifice" of this title is found in Naomi Sokoloff, "Transformations: Holocaust Poems in Dan Pagis' *Gilgul,*" *Hebrew Annual Review* 8 (1984): 216–217.

4. Rivkah Ma'oz, "Synonymous Texts: Intertextuality in the Poem 'Written in Pencil in the Sealed Boxcar' " (in Hebrew), *'Itton 77* 11, no. 90 (July 1987): 23.

5. Removing the *-on* suffix from *qaron,* which came into Hebrew from the Greek in the rabbinic period, leaves *qar,* which means "cold" in Hebrew. Although the transports took place in all seasons, this might imply that the scene invoked is the bleak, snow-covered landscape of winter.

6. A feminist reading of the connection between Eve and Mary may be found in Mieke Bal's *Lethal Love: Feminist Literary Readings of Biblical Love Stories* (Bloomington, Ind.: Indiana University Press, 1987), 128.

7. David G. Roskies, *Against the Apocalypse: Responses to Catastrophe in Modern Jewish Culture* (Cambridge, Mass.: Harvard University Press, 1984), 249.

8. This is typical of Pagis's approach in the poetry in *Metamorphosis*. As Hamutal Bar-Yoseph notes, "Dans la plupart des poèmes sur l'Holocauste, le destin du peuple juif n'est pas perçu comme un destin unique, mais comme un spécimen du mythe éternel de la bête féroce et de sa proie." Hamutal Bar-Yoseph, "Douze faces d'un poète: 'Douze faces,' anthologie rétrospective de Dan Pagis," *Yod*, no. 18 (1983): 88.

Sokoloff also comments that the use of Eve moves the poem "from the here and now into the eternal present of myth, and the effect of the biblical allusion is to universalize" (Sokoloff, "Transformations," 217). Had Pagis used the story of the Binding of Isaac as his intertext, as do other poets, the poem would have had a more Jewish resonance.

9. Plank discusses at some length the significance of "here" as a "simple deictic marker," but does not discuss it in conjunction with "this." Plank, "Scripture," 357. For him the "here" of the boxcar is distinct from the "there" of the intended reader of Eve's message. I would object that two "theres" exist in this poem. The reader of the poem is necessarily situated outside the boxcar, but the reader of Eve's message, assuming that it is written on the boxcar's wall, is equally necessarily inside it.

"The first word, *kan* [here], while it anchors us in present, does not clearly define a location in time and space." Sokoloff, "Transformations," 217. Further, opening with "*kan*" aurally, though not visually, starts with the opening and closing consonant of Cain.

10. Adam's absence here reminds the reader of his absence from Eve's encounter with the serpent (see chapter 2) and his marginalization at the time of Cain's birth (see below).

11. Perhaps a reference to the way in which during the Holocaust Jewish families were often divided either by the Nazis or trying to escape them.

12. See translation by Stephen Mitchell in Pagis, *Points of Departure*, 22–23. It should also be noted that the phrase "son of man" appears in the Christian Scriptures as an appellation of Jesus; see for example, Matthew 26:45.

13. For example, Ezekiel 37:3, 9. Pagis also refers to Ezekiel's vision of the dry bones in the following poem, "A Draft of a Reparations Agreement" (in Hebrew), lines 10–11, Pagis, *Metamorphosis*, 23.

14. Hebrew text in Hayyim Nahman Bialik, *Collected Poems 1899–1934: Critical Edition* (in Hebrew), edited by Dan Miron with Uzi Shavit, Ziva Shamir, Ruth Shenfeld, and Shmuel Trattner (Tel Aviv: Dvir and Katz Research Institute for Hebrew Literature, Tel Aviv University, 1990), 2:168–174; English text in David G. Roskies, *The Literature of Destruction: Jewish Responses to Catastrophe* (Philadelphia: Jewish Publication Society, 1988), 160–168.

15. Pagis explained that "the poem is based on writing or drawing by those being transported in the deathcars in Auschwitz on the walls of the cars, in order to inform their relatives and friends that they are alive." Report of an interview with the poet in New York, as reported in *Hado'ar*, March 29, 1981, as cited in Rivkah Ma'oz, "Synonymous Texts," 22.

16. Ibid.

17. Ma'oz claims that the possible addressees include Cain, but, unless Cain is a Nazi, he is an unlikely addressee; the odds are against a son's ending up in the same boxcar

that had previously held his mother. Further, the poem has a message to be delivered to Cain. Ma'oz, "Synonymous Texts," 23.

18. Plank avoids the most obvious possibility: her death ("Scripture," 358).

19. On Pagis's use of riddles, see Sidra Dekoven Ezrahi, "Dan Pagis—Out of Line: A Poetics of Decomposition," in *Prooftexts* 10, no. 2 (May 1990): 347 ff.

20. "As such, the witness's silence becomes a mode of listening to the difference of Eve and crafts a vessel through which its resonance may be heard in the world of Cain" ("Scripture," 361).

21. "Autobiography" appeared in Pagis's next collection of poetry, *Brain* (in Hebrew) (1975). For text, see Dan Pagis, *Collected Poems* (in Hebrew) (Jerusalem: Kibbutz Me'uchad, 1991), 165–166; for the translation, see Dan Pagis, *Variable Directions: The Selected Poetry of Dan Pagis*, trans. Stephen Mitchell (San Francisco: North Point Press, 1989), 5–6; for a discussion of the poem in relation to Pagis's Holocaust poetry and his real autobiography see Sidra Dekoven Ezrahi, "Dan Pagis," 335–363.

22. Ma'oz points out that this may be one of the paradoxes Pagis so enjoyed; the silence at the end of the poem lends itself to discussion among its readers, to communication. Ma'oz, "Synonymous Texts," 23.

23. The argument for considering the early chapters of Genesis a narrative unit is persuasively made by Ilana Pardes, who makes the point that one reason people tend to read only Genesis 1–3 is the centrality of the Fall to Christian theology. The biblical text, as Pardes indicates, does not include the notion of a Fall. Pardes, *Countertraditions in the Bible: A Feminist Approach* (Cambridge Mass.: Harvard University Press, 1992), 39–40.

24. There are those, including some of the classic Jewish biblical commentators, who opine that the conception and birth of Cain, or of Cain and Abel, actually preceded the exile from Eden. The ambiguity of the biblical verb tense and the rabbinic principle that events are not reported in chronological order in the Bible (see note 63 to chapter 2) allow for that possibility. I prefer to assume that the text here is linear and chronological. See Rashi ad loc. and *Pirqei Rabbi Eli'ezer*, below.

25. "In the opening verses of Genesis 4 we learn that Adam and Eve, after their banishment, make use of the 'knowledge' they acquired back in the Garden. . . . Knowledge, especially in its sexual sense, is no longer an abstract notion." Pardes, *Countertraditions*, 40.

26. Adam had already called the woman *ishah* (woman) (Genesis 2:23). See chapter 2.

27. The common formula is " s/he named called the child's name X; for s/he said . . . (the explanation of the name)." Pardes points out that Eve's giving the naming speech is not exceptional; more women than men give names in the Hebrew Bible and a higher proportion of the women namers give naming speeches. Pardes, *Countertraditions*, 41, 43, and 163 n.2.

28. As we have discussed in chapter 2, Adam's first naming speech represents the apex of his life and power. After that we hear his voice directly only in his blaming God and the woman for his eating the forbidden fruit (Genesis 3:13). His naming the woman Eve and the second report of the naming of Seth (Genesis 5:3) are recorded as indirect discourse.

29. "As name-giver, Eve maintains her prominence" (Kimelman, "Seduction," 20).

30. The Even-Shoshan biblical concordance lists 84 occurrences of this verb, most meaning "buy"; 15 meaning "acquire"; and 6 meaning "create." Genesis 4:1 is not listed in any of the specific meanings.

31. "In poetic diction, which naturally tends to preserve the archaic elements of a language, the full original signification of the root was also retained, especially in connection with two concepts: Divine creation and parental procreation" (*Commentary*, 201). Cassuto's suggestion that the name Cain (*Qayin*) is connected to the word for the blade of a sword (see 2 Samuel 21:16 where the term, a hapax legomenon, is translated as "bronze spear" in the NJPS) would render Cain's name as proleptic as is Abel's (*Commentary*, 1:197–198).

32. Pardes's claim that *qaniti* is derived from a different root—*q.y.n*—seems unnecessary to her argument; the meaning that she ascribes to it, "shape," can be subsumed under the creation meaning of *q.n.y* (*Countertraditions*, 41–42).

33. As discussed above, I do not see Adam as claiming a role in the creation of Eve (Genesis 2:23), but as acknowledging a relationship with her. This is supported by the following verse, which stresses the importance of the woman by predicting a matrilocal society. Pardes, on the other hand, sees Eve using *ish* in her naming speech to challenge the *adam*'s claim of procreative powers when he names her *ishah* by pointing "to the first man as another product of her creativity" (*Countertraditions*, 48).

34. In fact, the appearance of *ish* (man) in the first eleven chapters of Genesis is rare and to be noted. The only additional occurrence is in Lamech's strange speech where it is parallel to *yeled* (male child). Cassuto suggests that, in a sense, Lamech's boast is the antithesis of Eve's cry of jubilation. He is taking pride in having killed someone; she, in having created life (*Commentary*, 1:242–243). Alter's extended discussion of Lamech's song emphasizes the difference between *ish* and *yeled* in this verse. He concludes that *yeled* carries with it "a stress on the tenderness and vulnerability of the child" (*Art of Biblical Poetry*, 5–18, particularly 12).

35. Abel has no children and Cain's descendants are all wiped out in the Flood.

36. Pardes discusses the difference between God's role in Cain's birth and God's role in other contexts (*Countertraditions*, 44).

37. In truth, Pardes, while acknowledging her debt to Cassuto, goes far beyond his assessment. He says: "In light of the foregoing, it is possible to understand the verse with complete clarity: the first woman, in her joy at giving birth to her first son, boasts of her generative power, which approximates in her estimation to the Divine creative power" (*Commentary*, 1:201). Pardes's words here are quite unequivocal: "By defining herself as a creatress, she now calls into question the preliminary biblical tenet with respect to (pro)creation—God's position as the one and only Creator" (*Countertraditions*, 46). Pardes's approach would have Eve guilty of blasphemy; Cassuto's, only of pride.

38. Pardes, following Cassuto, emphasizes the similarity of this phrase to the title of "Ashera, the Ugaritic mother goddess: *qnyt ʾilm*, 'the creatress/bearer of gods.'" From Cassuto, reinforced by subsequent scholars, she concludes that "Eve is endowed with traits which in pagan works characterize the creatress" (*Countertraditions*, 45; Cassuto, *Commentary*, 1:200). While not challenging her evidence and agreeing that it may be "a trace from

an earlier mythological phase," I would read it a bit differently to note that Eve stakes her claim to the creation of a man, not a god, and recognizes God's partnership.

39. It is tempting to read into Eve's words some emotion: joy, surprise, shock, pride, and so forth, but the Hebrew Bible here characteristically provides the words without the tone.

40. There is a rabbinic line of reasoning, obviously motivated by the need to account for the females with whom first Cain and then Seth develop their lines, which posits that there were five births, as Cain and Abel were born with one and two sisters, respectively, represented by the word *et*. See *Genesis Rabbah* 22:2, 3, Theodor and Albeck 1:205–206, and below. Speculation can be tantalizing, but is not necessarily convincing.

41. See *Genesis Rabbah* 22:3; Theodor and Albeck 1:206.

42. Cassuto suggests that this may be a remnant of fratriarchy (*Commentary*, 1:202).

43. Ibid., 202; Pardes, *Countertraditions*, 164 n.8.

44. In legal sections of the Pentateuch, including those relating to sacrifices, there is a clear preference for the firstborn.

45. Jon D. Levenson proposes that the preference of Abel may reflect "the high regard for shepherds and the pastoral life" in ancient Israel ("Genesis," 18, vv. 3–5).

46. On the reversal of the biblical law of primogeniture in Genesis, see Alter, *Art of Biblical Narrative*, 6.

47. Pardes suggests that "the tragedy which befalls Eve's sons is meant, among other things, as a retributive deflation of her hubris. The son who was the object of her (pro)creative pride turns out to be the destroyer of her creation" (*Countertraditions*, 53). To this I would add that Eve's use of *ish* adds another layer to her offense.

48. The Hebrew word *ba'al*, here translated as "husband," also means owner, that is, the one who takes sexual possession of a woman.

49. Samma'el, who had been "the great prince in heaven" according to this midrash, rebelled against God and joined forces with the serpent. See *Pirkê de Rabbi Eliezer*, trans. and annotated by Gerald Friedlander (London, 1916. New York: Hermon, 1965), 92 and passim.

50. A term used for sexual intercourse.

51. Although some texts use "prophesied" here, I prefer, following other manuscripts, to use "looked," which better fits the portrayal of Eve.

52. Excerpted from *Pirqei Rabbi Eli'ezer*, chapter 21. Original text from Eshkol edition. Translation mine. See *Pirkê de Rabbi Eliezer*, chapter 21, 150–151 and 151 n.4 for manuscript variants.

53. *Genesis Rabbah* 22:2; Theodor and Albeck, 1:205.

54. This rabbinic solution is a minefield; it ends up implying an endorsement of incest that then has to be explained, as it is in *Pirkê de Rabbi Eliezer*, chapter 21 (Friedlander trans., 152) where it is linked to Leviticus 20:17 and explained as a situation that applied only in that first generation of humans born on earth.

55. *Genesis Rabbah* 22:7; Theodor and Albeck, 1:213–214.

56. The putative first Eve, who is not Lilith, is mentioned in *Genesis Rabbah* 18:4 (Theodor and Albeck, 1:163–164) in a statement attributed to the same Yehudah son of Rabbi. He suggests that initially God presented the newly created woman to the man who, seeing her covered with discharge and blood, was not interested. God then re-created her, leading Adam, upon seeing her, to exclaim: "This one, this time" (Genesis

2:23). Part of this midrash is also recorded in *Genesis Rabbah* 17:7 (Theodor and Albeck, 1:158), where it is attributed to R. Yose.

57. In terms of the Torah, sexual relations between siblings are also clearly banned as incestuous. Perhaps positing that the woman Cain and Abel are quarreling over is their sibling does not add a new layer of incest here, as it is widely assumed that Cain must have had relations with one of his sisters in order to have children.

58. See Genesis 21:8–10, 27:5–17, and 42–45, respectively.

59. If one accepts the biblical chronology, Seth was born when Adam was 130 years old (Genesis 5:3). Cain and Abel were born after the banishment from the Garden of Eden. There is no calculation of how many years intervened between the murder of Abel and the birth of Seth, but the detailed genealogy of Cain that intervenes might lead the reader to assume that a fair amount of time had elapsed.

The first time a notice of mourning is recorded in the Bible follows the death of Sarah (Genesis 23:2). *Pirkê de Rabbi Eliezer,* chapter 21 (Friedlander trans., 156) supplies a brief picture of parental mourning, obviously in response to both the halakhic and the emotional exigencies. "Adam and his helpmate were sitting and weeping and mourning for him, and they did not know what to do [with Abel], for they were unaccustomed to burial." A raven appears to show them what to do by burying a dead raven. Adam follows suit and buries Abel; Eve is not mentioned further.

In his poem "Autobiography," cited above, Dan Pagis, perhaps based on *Pirqei Rabbi Eli'ezer,* has the first-person narrator, who is Abel, claim:

"The raven taught my parents
what to do with me.

If my family is famous,
not a little of the credit goes to me.
My brother invented murder, my parents invented grief.
I invented silence."

(*Collected Poems* 165–166)

60. See *Genesis Rabbah* 20:11 or 24:6; Theodor and Albeck, 1:195–196 or 235–236.

61. The NJPS translation puts the words "for Cain had killed him" outside Eve's direct discourse, a choice for which, particularly given the emotional nature of Eve's speech, I find no textual basis.

62. Cassuto explains at greater length the way in which these verses parallel and complete the opening verse of the chapter with its description of the birth of Cain (*Commentary,* 1:190–191).

63. Cassuto seems somewhat conflicted in his reading of these verses. In his introduction to this section he characterizes them as providing the requisite happy ending in which "Adam and Eve found solace after losing their first two sons in one day and how they saw, despite the terrible calamity that befell them in the death of Abel and the banishment of Cain, the realization of the divine promise concerning procreation" (*Commentary,* 1:190–191). Yet, in his analysis of the specific verse, he states: "Eve's mood is one of mourning and sorrow for the family calamity" (ibid., 245–246). Pardes, disagreeing with Cassuto, says that it is "primarily a celebration of birth, even if toned down" (*Countertraditions.* 52).

64. "Unlike the wonder and joy expressed at that other birth, this statement is one of resignation and perhaps acceptance of the fact that the serpent's head may not be bruised soon." Kenneth R. R. Gros Louis, "Genesis 3–11," in *Literary Interpretations of Biblical Narratives*, Vol. 2 (Nashville, Tenn.: Abingdon 1982) 44.

65. Cassuto provides a chart drawing the parallels between these two verses concerning the birth and future progeny of Seth and the verse heralding Cain (*Commentary*, 1:245). Cassuto reads into the narrative the reaction of the grandparents, Adam and Eve, to the birth of Enosh: "But on the birth of Enosh, when Adam and Eve perceived that not only had a third son been born to them to replace the first two sons whom they had lost, but that, as additional compensation, they had been vouchsafed a grandson through their third son, forming the beginning of a new generation and bringing incipient hope for the future, they were comforted from their mourning" (ibid., 247). There is scant textual basis for this; none for Eve's having lived to see this grandson, as we have no indication of her lifespan or death.

66. See Pardes, *Countertraditions*, 51.

67. Perhaps in recognition of the traditional cantillation, which puts the break in the verse before the last clause, the NJPS puts the last clause of Genesis 4:25 outside the quotation marks indicating Eve's speech. I see no reason to assume that clause is an editorial explanation rather than part of Eve's naming speech.

68. A similar instance of the suppression of grief is in Leviticus 10:3 when Aaron is reported to have reacted to the death of his two sons, Nadav and Avihu, in silence.

69. By name and as the pronominal, accusative suffix of the verb *harag* (killed).

70. Maimonides defines true repentance as finding oneself in the same situation in which one had erred and acting correctly instead of repeating the error.

71. Pardes points to this parallel and to the divine naming of Adam in the previous verse (*Countertraditions*, 57). She reasonably enough attributes the many contradictions in these narratives to the difference between the *J* and *P* theologies and narratives.

Pirqei Rabbi Eli'ezer claims that not only was Cain "not of Adam's seed" but also that "until Seth was born, who was after his father Adam's likeness and image," Adam did not have a child in his "likeness and image." That leaves open the question of Abel's birth and the role in it that has already been ascribed to Adam (*Pirqei Rabbi Eli'ezer*, chapter 21; Friedlander trans., 158).

72. The genealogy verses that summarize Adam's life are quite detailed as they provide us with his age at Seth's birth, the number of years he lived after that birth, and the total number of years he lived (Genesis 5:3–5). The Bible does not mention his burial; burial description is first provided after Sarah's death. *Pirqei Rabbi Eli'ezer*, which fills in some of that detail, indicates that Adam built a mausoleum for himself before he died. The site was the Cave of Makhpelah where Sarah, Abraham, Isaac, Rebecca, Leah, and Jacob would later be buried. According to that text, based on earlier sources, Eve is also interred there (*Pirqei Rabbi Eli'ezer*, chapter 22; Friedlander trans., 148).

73. See Genesis 23:1–20; 49:31; 35:19. Of course, we do have the story of Eve's "birth" and not theirs.

74. Pardes, who deftly challenges Bal's omitting chapters 4 and 5 from her reading of Eve and thus missing Eve's rise to power through naming, understates her fall from power. "Contra Mieke Bal, the one feminist critic with whom I will engage in a more

extensive dialogue, I would argue that Eve's impressive comeback as a name-giver in Genesis 4—and not the emergence of the proper name Eve—is the final stroke in the formation of the first female character" (*Countertraditions*, 41). Pardes's assessment is also premature as she seems to recognize when, in examining the naming of Seth, she states: "Genesis 4:1 isn't quite the final note in the characterization of the first woman" (ibid., 51).

75. I saw the opera performed at the New York City Opera on November 15, 2001, and have a copy of the libretto. Unfortunately there is no nonarchival video copy.

76. *Lilith,* an opera by Deborah Drattell, libretto by David Steven Cohen (unpublished, April 17, 2000), 12.

77. Ibid., 25.

78. Ibid., 26.

79. Itzik Manger, *The Book of Paradise: The Wonderful Adventures of Shmuel-Aba Abervo,* trans. Leonard Wolf (New York: Hill and Wang, 1965), 95.

80. Ibid., 96.

81. Ibid., 98. The notion that the clothes have become impossible to remove may be a parody of the rabbinic tradition that the clothing God made for the man and woman (Genesis 3:21) is made neither from the skins of animals nor from the products of the skins of animals, for example, wool, but are actual human skin (B. Niddah 25a).

82. Manger, *Book of Paradise,* 98.

83. Ibid., 99.

84. Original from Miriam Oren, *After These Things* (in Hebrew) (Merḥavyah: *Sifriyat Po'alim,* 1962), 42. I have consulted the translation by Sue Ann Wasserman in her rabbinic thesis "Women's Voices through the Past and Present," Hebrew Union College-Jewish Institute of Religion, New York, 1987, as published in Ellen Umansky and Dianne Ashton, *Four Centuries of Jewish Women's Spirituality* (Boston: Beacon, 1992), 227.

85. Although Wasserman translates Oren's last word, *levaddo,* as "itself," I have used "alone," which serves as an accurate translation and replicates in the English the circular nature of the Hebrew original, where the last word of the first line is also the last line of the poem.

86. The context in Deuteronomy, a summary of the Israelites' experience in their desert wanderings, moves quickly to a description of the land to which they are going: a land that is reminiscent of Eden in that it has abundant water and fruit (Deuteronomy 8:7–9).

87. The rabbis read Exodus 21:10: "If he marries another [in addition to a wife who had been his father's slave], he must not withhold from this one her food, her clothing or her conjugal rights" as defining the basic, nonnegotiable obligations of a husband to a wife. Oren omits food, having previously mentioned bread, and replaces it with "the light of her eyes."

88. The contrast in English between the "righteous man" and the "strange woman" is less pronounced in the Hebrew where the masculine singular righteous one could be understood as the generic masculine in a language with no means of expressing a neuter. The word for wormwood, *la'anah,* appears eight times in the Hebrew Bible as the bitter taste of disaster (e.g., Deuteronomy 29:17, Jeremiah 9:14, Amos 5:7, Lamentations 3:15). I have chosen Proverbs 5:4 as the primary intertext because of its reference to

the woman and to the sword that recalls the angels with swords stationed to guard the approach to the Tree of Life after the banishment.

89. "She [Oren] writes about difficult things. About memories of madness, death, suicide." Ya'irah Ginossar, "To Tempt, To Tempt Death" (in Hebrew), 'Itton 77 9, nos. 60–61 (January–February 1985): 36. Translation mine.

90. See the list of Hebrew names in the *Even-Shoshan Dictionary* (in Hebrew) (Israel: HaMillon heHadash, 2003), 6:2061c.

91. The convention in modern Hebrew literature is to vocalize poetry, including titles, but not prose.

92. Hebrew from Yaakov Shai Shavit, *Mainly Love Poems: 1996–1997* (in Hebrew) (Jerusalem: Carmel, 1998), 110, translation mine.

93. *Genesis Rabbah* 20:11 records a similar rabbinic folk etymology for *Havvah* that takes the root in the direction of advising: Eve proved to be a poor adviser for Adam.

94. The gender of the first-person speaker cannot be definitively determined on the basis of the line spoken because it includes no gendered Hebrew word. Because the previous stanzas include a male and a female, and the "you" here is feminine, one may deduce that the speaker is male.

95. Marge Piercy, *The Art of Blessing the Day: Poems with a Jewish Theme* (New York: Knopf, 2000), 99–100.

96. See *Genesis Rabbah* 19:2.

97. Kimelman points to a number of similarities between the language used when God confronts and punishes Cain and the parallel verses when God responds to the behavior of the man and woman after their eating the forbidden fruit ("Seduction," 29). I see that as further evidence of the link between eating the fruit and the death of Abel as the punishment for that violation of the divine order.

98. It is worth mentioning that Eve is one of the very few women characters portrayed in the Pentateuch who does not have a fertility problem.

215

WORKS CITED

Alter, Robert. *The Art of Biblical Narrative.* New York: Basic Books, 1981.

————. *The Art of Biblical Poetry.* New York: Basic Books, 1985.

————. *Canon and Creativity.* New Haven, Conn.: Yale University Press, 2000.

————, trans. and commentator. *Genesis.* New York: Norton, 1996.

Anderson, Gary A. *The Genesis of Perfection: Adam and Eve in Jewish and Christian Imagination.* Louisville, Ky.: Westminster, 2001.

Annotated Midrash Rabbah (in Hebrew). Edited by members of the Annotated Midrash Institute. Jerusalem, 1984.

Aschkenasy, Nehama. *Eve's Journey: Feminine Images in Hebraic Literary Tradition.* Detroit, Mich.: Wayne State University Press, 1986.

————. *Woman at the Window.* Detroit, Mich.: Wayne State University Press, 1998.

Auerbach, Erich. *Mimesis.* Translated by Willard Trask. Garden City, N.Y.: Doubleday Anchor Books, 1953.

Bahat, Yaaqov. "The Bible in the Works of Yaakov Fikhman" (in Hebrew). In *Yaakov Fikhman: A Collection of Critical Essays on His Writings* [Hebrew], edited by Nurit Govrin, 133–141. Tel Aviv: Am Oved, 1971.

Bal, Mieke. *Lethal Love: Feminist Literary Readings of Biblical Love Stories.* Bloomington: Indiana University Press, 1987.

Bar-Ilan, Meir. *Some Jewish Women in Antiquity.* Atlanta, Ga.: Scholars Press, 1998.

Bar-Yoseph, Hamutal. "Douze faces d'un poète: 'Douze faces,' anthologie rétrospective de Dan Pagis" (in French). *Yod,* no. 18 (1983): 85–90.

Baskin, Judith R. *Midrashic Women: Formations of the Feminine in Rabbinic Literature.* Hanover, N.H.: University Press of New England/Brandeis University Press, 2002.

Bat-Miriam, Yokheved. *Figures on the Horizon* (in Hebrew). Tel Aviv: Maḥbarot lesifrut, 1942.

————. *Poems* (in Hebrew). Merḥavyah: Sifriyat Poʻalim, 1963.

Ben-Porat, Ziva. "The Poetics of Literary Allusion." *PTL: A Journal for Descriptive Poetics and Theory of Literature* 1 (1976): 105–128.

Beysé, K.-M. "ʻetsem." In *Theological Dictionary of the Old Testament,* edited by Johannes Botterweck and Helmer Ringgren, 11:304–309. Translated by David E. Green. Grand Rapids, Mich.: Eerdmans, 2001.

Bialik, Ḥayyim Naḥman. *Collected Poems 1899–1934: Critical Edition* (in Hebrew), edited by Dan Miron with Uzi Shvit, Ziva Shamir, Ruth Shenfeld, Shmuel Trattner. 3 vols. Tel Aviv: Dvir and Katz Research Institute for Hebrew Liberature, Tel Aviv University, 1990.

Bird, Phyllis A. "'Male and Female He Created Them': Gen 1:27b in the Context of the Priestly Account of Creation." *Harvard Theological Review* 74, no. 2 (1981): 129–159.

Bloom, Harold. *The Book of J.* Translated from the Hebrew by David Rosenberg. New York: Grove Weidenfeld, 1990.

Boyarin, Daniel. *Carnal Israel: Reading Sex in Rabbinic Culture.* Berkeley and Los Angeles: University of California Press, 1993.

———. *Unheroic Conduct: The Rise of Heterosexuality and the Invention of the Jewish Man.* Berkeley and Los Angeles: University of California Press, 1997.

Bratsiotis, N. P. "*ish, ishah.*" In *Theological Dictionary of the Old Testament,* edited by G. Johannes Botterweck and Helmer Ringgren, 1:222–235. Translated by John T. Willis. Grand Rapids, Mich.: Eerdmans, 2003.

Bronner, Leila Leah. *From Eve to Esther: Rabbinic Reconstructions of Biblical Women.* Louisville, Ky.: Westminster John Knox, 1994.

Brown, Francis, with S. R. Driver and Charles A. Briggs. *A Hebrew and English Dictionary of the Old Testament.* Oxford: Clarendon, 1907; reprinted and corrected, 1962.

Bueler, Lois E. *The Tested Woman Plot.* Columbus, Ohio: Ohio State University Press, 2001.

Cassuto, Umberto. *A Commentary on the Book of Genesis,* translated by Israel Abrahams. Part I, From Adam to Noah. Jerusalem: Magnes, 1978.

Chernin, Kim. *The Hunger Song.* London: Menard, 1983.

———. *Reinventing Eve: Modern Woman in Search of Herself.* New York: HarperPerennial, 1994.

Clements, R. E. "*zakhar.*" In *Theological Dictionary of the Old Testament,* edited by G. Joannes Botterweck and Helmer Ringgren, 4:82–87. Translated by David E. Green. Grand Rapids, Mich.: Eerdmans, 2003.

Cohen, Jeremy. "*Be Fertile and Increase, Fill the Earth and Master It*": *The Ancient and Medieval Career of a Biblical Text.* Ithaca, N.Y.: Cornell University Press, 1989.

Curzon, David, ed. *Modern Poetry on the Bible.* Philadelphia: Jewish Publication Society, 1994.

Douay-Rheims Bible. *The Holie Bible Faithfully Translated into English.* 1609–1610.

Drattell, Deborah. *Lilith* [opera]. Libretto, David Steven Cohen. Unpublished, April 17, 2000.

Easton, M. G. *Illustrated Bible Dictionary.* New York: Harper and Brothers, 1895.

Even-Shoshan, Avraham. *A New Concordance* (in Hebrew). Jerusalem: Kiryat-Sepher, 1990.

Even-Shoshan Dictionary (in Hebrew). Edited by Avraham Even-Shoshan and staff. Jerusalem: Even-Shoshan, 2003.

Ezrahi, Sidra Dekoven. "Dan Pagis—Out of Line: A Poetics of Decomposition." *Prooftexts* 10, no. 2 (May 1990): 335–363.

Fabry, Heinz-Josef. "*tsela*ʿ." In *Theological Dictionary of the Old Testament,* edited by G. Johannes Botterweck and Helmer Ringgren, 12:400–405. Translated by Douglass W. Stott. Grand Rapids, Mich.: Eerdmans, 2003.

Fikhman, Yaakov. *Ancient Images* (in Hebrew). Jerusalem: Bialik Foundation, 1948.

———. *The Concept of Modern Poetry and Other Essays* (in Hebrew). Israel: Hebrew Writers Association and Eked, 1982.

———. *A Corner of a Field: Poems* (in Hebrew). Tel Aviv: Schocken, 1944.

Fishbane, Michael. *Text and Texture: Close Readings of Selected Biblical Texts.* New York: Schocken, 1979.

Fonrobert, Charlotte. *Menstrual Purity: Rabbinic and Christian Reconstructions of Biblical Gender.* Stanford, Calif.: Stanford University Press, 2000.

Fox, Everett, trans., intro., commentary, and notes. *The Five Books of Moses*. New York: Schocken, 1995.

———, trans. and commentator. *In the Beginning*. New York: Schocken, 1983.

Frank, Sally. "Eve Was Right to Eat the 'Apple': The Importance of Narrative in the Art of Lawyering." *Yale Journal of Law and Feminism* 8, no. 1 (1996): 79–118.

Freedman, D. N., and M. P. O'Connor. "YHWH." In *Theological Dictionary of the Old Testament*, edited by G. Johannes Botterweck and Helmer Ringgren, 5: 500–521. Translated by David E. Green. Grand Rapids, Mich: Eerdmans, 1986.

Freedman, H., and Maurice Simon, eds. and trans. *Midrash Rabbah: Genesis*. 3d ed. London: Soncino, 1983.

"From the Editors." *Lilith* 1, no. 1 (fall 1976): 3.

Frymer-Kensky, Tikva. "The Dinah Affair." In *Reading the Women of the Bible*, 179–98. New York: Schocken, 2000.

———. *In the Wake of the Goddesses: Women, Culture, and the Biblical Transformation of Pagan Myth*. New York: Fawcett Columbine, 1st Ballantine ed., 1993.

Garr, W. Randall. *In His Own Image and Likeness: Humanity, Divinity and Monotheism*. Boston: Brill, 2003.

Geller, Stephen A. "Blood Cult: Towards a Literary Theology of the Priestly Work of the Pentateuch." *Prooftexts: A Journal of Jewish Literary History* 12, no. 2 (May 1992): 97–124.

Genesis Rabbah [Midrash Bereshit Rabba] (in Hebrew). Edited by Yehuda Theodor and Ḥanokh Albeck. 3 vols. Jerusalem: Wahrmann Books, 1965.

Gilat, Yitzḥak D. "Thirteen Years Old [and Subject] to the Commandments?" (in Hebrew). In *Meḥqerei Talmud: Talmudic Studies*, edited by Yaacov Sussman and David Rosenthal, 1:39–53. Jerusalem: Magnes Press, 1990.

Ginossar, Yaiʾirah. "To Tempt, To Tempt Death" (in Hebrew). *ʾItton 77* 9, nos. 60–61 (January–February 1985): 36.

Goldin, Judah. *The Fathers According to Rabbi Nathan*. New Haven, Conn.: Yale University Press, 1955.

Goldschmidt, Daniel, ed. *High Holy Day Prayer Book*. 2 vols. Jerusalem: Koren, 1970.

Greenstein, Edward L. "An Equivocal Reading of the Sale of Joseph." In *Literary Interpretations of Biblical Narratives*, edited by Kenneth R. R. Gros Louis, 2:114–125. Nashville, Tenn.: Abingdon, 1982.

———. "God's Golem: The Creation of Humanity in Genesis 2." In *Creation in Jewish and Christian Tradition*, edited by Henning Graf Reventflow and Yair Hoffman, 219–239. London: Sheffield Academic Press, 2002.

———. "Presenting Genesis 1, Constructively and Deconstructively." *Prooftexts: A Journal of Jewish Literary History* 21, no. 2 (winter 2001): 1–22.

Gros Louis, Kenneth R. R. "Genesis 3–11." In *Literary Interpretations of Biblical Narratives* (Nashville, Tenn.: Abingdon, 1982), 2:37–52.

Handelman, Susan A. *The Slayers of Moses: The Emergence of Rabbinic Interpretation in Modern Literary Theory*. Albany, N.Y.: State University of New York Press, 1982.

Hauptman, Judith. *Rereading the Rabbis: A Woman's Voice*. Boulder, Colo.: Westview, 1998.

Hecht, Anthony. "Naming the Animals." In *Modern Poems on the Bible: An Anthology*, edited by David Curzon, 61. Philadelphia: Jewish Publication Society, 1994.

Herrmann, Claudine. *Les Voleuses de langue.* Paris: des Femmes, 1976. (English: *The Tongue Snatchers.* Translated with introduction and notes by Nancy Kline. Lincoln: University of Nebraska, 1989.)

Heschel, Abraham Joshua. *God in Search of Man.* New York: Farrar, Straus, and Cudahy, 1955.

Hesiod. *Works and Days.* Translated by R. M. Frazer. Norman, Okla.: University of Oklahoma Press, 1983.

Howe, Irving, Ruth R. Wisse, and Chone Shmeruk, eds. *The Penguin Book of Modern Yiddish Verse.* New York: Viking, 1987.

Jacobson, David C. *Does David Still Play Before You? Israeli Poetry and the Bible.* Detroit, Mich.: Wayne State University Press, 1997.

———. *Modern Midrash: The Retelling of Traditional Jewish Narratives by Twentieth-Century Hebrew Writers.* Albany, N.Y.: State University of New York Press, 1987.

Kartun-Blum, Ruth. *Profane Scriptures: Reflections in Dialogue with the Bible in Modern Hebrew Poetry.* Cincinnati, Ohio: Hebrew Union College, 1999.

———. *Receding Horizons: Studies in the Poetry of Yokheved Bat-Miriam* (in Hebrew). Ramat-Gan: Massada, 1977.

Kasowski, Benjamin. *Thesaurus Talmudis Concordantiae Verborum* (in Hebrew). Vol. 32. Jerusalem, 1975.

Kimelman, Reuven. "The Seduction of Eve and the Exegetical Politics of Gender." *Biblical Interpretation: A Journal of Contemporary Approaches* 4, no. 1 (February 1996): 1–39.

Kugel, James L. *Ideas of Biblical Poetry: Parallelism and Its History.* New Haven, Conn.: Yale University Press, 1981.

———. *Traditions of the Bible.* Cambridge, Mass.: Harvard University Press, 1997.

Labovitz, Gail. "My Wife I Called 'My House': Marriage, Metaphor, and Discourses of Gender in Rabbinic Literature." Ph.D. diss., Jewish Theological Seminary, 2002.

Lachs, Samuel T. "The Pandora-Eve Motif in Rabbinic Literature." *Harvard Theological Review* 67 (1974): 341–345.

Lerner, Gerda. *The Creation of Patriarchy.* New York: Oxford University Press, 1986.

Levenson, Jon D. *Creation and the Persistence of Evil.* Princeton, N.J.: Princeton University Press, 1988.

———. "Genesis: Introduction and Annotations." In *The Jewish Study Bible,* edited by Adele Berlin and Marc Zvi Brettler, 8–101. New York: Oxford University Press, 2004.

———. *Sinai and Zion: An Entry into the Jewish Bible.* San Francisco, Calif.: HarperSanFrancisco, 1987.

Levinas, Emmanuel. *Du sacré au saint: cinq nouvelles lectures talmudiques* (in French). Paris: Editions de Minuit, 1977.

Levine, Molly Myerowitz. "The Gendered Grammar of Ancient Mediterranean Hair." In *Off with Her Head! The Denial of Women's Identity in Myth, Religion and Culture,* edited by Howard Eilberg Schwartz and Wendy Doniger (Berkeley: University of California Press, 1995), 76–130.

Lewis, Charlton T., and Charles Short. *A New Latin Dictionary.* New York: Harper, 1879.

Lighter, J. E., ed. *Random House Historical Dictionary of American Slang.* New York: Random House, 1994.

Maass, Fritz. "*'adam.*" In *Theological Dictionary of the Old Testament,* edited by G. Johannes Botterweck and Helmer Ringgren, 1:75–87. Translated by John T. Willis. Grand Rapids, Mich: Eerdmans, 1977.

Manger, Itzik. *The Book of Paradise: The Wonderful Adventures of Shmuel-Aba Abervo.* Translated by Leonard Wolf. New York: Hill and Wang, 1965.

——. *Clouds over the Roof* (in Yiddish). London: Alenenyu, 1942.

——. *Itzik's Midrash* (in Yiddish). Edited by Chone Shmeruk. Jerusalem: Hebrew University, 1969.

Ma'oz, Rivkah. "Synonymous Texts: Intertextuality in the Poem 'Written in Pencil in the Sealed Boxcar'" (in Hebrew). *'Itton 77* 11, no. 90 (July 1987): 22–23.

Mayer, Günter. "*'.v.h.*" In *Theological Dictionary of the Old Testament,* edited by G. Johannes Botterweck and Helmer Ringgren, 1:134–137. Translated by John T. Willis. Grand Rapids, Mich.: Eerdmans, 1977.

Meacham, Tirzah. "Woman More Intelligent than Man: Creation Gone Awry." *Approaches to Ancient Judaism,* n.s. 5 (1993): 55–67.

Meyers, Carol. *Discovering Eve: Ancient Israelite Women in Context.* New York: Oxford University Press, 1988.

Midrash Bereshit Rabba (in Hebrew). Edited by Yehuda Theodor and Ḥanokh Albeck. Berlin: Itzkovsky, 1912.

——. Edited by Yehuda Theodor and Ḥanokh Albeck. Jerusalem: Wahrman, 1965.

Midrash Rabbah: Genesis. Translated by H. Freedman. 2 vols. London: Soncino, 1983.

Mirkin, Moshe Aryeh, ed. *Midrash Rabbah.* 11 vols. Tel Aviv: Yavneh, 1956.

Miron, Dan. "About the Lyric Poetry of Yaakov Fikhman" (in Hebrew). In *Yaakov Fikhman: A Collection of Critical Essays on His Writings* (in Hebrew), edited by Nurit Govrin, 151–168. Tel Aviv: Am Oved, 1971.

Mitchell, Stephen, trans. *Genesis: A New Translation of the Classic Biblical Stories.* New York: HarperCollins, 1996.

New English Bible. New York: Oxford University Press, 1961.

The New English Bible with the Apocrypha. New York: Oxford University Press, 1971.

Norris, Pamela. *Eve: A Biography.* New York: New York University Press, 1999.

Oden, Robert A., Jr. "Jacob as Father, Husband and Nephew: Kinship Studies and the Patriarchal Narratives." *Journal of Biblical Literature* 102, no. 2 (1983): 189–205.

Oren, Miriam. *After These Things* (in Hebrew). Merḥavyah: Sifriyat Po'alim, 1962.

Ostriker, Alicia Suskin. *The Nakedness of the Fathers.* New Brunswick, N.J.: Rutgers University Press, 1994.

——. *Stealing the Language: The Emergence of Women's Poetry in America.* Boston: Beacon, 1986.

——. "A Triple Hermeneutic: Scripture and Revisionist Women's Poetry." In *Reading the Bible: Approaches, Methods and Strategies,* edited by Athalya Brenner and Carole Fontaine, 164–189. Sheffield: Sheffield Academic Press, 1997.

Pagis, Dan. *Collected Poems* (in Hebrew). Jerusalem: Kibbutz Me'uchad, 1991.

——. *Metamorphosis* (in Hebrew). Ramat-Gan: Makor, 1970.

——. *Points of Departure.* Translated by Stephen Mitchell. Philadelphia: Jewish Publication Society, 1981.

————. *Variable Directions: The Selected Poetry of Dan Pagis*. Translated by Stephen Mitchell. San Francisco, Calif.: North Point, 1989.

Papell, Helen. *Talking with Eve, Leah, Hagar, Miriam*. New York: Jewish Women's Resource Center, 1996.

Pardes, Ilana. *Countertraditions in the Bible: A Feminist Approach*. Cambridge, Mass.: Harvard University Press, 1992.

————. "Yocheved Bat-Miriam: The Poetic Strength of a Matronym." In *Gender and Text in Modern Hebrew and Yiddish Literature*, edited by Naomi B. Sokoloff, Anne Lapidus Lerner, and Anita Norich, 39–63. New York: Jewish Theological Seminary, 1992.

Pastan, Linda. *Aspects of Eve*. New York: Liveright, 1975.

————. *Imperfect Paradise*. New York: Norton, 1988.

Pelikan, Jaroslav. *The Christian Tradition: A History of the Development of Doctrine*. Vol. 1, *The Emergence of the Catholic Tradition (100–600)*. Chicago, Ill.: University of Chicago Press, 1971.

Piercy, Marge. *The Art of Blessing the Day: Poems with a Jewish Theme*. New York: Knopf, 2000.

Pinsker, Sanford. "Family Values and the Jewishness of Linda Pastan's Poetic Vision." In *Women Poets of the Americas: Toward a Pan-American Gathering*, edited by Jacqueline Vaught Brogan and Cordelia Chávez Candelaria. Notre Dame, Ind.: University of Notre Dame Press, 1999.

Pirkê de Rabbi Eliezer. Translated and annotated by Gerald Friedlander. London, 1916; reissued New York: Hermon, 1965.

Pirqei Rabbi Eli'ezer (in Hebrew). Jerusalem: Eshkol, n.d.

Plank, Karl A. "Scripture in a Sealed Railway-Car: A Poem of Dan Pagis." *Journal of Literature and Theology* 7, no. 4 (December 1993): 354–364.

Plato, *Symposium*. Translated with introduction and notes by Alexander Nehamas and Paul Woodruff. Indianapolis, Ind.: Hackett, 1989.

Pollitt, Katha. "The Expulsion." *New Yorker*, November 12, 2001.

Preuss, H. D. "*d.m.h, demut*." In *Theological Dictionary of the Old Testament*. edited by G. Johannes Botterweck and Helmer Ringgren, 3:250–260. Translated by John T. Willis and Geoffrey W. Bromiley. Grand Rapids, Mich.: Eerdmans, 2003.

Ringgren, Helmer. "*'elohim*." In *Theological Dictionary of the Old Testament*, edited by G. Johannes Botterweck and Helmer Ringgren, 1:276–284. Translated by John T. Willis. Grand Rapids, Mich.: Eerdmans, 1977.

————. *n.s.'*. In *Theological Dictionary of the Old Testament*, edited by G. Johannes Botterweck, Helmer Ringgren, and Heinz-Josef Fabry, 10:53–55. Translated by Douglas W. Stott. Grand Rapids, Mich.: Eerdmans, 1999.

Roskies, David G. *Against the Apocalypse: Responses to Catastrophe in Modern Jewish Culture*. Cambridge, Mass.: Harvard University Press, 1984.

————. Introduction to *The World According to Itzik: Selected Poetry and Prose*. Translated and edited by Leonard Wolf, xiii–xlvi. New Haven, Conn.: Yale University Press, 2002.

————. *The Literature of Destruction: Jewish Responses to Catastrophe*. Philadelphia: Jewish Publication Society, 1988.

Ross, Tamar. "Modern Orthodoxy and the Challenge of Feminism." In *Jews and Gender: The Challenge to Hierarchy*. Studies in Contemporary Jewry 16, edited by Jonathan

Frankel, 3–38. Oxford: The Avraham Harman Institute of Contemporary Jewry, Hebrew University of Jerusalem, and Oxford University Press, 2000.

Roth, Joel. "On the Ordination of Women as Rabbis." In *The Ordination of Women as Rabbis,* edited by Simon Greenberg, 127–187. New York: Jewish Theological Seminary, 1988.

Rubin, Nissan. *The End of Life: Rites of Burial and Mourning in the Talmud and Midrash* (in Hebrew). Jerusalem: Kibbutz Me'uchad, 1997.

Rukeyser, Muriel. *Breaking Open.* New York: Random House, 1973.

Sadan, Dov. "Controversy and Its Resolution" (in Hebrew). In Itzik Manger, *Medresh Itzik,* edited by Chone Shmeruk, xiii–xvi. Jerusalem: Hebrew University, 1969.

Sæbø, M. "*pa'am.*" In *Theological Dictionary of the Old Testament,* edited by G. Joannes Botterweck and Helmer Ringgren, 12:44–49. Translated by Douglas W. Stott. Grand Rapids, Mich.: Eerdmans, 2003.

Said, Edward W. *The World, the Text and the Critic.* Cambridge, Mass.: Harvard University Press, 1983.

Sarna, Nahum. *The JPS Commentary: Genesis.* Philadelphia: Jewish Publication Society, 1989.

Schüngel-Straumann, Helen. "On the Creation of Man and Woman in Genesis 1–3: The History and Reception of the Texts Reconsidered." In *A Feminist Companion to Genesis,* edited by Athalya Brenner, 53–76. Sheffield, England: Sheffield Academic Press, 1993.

Schwartz, Howard, and Anthony Rudolf. *Voices Within the Ark.* New York: Avon Books, 1980.

Seebass, Horst. "*bosh.*" In *Theological Dictionary of the Old Testament,* edited by G. Johannes Botterweck and Helmer Ringgren, 2:50–60. Translated by John T. Willis. Grand Rapids, Mich.: Eerdmans, 1977.

Shaked, Gershon. "Modern Midrash: The Biblical Canon and Modern Literature." *AJS Review* 28, no. 1 (2004): 43–62.

Shapira, Amnon. "On the Egalitarian Status of Women in the Bible" (in Hebrew). *Beit Mikra* 44, no. 4 (summer 1999): 309–337.

Shavit, Ya'akov Shai. *Mainly Love Poems: 1996–1997* (in Hebrew). Jerusalem: Carmel, 1998.

Smith, Barbara Herrnstein. *Poetic Closure: A Study of How Poems End.* Chicago: University of Chicago Press, 1968.

Sokoloff, Naomi. "Transformations: Holocaust Poems in Dan Pagis's *Gilgul.*" *Hebrew Annual Review* 8 (1984): 215–240.

Sommer, Benjamin D. "Inner-biblical Interpretation." In *The Jewish Study Bible,* edited by Adele Berlin and Marc Zvi Brettler, 1829–1835. New York: Oxford University Press, 2004.

Speiser, E. A. *The Anchor Bible: Genesis.* Introduction, translation, and notes by E. A. Speiser, xvii–lxxvi. 2d ed. 9th printing. Garden City, NY: Doubleday, 1964.

Spiegelman, Art. *In the Shadow of No Towers.* New York: Pantheon, 2004.

Stanton, Elizabeth Cady. *The Woman's Bible.* Amherst, N.Y.: Prometheus Books, 1999.

Stein, Dina. *Maxim, Magic and Myth: Pirqei Rabbi Eli'ezer in Light of Research in Folk Literature* (in Hebrew). Jerusalem: Magnes Press of Hebrew University, 2004.

Stendebach, F. J. "*tselem.*" In *Theological Dictionary of the Old Testament,* edited by G. Johannes Botterweck and Helmer Ringgren, 12:386–396. Translated by Douglas W. Stott. Grand Rapids, Mich.: Eerdmans, 2003.

Stern, David. "Midrash and Jewish Interpretation." In *The Jewish Study Bible,* edited by Adele Berlin and Marc Zvi Brettler, 1863–1875. New York: Oxford University Press, 2004.

———. *Midrash and Theory: Ancient Jewish Exegesis and Contemporary Literary Studies.* Evanston, Ill.: Northwestern University Press, 1996.

Strack, H[ermann] L[eberecht], and Günter Stemberger. *Introduction to the Talmud and Midrash.* Translated and edited by Markus Bockmuehl. 2d printing. Minneapolis, Minn.: Fortress, 1996.

Supowit, Sandy. "Things Eve Learned from the Serpent." *Jewish Women's Literary Annual* 4 (2000–2001): 21.

The Torah. Philadelphia: Jewish Publication Society, 1962.

The Torah, [The Prophets, the Writings]: A New Translation of the Holy Scriptures According to the Masoretic Text. Philadelphia: Jewish Publication Society, 1962–1968.

Trible, Phyllis. "Depatriarchalizing in Biblical Interpretation." In *The Jewish Woman: New Perspectives,* edited by Elizabeth Koltun, 219–221. New York: Schocken, 1976.

———. *God and the Rhetoric of Sexuality.* Philadelphia: Fortress, 1978.

Tyndale, William. *The First Book of Moses Called Genesis.* Antwerp: M. de Keyser, 1534.

Umansky, Ellen, and Dianne Ashton. *Four Centuries of Jewish Women's Spirituality.* Boston: Beacon, 1992.

Visotzky, Burton L. *Reading the Book: Making the Bible a Timeless Text.* New York: Anchor, 1991.

von Rad, Gerhard. *Genesis: A Commentary.* Rev. ed. Philadelphia: Westminster, 1972.

Walker, Barbara G. *The Woman's Dictionary of Symbols and Sacred Objects.* Edison, N.J.: Castle, 1988.

Wasserman, Sue Ann. "Women's Voices: The Present through the Past." Ordination thesis, Hebrew Union College-Jewish Institute of Religion, 1987.

Wegner, Judith Romney. *Chattel or Person? The Status of Women in the Mishnah.* New York: Oxford University Press, 1988.

Weinberg, Judith. "Lilith Sources." *Lilith* 1, no. 1 (fall 1976): 8, 38.

Weiss, Judy. "An Analysis of the Story of the Creation of Woman in the Palestinian Targumim." M.A. essay, Jewish Theological Seminary, May 2000.

Wentworth, Harold, and Stuart Berg Flexner, comps. and eds. *Dictionary of American Slang.* 2d supp. ed. New York: Crowell, 1975.

Wright, George T. "Hendiadys." In *The New Princeton Encyclopedia of Poetry and Poetics,* edited by Alex Preminger and T. V. F. Brogan, 515–516. Princeton, N.J.: Princeton University Press, 1993.

Zierler, Wendy. *And Rachel Stole the Idols: The Emergence of Modern Hebrew Women's Writing.* Detroit, Mich: Wayne State University Press, 2004.

Zuckoff, Aviva Cantor. "The Lilith Question." *Lilith* 1, no. 1 (fall 1976): 5–10, 38.

INDEX OF SOURCES

225

SUBJECT INDEX

Abel, 74, 142–46, 210n35; birth and naming of, 145–50, 154–55, 209n24, 209nn27–31, 211n59; murder by Cain of, 154–57, 165, 211–12n59, 213n68; personal qualities of, 151

Abigail, 69–70, 101–2

Abraham, 11, 171n7, 175n46, 193n236; Binding of Isaac, 116, 153; burial site of, 213n72; departure from home of, 190n188

Adam, 13, 171n7, 181–82n82; as counterpart to Jesus in Christian tradition, 172n12; death and burial of, 213n72; eating of the apple, 95–96, 200n96; fatherhood of, 144–55, 208n10, 211nn47–51, 211n59, 213nn71–72; genealogy records of, 155–57, 212n65, 213nn71–72; in modern poetic accounts, 77–83, 97, 121–26, 135–37, 162–65; reaction to creation of woman, 78. See also *adam*

adam, 180n65; absence in modern poetry, 31; androgynous nature of, 15, 24–25, 27–30, 37–38, 178nn35–37, 179n45; banishment from Eden of, 20–24, 113–15, 134–39; blessedness of, 61; as collective noun, 25; during Eve's dialogue with the serpent, 96–97; form of, 34–38, 181nn70–72, 181nn75–80, 181–82nn82–84; in the Garden of Eden, 20–24, 66–72, 191n209; grammatical gender of, 131, 174n39, 176n1, 202n137, 206n196; in midrashic accounts, 27–30, 179nn44–54; nakedness and clothing of, 114, 116, 158–59, 202n135, 214n81; naming of, 38, 125, 206n196; naming role of, 41–43, 73, 125, 130–34, 145–46, 154, 184nn112–15, 185n125, 206nn198–99, 209n26, 210n29; as plural male and female beings, 24–34, 37, 66, 69, 113–15, 178nn32–33,

181n70, 181–82nn82–84; purpose of creation of, 62–73, 74–75, 190–93nn191–233; purpose of woman, 66–69, 191–92nn211–214, 192n216; substance of, 38–39, 74–75, 182n89, 182n91, 182nn93–97; translations of, 5; trial and punishment of, 105–16, 140, 200–201nn110–112, 200n106. See also Adam; creation of woman; gender issues

"Adam" (Bat-Miriam), 121

Aeneid, 139

R. Aibu, 57–59, 100, 152–53

Alter, Robert, 6–7, 10; on *adam* as a term for humans, 25, 37, 131; on Eve in the Garden, 196n34; on Eve's test, 94, 197n45, 197nn47–48; on Lamech's song, 210n34; on naming of *ishah*, 42, 184n112

alterity of women, 45–52, 185–87nn135–157

"Apple Sauce for Eve" (Piercy), 163–65, 215n95

approaches to literary analysis, 4–5, 172nn10–11; feminist biblical revisionism, 5; scholarly focus on Eve, 11–13

Aschkenasy, Nehama, 12, 200n104

"Aspects of Eve" (Pastan), 52–56

"Autobiography" (Pagis), 146, 208n21, 211–12n59

Bal, Mieke, 11, 189n178, 213n74

banishment of Eve from the Garden, 20–24, 113–15, 134–39

R. Bannayah, 56–60

basilisk, 138, 206n210

Baskin, Judith R., 12, 173n28; on *adam*, 29–30, 179n45, 180nn52–53; on alterity of women, 45, 186n140, 187n153; on gender hierarchy, 65, 191n199; on women's blood-related taboos, 120; on women's *mitsvot*, 203n152, 203n154

modern poetic accounts, 2–7, 12–13, 168–
69; audience of, 7; of banishment from
Eden, 135–41; comparisons of, with
rabbinic writings, 172n16, 193n240; of
creation of woman, 31–34, 52–56, 74–
76; degendering of God in, 32–33; of
Eve's life in the Garden, 77–83, 121–30;
of Eve's motherhood, 142–46, 157–65,
207nn1–2, 208nn10–11; of Eve's test,
83–90; gender roles in, 3–4; Holocaust
imagery in, 142–46, 165, 207n2, 207n8,
208n11, 208n15; language of, 6–7; polemical aspects of, 6–7; polysemy of,
2–3, 169; traditional "rib" accounts in,
52–56, 75–76; translations of, 194n1
monotheism, 22–24
Moses, 193n236
motherhood of Eve, 142–65, 211n59,
215n98; in biblical accounts, 146–51,
153–55, 209–10nn23–39; birth of Cain
and Abel, 145–47; birth of Seth, 153–55,
167, 210n40; fratricide of Cain and
Abel, 142–46, 149–50, 153–55, 211nn44–
47, 211–12n59, 212n63, 213n68; hubris,
149–50, 155, 164–65, 167–68, 210nn37–
39, 211n47, 213n74; marginalization by
adam's lineage, 155–57; in midrashic accounts, 150–53, 210n40, 211nn48–51; in
modern poetic accounts, 142–46, 157–
65; naming role, 145–48, 155, 167–68,
209n27, 209n29, 210nn33–34; unnamed
daughters of, 210n40, 211n57

Nabal, 69–70, 101–2
R. Naḥman ben Yitzḥak, 179n50
naming, 130–34, 176n1; of adam, 38, 125,
206n196; adam's role, 41–43, 72, 125,
130–34, 145–46, 154, 184nn112–15,
185n125, 206nn198–99, 209n26,
209n29; of Cain and Abel, 145–48, 154–
55, 209–10nn27–33, 211n59; of Eve, 41–
43, 72, 125, 132–34, 145–47, 184nn112–15,
184n125, 206n202, 209n26, 209n28;
Eve's role, 145–48, 155, 167–68, 209n27,
209n29, 210nn33–34; of ishah, 41–43,

72, 132, 147–48, 184–86nn112–126,
206n202, 209n26; of Seth, 153–55, 167,
209n28, 210n40, 213n71; unnamed biblical women, 151–52, 206n197, 210n40,
211n54
Noah, 156, 171n7, 191n211
Nod, land of, 154
Norris, Pamela, 12
number. See plural nature of adam

operatic accounts, 158
Oren, Miriam, 159–61, 214nn84–89
Ostriker, Alicia Suskin, 5, 32–33, 52, 61,
180n59

P (Priestly) tradition, 9–10, 157
Pagis, Dan, 142–46, 161, 165, 207nn1–3,
207n8, 208–9nn15–22, 211–12n59
Pandora, 102–4
Papell, Helen, 88–90, 196n29
Pardes, Ilana, 11, 157, 193n234, 204n164; on
adam's naming role, 213n71; on biblical
accounts of Eve, 209n23; on chronology of creation, 193n234; on Eve's hubris, 211n47, 213n74; on Eve's mother-
hood, 212n63; on meaning of "create,"
210nn32–33, 210nn36–38; on naming of
ishah, 43
Pastan, Linda, 52–56, 188nn160–64
Paul the Apostle, 73
Philo, 11, 171n5
Piercy, Marge, 163–65, 215n95
Pinsker, Sanford, 53
Pirqei Rabbi Eli'ezer, 7–8, 173nn25–26. See
also midrashic accounts
Plank, Karl A., 146, 207n9
plural nature of adam, 24–34, 37,
178nn32–33
poetry. See modern poetic accounts
Pollitt, Katha, 135–39, 141
polysemous writing, 2–4, 171n6; in biblical accounts, 17–19, 66–67; in modern
accounts, 55, 74–76, 169
pregnancy and childbirth, 110–13, 118–19,
201nn121–27

(continued from page iv)

(in Hebrew) by Yaakov Fikhman. Copyright © 1944 by Schocken Publishing House Ltd., Tel Aviv, Israel. Used by permission of the publisher. Excerpts from "Khaveh un der Epplboym," from *Itzik's Midrash* (in Yiddish) by Itzik Manger. Copyright © 1969 by Magnes Press. Used by permission of Magnes Press, Hebrew University. "Ḥavvah," from *After These Things* (in Hebrew) by Miriam Oren. Copyright © 1962 by Sifriyat Poalim. Used by permission of Hakibbutz Hameuchad Publishers Ltd. and Sifriyat Poalim. Excerpts from "In the Beginning the Being," from *The Nakedness of the Fathers* by Alicia Suskin Ostriker. Copyright © 1994 by Alicia Suskin Ostriker. Reprinted by permission of Rutgers University Press. "Katuv be'ipparon bakaron," from *Collected Poems* (in Hebrew) by Dan Pagis. Copyright © 1991 by Hakibbutz Hameuchad. Used by permission of Hakibbutz Hameuchad Publishing House and the Bialik Institute. "Tree of Knowing," from *Talking with Eve, Leah, Hagar, Miriam* by Helen Papell. Copyright © 1996 by Helen Papell. Used by permission of the author. "Aspects of Eve," from *Aspects of Eve* by Linda Pastan. Copyright © 1970, 1971, 1972, 1973, 1974, 1975 by Linda Pastan. Used by permission of Liveright Publishing Corporation. Excerpts from "Apple Sauce for Eve," from *The Art of Blessing the Day* by Marge Piercy. Copyright © 1999 by Middlemarsh, Inc. Used by permission of Alfred A. Knopf, a division of Random House, Inc. "The Expulsion," by Katha Pollitt. Copyright © 2001 by Katha Pollitt. Used by permission of the author. "Ḥavvah," from *Love Poems* (in Hebrew) by Yaacov Shai Shavit. Copyright © 1998 by Yaacov Shai Shavit. Used by permission of Carmel Publishing House. "Things Eve Learned from the Serpent," by Sandy Supowit. Copyright © 2000 by Sandy Supowit. Used by permission of the author. Parts of chapter 1 are also included in Anne Lapidus Lerner's "Rib Redux" that appears in *Bringing the Hidden to Light: The Process of Interpretation—Studies in Honor of Stephen A. Geller,* edited by Kathryn Kravitz and Diane Sharon (Winona Lake, Ind.: Eisenbrauns, 2007), pp. 129–47, and is here reprinted with permission of the publisher.